STUDIES ON THE CHINESE ECONOMY

General Editors: Peter Nolan, Sinyi Professor of Chinese Management, Judge Institute of Management Studies, University of Cambridge, and Fellow of Jesus College, Cambridge, England; and Dong Fureng, Professor, Chinese Academy of Social Sciences, Beijing, China

This series analyses issues in China's current economic development, and sheds light upon that process by examining China's economic history. It contains a wide range of books on the Chinese economy, past and present, and includes not only studies written by leading Western authorities but also translations of the most important works on the Chinese economy produced within China. It intends to make a major contribution towards understanding this immensely important part of the world economy.

Titles include:

Thomas Chan, Noel Tracy and Zhu Wenhui
CHINA'S EXPORT MIRACLE

Xu Dixin and Wu Chengming (*editors*)
CHINESE CAPITALISM, 1522–1840

Christopher Findlay and Andrew Watson (*editors*)
FOOD SECURITY AND ECONOMIC REFORM

Samuel P. S. Ho and Y. Y. Kueh
SUSTAINABLE ECONOMIC DEVELOPMENT IN SOUTH CHINA

Kali P. Kalirajan and Yanrui Wu (*editors*)
PRODUCTIVITY AND GROWTH IN CHINESE AGRICULTURE

Bozhong Li
AGRICULTURAL DEVELOPMENT IN JIANGNAN, 1620–1850

Alfred H. Y. Lin
THE RURAL ECONOMY OF GUANGDONG, 1870–1937

Dic Lo
MARKET AND INSTITUTIONAL REGULATION IN CHINESE INDUSTRIALIZATION

Jun Ma
THE CHINESE ECONOMY IN THE 1990s

Guo Rongxing
HOW THE CHINESE ECONOMY WORKS

Sally Sargeson
REWORKING CHINA'S PROLETARIAT

Ng Sek Hong and Malcolm Warner
CHINA'S TRADE UNIONS AND MANAGEMENT

Michael Twohey
AUTHORITY AND WELFARE IN CHINA

Wang Xiao-qiang
CHINA'S PRICE AND ENTERPRISE REFORM

Xiaoping Xu
CHINA'S FINANCIAL SYSTEM UNDER TRANSITION

Yanni Yan
INTERNATIONAL JOINT VENTURES IN CHINA

Wei-Wei Zhang
TRANSFORMING CHINA

Xiao-guang Zhang
CHINA'S TRADE PATTERNS AND INTERNATIONAL COMPARATIVE ADVANTAGE

Studies on the Chinese Economy
Series Standing Order ISBN 0–333–71502–0
(*outside North America only*)

You can receive future titles in this series as they are published by placing a standing order. Please contact your bookseller or, in case of difficulty, write to us at the address below with your name and address, the title of the series and the ISBN quoted above.

Customer Services Department, Macmillan Distribution Ltd
Houndmills, Basingstoke, Hampshire RG21 6XS, England

International Joint Ventures in China

Ownership, Control and Performance

Yanni Yan
Lecturer in International Business and Management
University of Essex

palgrave
macmillan

Published by PALGRAVE MACMILLAN
Houndmills, Basingstoke, Hampshire RG21 6XS and
175 Fifth Avenue, New York, N. Y. 10010
Companies and representatives throughout the world

PALGRAVE MACMILLAN is the global academic imprint of the Palgrave Macmillan division of St. Martin's Press, LLC and of Palgrave Macmillan Ltd. Macmillan® is a registered trademark in the United States, United Kingdom and other countries. Palgrave is a registered trademark in the European Union and other countries.

Outside North America
ISBN 0–333–73454–8

In North America
ISBN 0–312–22301–3

This book is printed on paper suitable for recycling and made from fully managed and sustained forest sources.

A catalogue record for this book is available from the British Library.

Library of Congress Catalog Card Number: 99–22106

Transferred to digital printing 2002

Printed and bound in Great Britain by
Antony Rowe Ltd, Chippenham and Eastbourne

This book is dedicated to my parents

Kong Xing Yan *and* ***Li Qing Lin***

Contents

List of Figures

List of Tables

Abstract

A longstanding issue in the area of corporate governance, namely the relationship between the ownership and control of firms, takes on new dimensions in the case of international joint ventures. One dimension is that such ventures often have only two owners, and another, particularly relevant to the case of China, is that the question of control is bound up with the extent to which host government development policy is served by foreign-invested joint ventures. The literature on the ownership–control relationship in developing counties is limited. The present study contributes a new examination of this relationship, first through its conceptual refinement, and second through original empirical research. It develops a conception of ownership suited to the joint venture as opposed to the conventional firm, in which account is taken of non-capital resourcing by partners, on both a contractual and a non-contractual basis. Account is also taken of a joint venture's transactional resource dependence on the partners.

Following a review of relevant literatures, an analytical model is developed. The research models articulate postulated relationships for joint ventures between partners' objectives, the resourcing they provide as owners, their levels of control and joint venture performance. The empirical study used a sample sufficiently large to permit the testing of the models – sixty-seven Sino-foreign joint ventures. Data were collected by means of interviews within each joint venture of Chinese and foreign managers, using a structured checklist. The criteria for selecting a joint venture for study was that it should have a minimum of two years' operation, and that at least one expatriate manager should be working in it. All the joint ventures were located within the electronics and fast-moving consumer goods sectors.

The more significant findings are that (1) equity is a stronger lever for strategic control than it is for operational control, (2) contractual resourcing by partners is a generally weak lever for control over joint venture operations, and (3) the provision of resourcing on a non-contractual basis adds to parent company control over a wider range of joint venture management activities, especially with respect to operational matters. Moreover, the degree of fit between resourcing and control is associated with levels of joint venture performance.

It is concluded that the ability to predict levels of partner control in any joint venture is enhanced by applying the broader concept of ownership adopted in this study. It also appears that Western theory on the subject can usefully be applied to China, despite the differences in context.

Acknowledgements

This study has benefited very greatly from the encouragement and support generously given by a number of people. I should like to thank them all most sincerely.

First and foremost, my deep gratitude goes to Professor John Child, who has throughout given me guidance and continuous feedback. The final writing of this book gained a great deal from comments and suggestions generously given by Dr John R. Fawn, Professor Malcolm Warner, Professor Ingmar Bjorkman, Professor Aimin Yan, Dr Yuan Lu, Professor Peter Nolan, Dr Zhiping Chen and Dr Robert Pitkethly. I owe a debt gratitude to all these colleagues and friends.

My thanks also go to the numerous expatriates and Chinese managers of the joint ventures in China who provided the data on which this study is based. Without their cooperation there would be no research findings to report. Colleagues in the Cambridge–PRC State Council project team contributed ideas about joint ventures and field work methods, as well as assisting with access to companies. These colleagues are Professor Linzhu Chen, Shiquan Zhang, Xinjian Wang and Yaobin Lu from the State Council, and Professor John Child and Dr. Yuan Lu from the University of Cambridge. In addition, I give special thanks to Keith Povey, the copy-editor, for his helpful suggestions.

I am very grateful to various institutions that provided their sponsorship for this study. United Distillers Asia Pacific, Rothmans Charitable Trust, the School of Business, at Hong Kong University, Churchill College, Cambridge and University of Essex provided various funds to cover research costs and conference travel.

Last, but certainly not least, I must record my debt to those at home. During the time in which this book has taken shape, I have been the fortunate beneficiary of constant support from my family, especially the love and encouragement of my parents, Gongxin Yan, and Liqin Lin. My brother, Keguo Yan, sister, Mingxia Yan, and uncle, Gongbiao Yan, also gave their encouragement. In particular, Rungan Zhang, my husband, and Zichao Zhang, our son, have given of their patience, tolerance and, above all, love throughout my studies in Cambridge and Essex.

YANNI YAN

Part I
The Background

1 Introduction

The subject of creating equity joint ventures or wholly owned subsidiaries in developing countries has attracted the attention of many international business researchers. The effects or determinants of full or shared ownership options have been some of the most important strategic issues to be decided in foreign direct investment (FDI) areas over the last thirty years. Full equity ownership has been the preferred mode of entry for most multinational corporations (MNCs) in developing countries, because many foreign managers prefer to hold tight to managerial control rather than to relinquish authority to host country managers (Holt 1998). Full equity ownership characterises the ultimate form of international management involvement in countries, and represents the risk profile of available control options.

The longstanding central issue of corporate governance, namely the relationship between the ownership and the control of firms, takes on a new dimension in the case of international joint ventures (IJVs). The question of the relationship between ownership and control of IJVs has a direct impact upon the understanding of a developing country's industrial and FDI policy. The literature on the determinants of ownership in developing countries is somewhat limited. Host governments may wish to maintain some control over joint ventures, even if they are not in a financial position to contribute the major share of equity capital. Their wish to maintain control may stem from their desire to ensure that there is effective technology transfer and also to avoid possible exploitation by powerful international partners in matters such as transfer pricing. A further aspect of IJV control stems from the desire of developing country governments to encourage local participation in joint venture ownership, thereby facilitating technology transfer and the acquisition of managerial expertise. In such circumstances, government agencies may also decide to exercise quasi-ownership rights. For these reasons, the relationship between ownership and control of those IJVs that are located in developing countries may take a different form from that analysed in the more conventional literature (Beamish 1988).

The ownership and control issue may also be significant for foreign investing companies. The issue is associated with the extent to which foreign investing companies believe they can manage uncertainty and risk in host country environments, and also the extent to which they perceive they can introduce best practice into their joint ventures. Equally, from the practical point of view, it is clearly interesting to discover what are the most effective levels for control, and it is important to know, in a very different market environmental context, how much ownership factors actually contribute to control. This obviously raises the further question of whether Western theory and research findings on ownership and control will apply to a developing country.

As well as being the largest host for FDI among developing countries, China, as a context for joint ventures, raises special issues for both theory and practice. China is a good case for testing the generalisability of those theories concerning ownership and control that have been derived from Western experience, because it has a long-standing culture and is still nominally a socialist country whose government plays an active role in business affairs. Chinese government intervention in business, through the state-owned enterprise partnership of joint ventures or via regulation, may qualify the formal right of foreign majority owners to control the joint venture management.

THE INTERNATIONAL JOINT VENTURE

An IJV is a quasi-independent organisation, the legal child created by the partnership of two or more parent companies. Joint ventures are hybrid in nature, but have their own identifiable structures, working procedures, economic transactions and management personnel. Each partner may take an active role in the decision-making activities of the joint venture. They receive a proportionate share of its dividend, and can expect to be represented on the joint venture's board of directors. An IJV has its own independent assets and liabilities, and it pays taxes to the host nation, China. The arrangement can be an advantage if the foreign tax rate is less than that in the home country, that is, the foreign partner's country of origin.

An IJV can be expanded rapidly, and risks and costs can be reduced effectively, through inter-partnership, simply because local equity partners assume some financial risk. By setting up an IJV with an existing host company, foreign firms can immediately penetrate trade barriers. IJV partnerships provide access to complementary technologies and create synergies. In advanced-technology industry sectors, such as electronics, the reason for setting up an IJV partnership typically includes greater technological synergies, faster innovation, accessing tangible and intangible resources and reducing the costs and risks associated with R&D. In capital- and labour-intensive industry sectors, such as fast-moving consumer goods (FMCG), the resources from an IJV partner can provide an opportunity to strengthen technological capabilities and move more rapidly towards a higher-value-added product range.

Four general characteristics of joint ventures are often identified in the literature. First, the joint venture objectives usually derive from a combination of objectives held by the partners and, in the case of an international joint venture, in combination with those of the host country government. The formation of a joint venture can be used to achieve a number of advantages: to share business risks and costs (Contractor and Lorange 1988, Harrigan 1988, Teece 1992); to achieve economies of scale (Collis 1991); to secure complementary contributions of technology or know-how (Teece 1992); to overcome market barriers in a foreign country (Hamel 1991); to acquire/develop new competencies to improve management by transferring tacit knowledge (Prahalad and Hamel 1990; Hennart 1988); to increase local managerial autonomy and flexibility (Doz 1986); and to acquire raw materials at a low cost for use or sale (Root 1988).

Second, a joint venture links ownership resources and organisational systems as a means by which two or more firms can establish a partnership. Ownership resources are defined as the combined capital (equity) and non-capital (on both a contractual and a non-contractual basis) resourcing provided by the partners. Within a joint venture, partners can contribute and exchange either tangible resource such as assets, and/or intangible properties such as knowledge, skills, training, and information. The value of this partnership lies in having a control mechanism through which parent companies endeavour to create a synergistic context within which the joint venture can draw upon their organisational systems, and resources. On the one hand, this should provide an opportunity to generate competitive advantages for the joint venture. On the other hand, as Borys and Jemison (1989) note, the boundaries between partners become blurred, though each partner maintains its sovereignty as an independent organisation.

Third, a joint venture often involves partners from different countries. The resources contributed by each partner must be sufficiently distinctive to confront markets and operating conditions that are strikingly unlike those of the home country. Different partner nationalities and organisational cultures create additional contrasts between the partners (Parkhe 1991). Therefore, conflicts can be generated not only by the distinct objectives and operational requirements of each of the partners, but also by their particular social and cultural characteristics.

Finally, the management control of joint ventures is problematic, because there are complications that are embedded in both the inter-partner and the parent–joint-venture relationships. Each partner may have incongruent objectives, and their criteria for the joint venture's performance may diverge (Geringer and Hebert 1991). The parent companies share the joint venture's formal ownership according to their equity investment. Each equity-holding parent firm has a legitimate right to derive revenues and to share in control (Buckley and Casson 1988, Kogut 1988). In addition to this formal definition of control rights, differences in the partners' management styles, cultures and managerial perceptions are also likely to mould the joint venture's behaviour.

OWNERSHIP EQUITY EVALUATED IN A BROAD CONTEXT

International management research on ownership equity has received much attention. Evaluating a portfolio of core contributions to the management and the technology of joint ventures has been shown to be particularly problematic in previous research (Yan and Gray 1994a). Managing and controlling the equity investment made by the partners in joint ventures raises even greater problems. The choice of the investment involves a two-step process. First, there is the determination of the investing companies' preferred ownership stakes in the joint venture. Second, there is alignment of one owner's resource profile with that of a suitable partner. The ownership equity outcome depends on the interaction between these two steps.

In establishing joint ventures to exploit common advantages, the IJV partners provide resources, skills and knowledge that are assets in the possession of partner firms. They have intrinsic value, and amount to ownership inputs with property rights. Equity as the provision of a capital resource to a joint venture is contributed by its partner companies. This is usually financial, but sometimes comprises land, buildings and plant (Child *et al.* 1997). The distinction between the types of resource is important, because assets such as technology, market channels and management expertise have become increasingly recognised as ownership factors, especially in the formation of IJVs, where they may constitute complementary assets that are more important than purely financial contributions. Prahalad and Hamel (1990) suggest that it is possible to conceive of a firm as a portfolio of core competencies on the one hand, and encompassing disciplines on the other. There is, nevertheless, considerable ongoing debate about the effects of the range of resources contributed by the partners to the performance of a joint venture.

WHY STUDY THE SUBJECT?

The objective of this book is to make a contribution in the relatively unexplored conceptual territory of the relationship between the objectives, ownership, control and performance of Sino-foreign joint ventures. The intention is to develop a categorisation of ownership resourcing, based upon the distinction between contractual and non-contractual resources, which may add to our understanding of the differences between conventional companies and joint ventures in China. The study also explores the applicability of established Western theories to the Chinese business environment. Undertaking the study reported in this book was worth while for the following main reasons:

1. There was little research on international joint venture ownership and control issues, in the Chinese context, when the study was first planned. Even after the recent important contributions of Yan and Gray (1994b), there is still far more speculation than sound research. There is scope both for conceptual development (especially the nature of ownership) and for adding to the empirical base. It is believed that further exploration of the issue will yield returns to both theory and policy.
2. There is a need to develop a conception of ownership suited to the joint venture as opposed to the conventional firm. It is generally recognised that the joint venture is (a) founded on a resource base of a range of complementary *direct* owner resourcing inputs over and above equity capital; (b) likely to engage owners much more closely in the management; and (c) a hybrid organisation whose control could be affected by proportions of equity held by each partner in the joint venture. Hence, the ownership concept and the basis for the owner–control relationship require re-examination in the context of the joint venture, because both the scope of ownership resourcing and the degree of owner involvement in control are likely to be greater.

3. There is the opportunity to carry out an empirical examination of the contribution of available theories to these issues and thus to establish areas where further theoretical development would be advantageous.
4. Those firms that are considering developing their operations through joint ventures need to be able to evaluate thoroughly the conditions and consequences of their ownership resourcing before coming to an investment decision. There are questions as to whether an essentially Western theoretical literature can yield perspectives useful in understanding the ownership and control of international joint ventures in China, where distinctive institutional and cultural backgrounds may play an important role.
5. There is a need to understand how the control mechanisms in Sino-foreign joint ventures adopted by foreign and Chinese parent companies vary according to the level and type of their equity investments.

A GUIDE THROUGH THIS BOOK

This book consists of three parts. The chapters in Part I (Chapters 1 to 4) develop the conceptual and theoretical basis for the research. Chapter 1 reviews the literature on the development of international joint ventures and provides a guide for the book. Chapter 2 discusses the main characteristics of the Chinese context in which the joint ventures are evaluated and located. In particular, the history of relevant legislation and key aspects of Chinese government policy are highlighted, followed by an examination of the general characteristics of foreign-funded ventures in China. Chapter 3 draws upon available literature to consider two aspects of the relationship between ownership and control. In the first part, the general concepts of ownership and control are applied to the specific case of a joint venture. In the second part, seven widely accepted international business theories are used to help identify the different dimensions relevant to the relationship between ownership and control of joint ventures. Chapter 4 presents a formation model, a universalistic model and a contingency model. The implications of the three models are used to identify the main objectives for joint venture formation, the resources contributed by joint venture owners and the fit between ownership and control.

Part II (Chapters 5 to 8) focuses on an empirical study undertaken by Cambridge University in conjunction with the State Council of

China and the methodology used. Chapter 5 provides an overview of the research employed in the study. This is primarily quantitative in nature, but is complemented by some qualitative evidence. Chapter 6 profiles the configuration of objectives, ownership and control that emerged from the cases of sixty-seven Sino-foreign joint ventures. Chapter 7 examines the relationships between partner objectives, ownership and control. Chapter 8 overlooks the effects of ownership and control on the performance of joint ventures.

Part III comprises one chapter, Chapter 9, which summarises and draws together the findings that have been derived from applying the research framework to the sample of joint ventures. Comparison with previous research permits a discussion of this study's contribution to theory development and of how far the findings for joint ventures in China fit the Western case or require a separate analysis. This also permits some suggestions for further research that might follow on from the present study. The chapter finally draws some policy implications for Sino-foreign joint ventures.

SUMMARY

The research presented in this book is concerned with the relationship between partner objectives, ownership, control and performance in IJVs. The specific focus of this study is foreign direct investment in China, through joint ventures with local Chinese partners. The book presents findings from a study of sixty-seven Sino-foreign joint ventures undertaken in 1994–5. It investigates the relationship between various dimensions of ownership and management control in the joint ventures. This investigation is made with reference to the objectives of the foreign and Chinese owning companies, as well as the resources they contribute to their joint ventures. In addition to investigating the relationship between ownership and control, the study also examines whether the fit between these factors has any relevance to joint venture performance.

2 Sino-Foreign Joint Ventures

INTRODUCTION

FDI plays a major role in linking China's national economy to the global economy. The World Investment Report (UN 1997) records that among developing countries China has been the recipient of the largest FDI inflow, amounting to some $57 billion in 1997. FDI has made a significant contribution to the Chinese economy by improving local production, management and marketing systems. This is achieved through a portfolio of inputs, which include capital, technology, management and marketing know-how. The success of China in attracting FDI lies in an investment climate characterised by growing markets, increasingly favourable regulatory frameworks and the possibility of establishing joint ventures (Beamish 1983).

China has already become the world's third largest economic power in terms of GDP. This achievement is based on rapid growth, a huge population and a large domestic market. IJVs are encouraged by the Chinese government, as they present an ideal form for securing rapid access to capital, technology and export markets within a competitive and rapidly changing global economy (Harrigan 1986). During the last 20 years, 195 000 foreign-funded enterprises have come into operation and 360 000 projects have been approved in China. A total of over US$ 300 billions of foreign direct investment had been committed in China by the end of 1997. Surveys, reported by Zhou (1997), suggest that most foreign investment companies are satisfied with the performance of their joint ventures, as they are meeting the financial objectives originally envisaged. As the joint venture is becoming a favourable investment entry mode and is making a significant contribution to the Chinese economy, it has become particularly relevant to gain a greater understanding of its nature. Joint ventures in China have their own distinctive characteristics, covering almost the whole range of business sectors and engaging partners of many different foreign nationalities. They range from relatively minor foreign equity stakes in short-term alliances through 50: 50 investments to majority foreign equity stakes in investments of a long-term nature.

The Chinese government favours the development of joint ventures with foreign investment companies, and has indicated its preferences with a combination of economic incentives and restrictive regulations (Carver 1996). Among the latter are legal provisions and restrictions on foreign equity holding that are imposed in certain strategically important sectors by the Chinese government. Central and local Chinese authorities are therefore able to exercise considerable influence over foreign investments in partnerships, with state- and collective-owned enterprises remaining under their control. Beamish (1993) notes that China remains a state-dominated country, and the government has not encouraged the private sector to form joint ventures with foreign firms. In China, a state-owned enterprise possesses political clout, which provides its higher authorities with some bargaining power over the foreign investor (Nolan 1995).

The attraction of accessing the huge Chinese market provides for many foreign investing companies the most important objective when engaging in a joint venture there (Shenkar 1990). However, the management of joint ventures in China presents some unusual challenges that are associated with the intervention of the governmental bureaucracy, highly specific legal frameworks, an important local government role, the impact of traditional Chinese ways of doing business, Chinese management practices, the underdeveloped state of the Chinese market and the problematic availability of raw materials.

In order to achieve the full strategic and economic potential of their Chinese IJVs, many foreign firms have come to the conclusion that they need to strengthen their control in a number of key areas, such as technology transfer, marketing and finance (Meier *et al.* 1995), because these areas are likely to be located primarily within the foreign company. The introduction of relevant standards in the areas of technology, marketing and finance, together with the imposition of foreign reporting mechanisms, often means that the foreign partner of an IJV has influence over its management. These considerations suggest that the relationship between ownership and control has a greater priority for the foreign partners in equity joint ventures, and this can cause problems for the partnership.

This chapter is divided into four sections. The first section highlights the history of legislation and key aspects of Chinese government policy on foreign direct investments, and therefore indicates how

Chinese legal institutions impact on joint ventures in China. This is followed by a summary of joint venture development in the economic reform period. The third section is concerned with identifying the influence of the Chinese and foreign parties on the nature of Sino-foreign joint ventures and a discussion of whether China is different from the West. The last section discusses the objectives of foreign and Chinese partners.

THE DEVELOPMENT OF CHINESE LEGISLATION AND GOVERNMENT POLICY

Joint ventures operate in environments that can put at risk those rights of ownership commonly accepted as normal in Western countries. In China, restrictions have been imposed on the use and management of foreign direct investment (Pearson 1991), but these have been reduced since the original opening up of the economy in the mid 1970s. The evolving definitions of ownership rights have played an important part in China's successful policy of encouraging joint ventures.

The development of Chinese laws and regulations on foreign investment in China over the past twenty years has reflected a basic tension between encouraging foreign business activities and the desire to maintain state control over them. The Chinese legal regime for foreign investment has evolved significantly since its inception following the third plenum of the eleventh central committee of the Chinese communist party in 1978. Foreign investment laws have been enacted on contracts, taxation, foreign exchange and other matters. The taxation system is currently undergoing reform to harmonise the treatment of Chinese and foreign firms. More recently, efforts have been made to remove disparities in the legal treatment of Chinese and foreigners. The recent PRC enterprise law heralds an effort to unify the corporate legal status of Chinese and foreign businesses.

The Chinese authorities distinguish four main types of foreign direct investment: (1) equity joint ventures; (2) cooperative enterprises, namely contractual joint ventures; (3) wholly foreign-owned enterprises and (4) offshore oil development projects. Equity joint ventures have the status of separate legal entities. Chinese and foreign partners contribute to their registered capital and take profits, risks and losses in proportion to that contribution.

The legal status of equity joint ventures is defined by a host of laws and regulations that have general application: the 1979 Joint Venture

Law, the 1983 Implementing Regulations, the 1986 State Council Provisions, the 1990 Amendments to the Joint Venture Law, the 1993 PRC Company Law, the 1994 PRC Foreign Trade Law and the 1996 Tax Law.

The 1979 Joint Venture Law contains fifteen articles. It sets out the general principles governing the establishment and operation of joint ventures. These deal with approval procedures, capital structure, forms of equity contribution, profit distribution, general management structure, foreign exchange and remittance of funds abroad, action in the case of losses, labour relations and the settlement of disputes. The law clearly states that each joint venture is to have a board of directors, with a chairman appointed by the Chinese side and one or two vice-chairman appointed by the foreign side. Managerial autonomy is granted to the board on issues of business programmes, expansion, finance, personnel policy, procedures and the hiring and remuneration of senior officers. Lin (1996a) reports that this joint venture law is supposed to serve the development of China's centrally planned economy. The Chinese authorities intend to use joint venture laws and regulations in order to absorb foreign investment into the Chinese national economy. These laws and regulations are designed to guarantee that the Chinese side can still exert strong control and influence in the context of Chinese institutional settings. Most of the Chinese partners are state-owned or collective enterprises. In order to seek Chinese partners, the reality is that foreign investment companies have to ask for help and support from the Chinese government.

The Regulations for the Implementation of the Law on Joint Ventures were promulgated by the State Council in September 1983. They were designed to improve the investment climate by clarifying the legal position so as to give foreign investors greater confidence. They provide greater detail on questions of profit repatriation, technology transfer, foreign exchange and labour management. The Implementation Regulations stipulate that government departments should not interfere in the production and operating plans of joint ventures. The authority to approve the establishment of small joint ventures, with a total investment of $5 million or less, was decentralised to municipal, provincial or autonomous regional governments. The limits on the sectors in which joint ventures are permitted to operate were clarified in the Implementation Regulations. These were sectors where technology, advanced management, natural resources and products for export are urgently required. Moreover, joint ventures are allowed to sell products and services primarily on the domestic market if the authorities consider there is an urgent need for such products. The Implementing Regulations also specify the rules of accounting, fiscal reporting from joint ventures and allocations to expansion funds, reserve funds and bonus/welfare funds that must be made before profits are distributed between partners.

The Foreign Economic Contract Law was promulgated in March 1985 and contains forty-three articles. It further clarified the rights of the parties to economic contracts involving foreign interests, a clarification intended to improve the environment for foreign investment (Child 1994). In 1980, the Chinese authorities created the four special economic zones (SEZs) of Shenzhen, Zhuhai, Shantou and Xiamen. The province of Hainan inland was also designated and opened as the largest SEZ in China in 1988. The establishment of the SEZs was predicated on their role as export platforms for foreign firms. The subsequent designation of fourteen municipalities as open coastal cities and the establishment of economic and technology development zones (ETDZs) centre mainly on technology development, although export-oriented production is also emphasised. Tax incentives are provided for businesses located in the SEZs and ETDZs, including a provision that all foreign investment enterprises scheduled to operate in the production sector for more than ten years received the five-year tax holidays previously extended only to equity joint ventures. The use of SEZs and ETDZs indicates an effort to concentrate foreign investment in particular location, and the focus of control over SEZs and ETDZs has shifted from the central to the local government, while the focus on the importance of exports and the acquisition of technology continues unabated. The Foreign Economic Contract Law also goes into detail on the formation, amendment and termination of contracts.

The State Council in October 1986 issued twenty-two further Provisions for the Encouragement of Foreign Investment (known as the 'Twenty-Two Articles'), targetting foreign investment enterprises engaged in export activities and advanced technology production. These regulations attempt to steer foreign investment towards the establishment of export industries and the acquisition of advanced technology. The importation of technology is encouraged by those articles among the twenty-two articles that permit industrial property rights to be contributed as capital by foreign investors. Approval of joint ventures is contingent on their ability to satisfy criteria that emphasise the areas of export and technology development. Incentives in the form of tax holidays are offered in an effort to induce foreign investors to comply with these requirements. Similarly, those of the twenty-two articles that govern wholly owned subsidiaries emphasise that approval by the Chinese government is conditional upon their use of advanced technology or upon exporting all or most of their products.

Joint ventures that satisfy the conditions for designation as a 'technological advanced enterprise' can extend their initial three years' tax holiday by an additional three years. Foreign participants in technologically advanced enterprises and export enterprises are also exempt from the withholding tax on profits remitted outside China. Special incentives are offered for export-oriented and technologically advanced enterprises, thus targeting the government's priority areas. These enterprises pay reduced fees for labour and for land use. They are to be given priority in the allocation of infrastructure services, and also in the granting of funds for working capital. Under these provisions, foreign-invested enterprises whose export production value is 70 per cent of total production value are to be considered 'export-oriented enterprises', eligible for a 50 per cent reduction in enterprise income tax, with additional reductions also possible. The Twenty-Two Articles further guarantee the autonomy from external bureaucratic interference of those enterprises, that have foreign investment, and promise that they will receive more positive support from government departments.

The Chinese government has made clear its intent to supervise foreign business activities closely. Since Chinese policies enacted in 1978 permitted China to develop greater ties with the international systems of commerce and finance, state control over foreign business has remained a singular norm of the regulatory regime. The conduct of investment transactions with the PRC is subject to a host of laws and regulations, which seek to strengthen state control as a precondition for economic ability in China. The proposed extent of state control is evident in regulatory requirements governing the formation of joint ventures. The approval of joint ventures entails a significant degree of state control. The foreign investment contract and the articles of association that represent the rules for operation of the joint venture must receive approval from the Ministry of Foreign Trade and Economic Cooperation (MOFTEC). These documents then provide the basis upon which the State Administration for Industry and Commerce (SAIC) issues the project's business licence. Once in operation, joint ventures are subject to an additional range of regulatory controls on matters such as environmental protection and labour management. Government financial control has also been maintained through the tax reporting system.

The role of the state in China's development can be assessed from a range of perspectives. More laws were promulgated in the early 1990s, including the copyright law and also provisions for strengthening the property rights of foreign businessmen. There are regulations concerning land rights in urban areas for the development and management of land by foreign investors. The Chinese government decided to abolish as from 1 April 1996 all tax exemptions on the import of foreign goods to China. This means that foreign joint ventures had to pay a 40 per cent duty plus 17 per cent VAT on imported machinery and equipment. On the one hand, the Chinese authorities rely on formalistic and authoritarian legal systems in order to retain control, and to establish legal regimes aimed at pursuing national development objectives. On the other hand, they have largely reduced the measures that protected the monopolies of the state-owned enterprises, and have encouraged fair competition between enterprises with alternative forms of ownership.

The Chinese authorities are very determined to meet the requirements of a 'socialist market economy' that is supposed to be compatible with the international market system. More and more internal Chinese documents (*neibu*) on particular political, economic and technical issues have been replaced by a host of explicit laws and regulations. State control has been strengthened through the Chinese investment incentive system and a more transparent investment environment. Reliance on tax preferences permits increased state monitoring over foreign investments. In order to access tax preferences, foreign investment enterprises must submit documentation indicating income and tax due before the incentive adjustments are made. Similarly, in order to receive 'export-oriented' or 'advanced technology' status, such enterprises must establish export figures and the capabilities of the technology in use. Thus, even as it grants incentives for foreign investment, the Chinese state seeks to strengthen its capacity to obtain information on the financial condition and sales activities of joint ventures.

THE DEVELOPMENT OF JOINT VENTURES IN CHINESE BUSINESS SECTORS

The Chinese government intends that foreign-funded joint ventures should be directed into those business sectors that are regarded as crucial to China's rapid modernisation. Foreign investment companies established in these sectors are expected to provide advanced technology, foreign exchange or export capability. However, in the early 1980s there appeared to be no specific policies to identify the industrial priorities in establishing joint ventures. Before 1985, inward investment was heavily biased towards those industrial sectors with short-period investment cycles, such as tourism, hotels and low-tech assembly activities. The agriculture and infrastructure sectors received a minimal share. Since the beginning of the 1990s, the service sector has re-emerged as a substantial recipient of joint venture investment. The government formed a new policy for joint ventures in the tertiary industry by opening a wide range of tertiary sectors, such as retailing, tourism, finance, insurance, accounting and law services, real estate development, transportation, aviation and communication (China Economic News 1995). Real estate development is now discouraged.

In fact, the sectors of transportation communication and real estate were ranked as the fastest-developing sectors in 1992 in terms of the growth rate based upon utilising joint venture activity. Concerning the development of joint ventures in the manufacturing sectors, the Chinese government had decided to open the domestic market wider so as to attract more and more foreign companies to invest in the industrial sectors with advanced technologies, such as machinery and electronics. After 1990, the government started to relax its policy on industrial priorities and distribution. Some small foreign investment projects, in which production is only labour-intensive, are now also encouraged and welcomed by the government. Lin (1996b) observes that in the 1980s most joint venture investment went to the manufacturing and related sectors in 1980s. After 1990, real estate and public utilities, including tourism and hotels, appeared to be the second largest joint venture recipient. In 1995, further guidelines were issued as to sectors and regions where FDI is currently favoured.

The distribution of equity ownership in particular business sectors is reflected both by what the investment companies want and by what they cannot receive from the local side (Gomes-Casseres 1990). The unique characteristics of equity joint ventures in China's business sectors are generally identified by the differences in business practices between regions, the level of state ownership involvement, the degree of favourable policies enjoyed in areas such as coastal cities and SEZs, and the equity holding restrictions in the sectors.

Joint ventures are considered an important way of facilitating the adjustment of the national industrial structure. Foreign investment companies targeting a particular sector with specific high-technology advantage may still need to get permission from the Chinese government. The rationales of government policies on joint venture development with respect to its industrial distribution and priorities across the different Chinese regions reflect objectives regarding the acquisition of technology, of capital and of export capabilities. Shenkar (1990) stated that the government's policy is often the basis of bargaining power for the local partner. Pan (1996) reported that a local Chinese firm owned by a higher level of government has greater bargaining power when dealing with foreign partners than has a lower-level Chinese firm. It is recognised that the management control of joint ventures and the implementation of joint ventures in certain strategically important sectors could affect China's industrial structure and her national development policies.

With respect to sectoral investment in China, foreign investment companies were extremely cautious in the early 1980s compared with the 1990s (Beamish 1993). Evidence on foreign investment preferences as between different Chinese industrial sectors remains very limited. Many of the problems expressed by foreign investing companies in the present study reflect a frustration with Chinese sectoral arrangements, in terms of restriction on foreign equity holding, duration of contracts and specific technology previsions. When foreign investing companies are capable of contributing more to the initial capital, technology and management of joint ventures, they are in a stronger position to negotiate a higher equity share (Fagre and Wells 1982). Foreign investing companies are also likely to demand a higher level of control to safeguard their equity investment (Harrigan 1985).

THE MAIN INFLUENCES ON SINO-FOREIGN JOINT VENTURES

There are two kinds of influences over joint ventures in China relevant to the relationship between ownership and control. First, the influence from the Chinese government over joint ventures is examined through the Chinese constitutional context and the government rules over joint ventures. Second, the influence from the foreign investing companies on joint ventures is identified via the process of FDI in China.

Influence of the Chinese Government on Joint Ventures

The management of joint ventures is very much affected by the changes in economic policies, laws and regulations that have accompa-

Figure 2.1 Changes under the Chinese economic reform and FDI

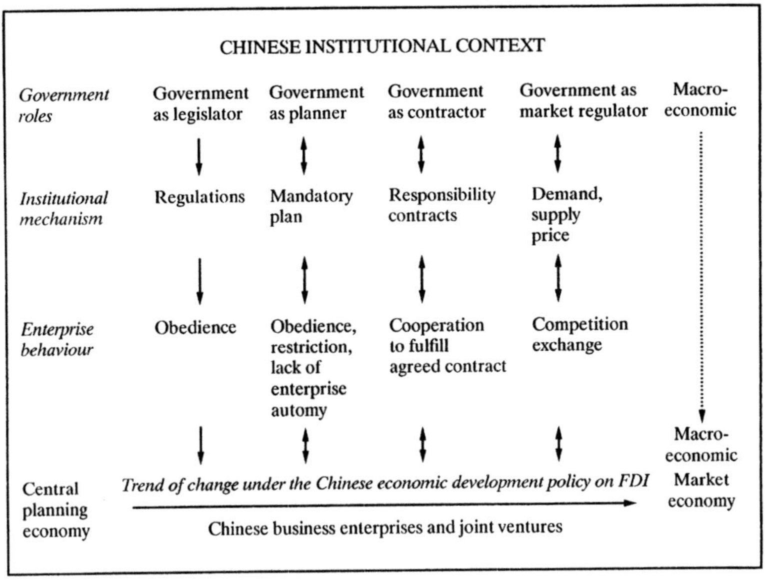

nied the Chinese economic reform. China's economic internationalisation strategy has raised many issues in connection with the increasing numbers of joint ventures. As shown in the Figure 2.1, there are two dimensions to the changes in Chinese management practice that arise as a result of government policies, laws and regulations on inward foreign direct investment.

In the figure, vertical dimension depicts the ways government policies affect the behaviour of enterprises through intermediate institutional mechanisms. Most Chinese companies until the mid 1980s operated within a central planning system under which quotas for inputs and outputs were imposed on them. Child and Lu (1996:2) state that:

> Chinese managers had to involve themselves closely with the higher governmental officials upon whom they were dependent, giving rise to a system of personal rather than formalised relations and roles. Chinese managers were generally political appointees. They had to reach physical performance targets and their decisions had to take account of multiple criteria which derived from social and political considerations as well as economic requirements.

Over the period of the Chinese economic reform, most Chinese joint venture partners were subject to strong governmental influence. However, the role of government has been changing from operating as legislator to performing as market regulator. The authorities and controlling system at institutional level have also experienced tremendous changes, from a heavy vertical dependency to primary reliance on market information guidance. The laws, regulations and policies of government continue to contribute to the unique characteristics of Chinese management practice.

The second and horizontal dimension in Figure 2.1 refers to the changes in relationship in the transition from the central planning economy to the market economy. Liu (1986) mentioned that adjustment and improvement in the relations of ownership is a necessary condition for the reform of the mechanisms of economic activity. The main area of adaptation in the Chinese economic reform process has been to permit enterprise managers to develop their own strategic management thinking. Joint ventures formed in the earlier stage of Chinese reform tended to face significant challenges in terms of poor infrastructure, poor service, low-quality suppliers, insufficiency of market information, counterfeiting, copyright piracy and poor-quality human resources, which set limits to the degree of available strategic choice. Joint ventures set up in the earlier 1980s also faced a management challenge, as most Chinese partners of joint ventures tend to lack any experience of strategic and long-term thinking.

Several implications can be derived from the analysis presented in Figure 2.1. First, consolidation and further adjustment in the institutions of China's emerging socialist market economy are desirable for both Chinese and foreign partners, because an improved structure of economic governance will greatly benefit the development of joint ventures. Second, economic efficiency is encouraged by fair market competition and a reduced cost of business transactions. The indications are that joint ventures formed during the 1990s have benefited greatly from the improved efficiency of the Chinese economy, compared with joint ventures formed in the early 1980s. Although great changes have taken place over the reform period, both Chinese management practices established in the previous system of industrial governance and local ways of doing business will continue to retain some influence over joint ventures. Third, a bundle of rights that the joint venture is empowered to exercise over its assets are higher now than before. Local managers have gained autonomy as a result of the liberalisation of the Chinese economy. However, the actual changes in Chinese management practice are more likely to be slow and time-consuming. Fourth, as the government had no previous experience and practices to follow, the way to safeguard Chinese national interests has been to draw upon internationally recognised business laws, policies and regulations, which will impinge to some extent on the realisation of any foreign investment company's strategic intentions. Finally, joint ventures funded at different stages of Chinese economic development may differ in terms of foreign equity level, management commitment, human resource management, financial accounting, technical control and quality control.

Although some general Chinese management policies on joint ventures can be traced back to influence of the Chinese economic reform, analysis of the relationships between ownership and control in Chinese industry and in Sino-foreign investment projects demonstrates in a broader perspective that the Chinese investment context differs from that of most other developing countries. Policies on the ownership system in industry have their own unique characteristics, which can be traced back to the Chinese traditional way of doing business, Chinese management practices, cultural influences and the Chinese economic institutional context. Overall, as summarised and shown in Table 2.1, the relationships between ownership and control in Chinese industry and FDI projects have contributed their own degree of influence on the Chinese investment environment.

In Chinese industry, state-owned enterprises are nominally owned by the whole people. Before 1978, they had become increasingly controlled by a series of jurisdictions ranging from the central state to provinces, municipalities and local countries (Potter 1995, Warner 1996a). In 1983, the respective roles of the local party secretary and the manager were legally separated. Management had gained more freedom to purchase inputs, but in practice managers often lacked discretion over the employment of capital and labour (Warner 1986, 1993). In late 1987, the contract responsibility system was introduced. The objective was to increase productivity within the framework of continued state ownership by further separating the ownership of assets by the state from the management of the enterprise. By the early 1990s, most investment in state-owned enterprises was financed by bank loans and retained earnings. The reform gave enterprise managers the right to retain portions of the profits within their enterprise, and to make many decisions regarding production and input use. The main changes resulting from the 1993 third plenum, specifically concerning the state-owned enterprise (SOEs) sector, related to ownership. The government favours SOEs becoming corporations with issued shares. Shares in centrally controlled SOEs are to be held by

Table 2.1 Comparison of ownership and control in Chinese industry and in Sino-foreign investment projects

Chinese industry	*Ownership*	*Control*
• State enterprise	State: 'owned by whole people'	Planning authorities act on behalf of state ownership (now delegated)
• Collective enterprise (township)	Capital and non-capital resources owned by localities	Managed by the district localities
• Private	Individual	Managed by the individual
Sino-foreign investment projects		
• Wholly owned	Owned by foreign investment companies	Foreign investment companies
• Joint ventures	Shared	Boards of director act on behalf of shareholders
• Cooperative ventures	Partner	Based on the contract
• Offshore project	Individual contract rights	Managers act on the individual project contract

the state, but there is the intention of distributing them gradually to provincial and local governments, state firms and banks.

Over the past twenty years FDI has achieved great success in terms of the acquisition of technology and capital from foreign investment companies. The open-door policy has attracted foreign investors from more than 110 countries and regions. A synergistic pooling of resources between foreign and Chinese firms is obviously highly desirable from the Chinese government's point of view. The combination of Western product know-how and technical and management expertise, with the Chinese partner's local assets, management skills, existing plants, marketing expertise and knowledge of the environment can result in more efficient and productive ventures than could be achieved by either partner on its own.

However, Chinese industrial and FDI sectors have developed different ownership resourcing inputs, governance structures and reward systems. Joint venture development has taken place in the industrial sector. Figure 2.2 indicates the changes in the nature of competition in

Figure 2.2 Share of national output by types of ownership

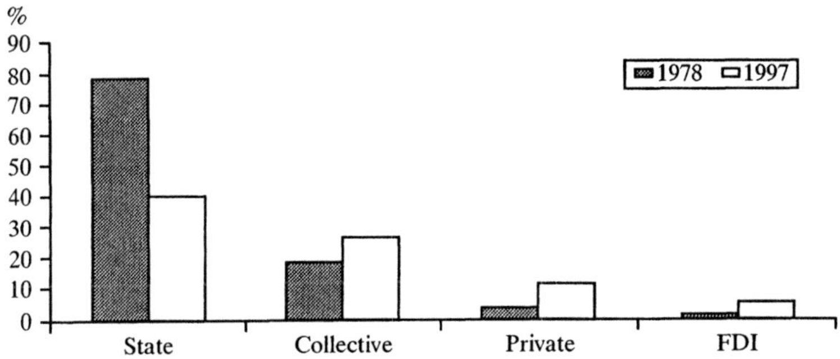

Source: 1997 *China Statistical Year Book.*

the Chinese domestic market by presenting further information on the share of national output contributed by four types of Chinese enterprise over the period from 1978 to 1997. State-owned enterprises accounted for 78 per cent of China's industrial output in 1978. By 1998, they still dominated industrial employment in China, but their share of industrial output had fallen to just over 40 per cent, and the Chinese authorities estimate it will be only 25 per cent by the year 2000. Other sectors, such as collective, private-owned and foreign-funded businesses, now make a significant and growing contribution to the national economy.

Chinese influence on joint ventures stems from the institutional setting, the changes in the ownership patterns of industry and FDI, and the role of the state in industrial governance. This influence takes a number of forms. First, the Chinese government favours joint ventures as the market entry mode to China, but wishes to direct joint ventures to priority Chinese industrial sectors and regions. With a substantial foreign ownership involved in equity joint ventures, and the large degree of autonomy granted to joint ventures, the government has tended to acquiesce in joint venture governance that has been consistent with the interests of foreign owners. Nevertheless, despite considerable control of key aspects of technology and management by foreign investing companies, joint ventures can still prove to be successful from the standpoint of the local partners. Even in a joint venture where the foreign partner controls certain key management functions, local partners can control other aspects of the business. Such factors can allow local partners to expand their control over time as they gain technical, production, marketing, financial, organisational and other competencies. Local partners will also normally receive a better financial return from a successful joint venture than they would have secured from further investment in their own state- or collectively-owned enterprises.

Second, the Chinese policies that have developed over the years of economic reform since 1978 have led to local joint venture managers gaining additional autonomy to make investment, personnel and marketing decisions. This autonomy may still be offset by changes in government laws, policies and regulations. As Chinese economic reform pursues its objective to move from hierarchical to market governance of economic transactions, authority at both governmental and intermediate institutional levels are is gradually being withdrawn from the direction of individual Chinese companies. This enables the local Chinese partner to enjoy legitimate autonomy in the making of business decisions, but it now lacks direct support from its higher authorities in terms of technology, management and resources.

Third, the industrial governance structure of state-, collective- and individual-owned business provides an insight into Chinese organisational power structure. The Chinese authorities press for more joint ventures to be established with state-owned enterprises as partners. State enterprises are viewed primarily as a response to the system of industrial governance within the Chinese informational and cultural environment. Moreover, the establishment of a joint venture still requires a substantial adjustment in rational, material and local management practices. The main characteristics still remaining in state enterprises are their relationship with higher authority, involving mutual support, reciprocal favours, resource lobbying and price bargaining.

Influence of Foreign Investment on Joint Ventures

During the early 1990s, foreign investing companies experienced a changing government attitude towards the use of the joint venture. A shift in Chinese government policy has been emerging that has moved away from requiring joint ventures as the method of FDI to permitting wholly owned subsidiaries. Nevertheless, the preference for the use of joint ventures in China is very high. The implication is that the joint venture form is better able to align Chinese policy on equity participation with foreign companies' objectives in entering the Chinese market. Campbell (1986) stated that a-third of the firms felt that an equity joint venture was the only way to secure a long-term strategy

Table 2.2 Foreign direct investment in China

	Number of contracts	*Contracted (US$)*	*Utilised (US$)*
Direct investment	47 549	82.68 bn	33.77 bn
Joint ventures	54 003	40.19 bn	n.a.
Cooperative ventures	10 445	20.30 bn	n.a.

n.a. = not available.
Sources: *China Statistical Year Book* 1997.

for the PRC. As shown in Table 2.2, only a third of joint venture contracts have been utilised. The gap between contracted investment and utilised investment is the result of several factors (Pearson 1991). First, there is an inevitable time-lag between signing and start-up, which is due in part to the Chinese bureaucracy. Second, some of the Chinese partners have encountered difficulties in obtaining even small amounts of foreign exchange to invest in equity. Third, many of the proposed joint ventures are very small, and thus more vulnerable to economic fluctuations, which can delay IJV implementation.

The joint venture remains one of the key strategic arrangements in international management. Joint ventures in China present a challenge as how to fit the endemic features of foreign management to Chinese management traditions. Much of the adjustment that has to be achieved in joint ventures with Chinese partners lies in the acquisition of local knowledge, in marketing, distribution, and in understanding the Chinese social welfare structure and personnel system. The adjustment presents a great challenge, because it is necessary to face existing Chinese management realities and to accommodate changes in the present Chinese management system, as it moves from the mind-set of Chinese socialism to the Western market-driven ideology.

Second, joint ventures in China rely heavily on technology and management expertise contributed by foreign partners, which offer them more bargaining power on IJV's operational decisions.

Significant foreign influence derived from their investments on joint ventures can be identified in institutional norms.

First, technology transfer contributed by foreign investment companies to joint ventures is tied to the nature of decision-making on strategic transactions. When Chinese and foreign partners have dissimilar orientations or interests, they appear to utilise different methods of technology transfer into joint ventures. Most foreign investment companies tend not only to commit 'hard' technology to their joint venture, but also to include 'soft' technology such as technology support and management procedures. The intention of most foreign investing companies is to gain more power and control by introducing more features oriented to the market economy and their own management practices into joint ventures. Second, joint ventures in China rely heavily on technology and management expertise contributed by foreign partners. It has been noted that many foreign investment companies have the intention of introducing the same management and technology systems into joint ventures in order to fit their structures to the parent company organisation. Third, the national distinctiveness of joint venture foreign partners is demonstrated by the differences in their preferences for particular forms of control.

OWNERSHIP RATIONALES OF FOREIGN INVESTMENT COMPANIES IN CHINA

Beamish (1985, 1993) has stated that the frequency of association with government partners is high in China. The high probability of having a government partner in China means that the foreign partner cannot make the same assumptions about the partner's profit motivation, speed of decision-making, desire for employment efficiency and so forth that would apply elsewhere. Without a radical Chinese policy shift, the very high frequency of association with government partners is likely to continue. The Chinese government has also imposed performance requirements on joint ventures with respect to employment, management, local content, exports and R&D.

Beamish and Wang (1989) compared the characteristics of joint ventures in China with joint ventures in other developing country market economies. The characteristics of Sino-foreign joint ventures derived from twelve studies, and indicated that joint ventures are created because of Chinese government pressure. They are often formed with partners from ethnically related countries. Many intended joint ventures are never implemented, and those that are implemented have often been set up for a predetermined duration. The foreign partner most commonly has a minority equity position, and those that have used split control have seen stronger performance. Overall, the rate at which joint ventures have been established has been high, but it is expected to decline in the future. Foreign partners' satisfaction with the performance of joint ventures in general is low.

Kogut and Singh (1988) categorise 228 market entries into the United States to illustrate a striking difference among countries regarding their access to joint ventures. The relationship between culture and entry choice, as an explanation of country patterns of ownership rationales, can be extended in this study. With regard to increasing numbers of ethnic Chinese, Japanese, Continental European and Anglo-Saxon (USA/UK) firms' investment in China, the ownership rationales in those groups are quite different. Chinese official government statistics point to ethnic Chinese groups as the primary source of joint venture investment in China. Child *et al.* (1990) reported that small ethnic Chinese investing companies tended to engage in manufacturing, using labour-intensive technology to produce and market standardised products at lower costs. Hong Kong, Taiwan and Singapore investment companies have joint ventures with Chinese partners anxious to obtain capital and management. Taiwan investment companies have used a number of parent firm managers to manage their joint ventures and have granted considerable autonomy to them. Hong Kong is not only in close geographic and cultural proximity to the southern region of China, such as Guangdong province and Shenzhen, but also shares with it a common language. Hong Kong business people would be expected to have a keen interest in establishing their business operations in this part of the country. Schroath *et al.* (1993) reported that Hong Kong has only 15.1 per cent of its joint ventures in the major business centres of China. The investment pattern may be explained by the fact that Hong Kong business people tend to operate efficiently in the smaller cities in southern China, as they are already armed with Cantonese language skills and formal connections. With geographical advantage and cultural closeness, a high percentage of joint ventures are formed in the south of China with ethnic Chinese such as those from Hong Kong, Taiwan and Singapore.

Japanese foreign investment companies have shown their preference for joint ventures where labour and other resources are abundant (Wei 1994). Small and medium Japanese firms accounted for about half the Japanese joint ventures in manufacturing up to the mid 1980s. The ownership pattern of Japan-based investment companies is explained particularly by the fact that their joint ventures in China have been primarily for producing fairly standardised products, such as consumer electronics. Japanese investment companies have been involved in many of the joint ventures in China, helping small and medium-sized firms by providing capital, by financing and by handling exports to and from the affiliates. By engaging in these joint ventures, Japanese investment companies share the start-up risks, while obtaining management, control, particularly in marketing, and gaining knowledge of local customs and political situations in the developing countries. In a number of cases, Japanese investment companies have had ventures with more than one local Chinese partner. Although the Japanese have used local managers, particularly in sales to maintain contacts with governments of host countries, they have generally controlled the key strategic and operational decisions of joint ventures. Schroath *et al.* (1993) indicated that about 48 per cent of Japan's investments are in the geographically proximate north-eastern region of China.

American and European foreign investment companies that are leaders in their industry, with high technology and a developed marketing-oriented approach, tend to show the same preference for majority ownership in China. Examples are Nestlé, the Swiss food manufacturing corporation, Procter & Gamble, a major US company, and Siemens, Ericsson and NEC, all multinational electronic companies. Most of the world's leading technology and marketing-oriented companies have an ownership strategy that seeks majority ownership in China. They all endeavour to deal with strong Chinese nationalism by contributing to economic development. When the Chinese authorities require that sound commercial reasons exist, these companies will accept joint ventures with local partners, but majority ownership is generally preferred in order to control key aspects of management and marketing.

OBJECTIVES OF FOREIGN AND CHINESE PARTNERS

Joint ventures are intended to foster the achievement of major objectives by both the foreign and the Chinese sides. The major objective of foreign investing companies is to enter into the large foreign market, which has growth potential, reasonable risk, and an opportunity for a satisfactory rate of return in the medium or longer term. Daniels *et al.* (1985) indicated that investing companies usually engage in foreign direct investment for two main reasons, namely either to expand their markets by exporting abroad, or else to acquire foreign resources (for example, raw materials, production efficiency and knowledge). When governments are involved in direct investment, an additional objective may be to attain some political advantage. These objectives may be pursued in turn by any of the different forms of foreign involvement. Child (1994) explained that the first constellation of reasons includes expansion into new markets, avoidance of barriers around markets, and pre-empting entrance to new markets by competitors. The latter includes gaining access to new or cheaper labour, materials or transportation routes, and responding to attractive host country investment incentives.

Foreign Objectives

Beamish *et al.* (1994) summarised four basic purposes that lead companies to the creation of joint ventures: (1) to strengthen the firm's existing business; (2) to take the firm's existing products into new markets; (3) to obtain new products that can be sold in the firm's existing markets; (4) to diversify into a new business. Foreign investment companies using joint ventures for each of these purposes will have different concerns and be looking for partners with different characteristics. Among the most important types are joint ventures formed to achieve economies of scale, joint ventures that allow the firm to acquire needed technology and know-how, and ventures that reduce the financial risk of major projects. Joint ventures formed for the latter two reasons may have the added benefit of eliminating a potential competitor from a particular product or market area.

The dominant objective for foreign investment companies wishing to invest in China has been the prospect of gaining access to what they perceive as the potentially huge Chinese market. Most foreign investors have taken a long-term view that an early presence in Chinese market might lay the basis for a substantial market share, and at the same time prevent international rivals from squeezing them out. The required scale of production must be considered in relation to the size of the Chinese market being served. Research by Yan and Gray (1994b) revealed that most joint ventures prefer to sell their products only in China because of the enormous significance of the Chinese market. Moreover, the protection of Chinese domestic industry and the avoidance of imports do not apply equally to all foreign investment companies. Some products or services introduced that were either new to China and/or used local materials have received preferential treatment. A case-study prepared by Morrison (1986) indicated that the success of Kentucky Fried Chicken (KFC) in China is due to the large market for its highly branded and promoted Western food. The very high profit achieved by KFC was helped by the ease of location of its facilities and the availability of local raw materials. Porter (1980) suggested that in an environment of short product life cycles and global competition, timing is a critical issue driving joint venture formation. First-mover advantages exist, allowing pre-emptive access to resources and the establishment of an early reliable market share, enabling exploitation of learning and experience curves.

Previous research shows that large foreign investment companies often make decisions to invest in the Chinese market in order to prevent their competitors from using high profits obtained there to invest and compete in other parts of the world, particular in the Asia-Pacific region. For example, China Hewlett Packard not only serves the Chinese domestic market, but also targets the total Asia-Pacific market. Daniels *et al.* (1985) found that by far the great part of American companies' investment in China was to establish a long-term position in a country with a potentially strong growth market and as an operating base within the Asia region. Foreign investment companies from a developed country are usually seeking market expansion because of the increasing saturation of the home market, whereas the Chinese partner typically expects to acquire new technology and to earn much-needed foreign exchange.

Joint ventures are seen as an attractive mechanism for hedging risk, because neither the Chinese nor the foreign partner bears the full risk and cost of the joint venture activity. Foreign investment companies learn how to do business in China at a reduced cost through a joint venture that gives them access to local Chinese expertise and facilities. Contractor and Lorange (1988) have identified the ways a joint venture can reduce a partner's risk. These include: (1) spreading the risk of a large project over more than one firm; (2) enabling product diversification and the faster establishment of a presence in the market, which in turn allows a more rapid payback of investment; (3) cost subaddivity – that is, the cost of the partnership being less than the cost of investment undertaken by each firm alone. A survey of over a hundred United States transnational corporations conducted in 1980–1 showed that about two-thirds of the firms were willing to enter into joint ventures in developing countries. The transnational corporation actively seeks possible joint ventures in order to take advantage of emerging opportunities, to reduce risk and to deal with strong nationalism in countries such as China. There can be cost advantages from direct investment relating to labour, land and other resources. These are particularly attractive to labour-intensive firms. Child *et al.* (1990:27) reported that:

> Many investors from Hong Kong and Macau, together with Japanese firms, have looked for more immediate profits through low-cost unskilled labour and land which had become a scarce resource in their own territories. Many of the joint ventures from Hong Kong, Taiwan, Singapore and Macau have been in small, low technology processing and assembly plants. In keeping with the greater emphasis of these ethnic Chinese investors on short term profits and their limited technological commitment, the average contract term of joint ventures with Hong Kong is shorter.

Hong Kong and Macau partners tend to have a shorter-term commitment to joint ventures in China than do Western and Japanese investors. The availability of cheap labour, raw materials and adequate production standards may allow this type of joint venture to carry smaller inventories and spend less on promotion. It may also permit considerably greater flexibility in shifting funds, taxes and profits from their own country to China. Advantages of vertical integration may accrue to such joint ventures through supply-oriented investments in other nearby countries.

The willingness of foreign investors to commit capital and transfer technology to China, and to use local resources, is quite compatible with Chinese objectives. The Chinese government frequently encourages direct investment inflows by offering tax concessions or a wide variety of other subsidies. Direct assistance incentives include tax holidays, accelerated depreciation, low-interest loans, loan guarantees, subsidised energy or transport and the construction of roads to serve the facility. Such incentives obviously affect the comparative cost of production among countries, and attract companies to invest at one particular location to serve the market. The foreign desire to produce for the Chinese market may present few problems if the joint venture's products are new to the country and/or if the market is growing rapidly. Equally, many foreign companies are willing to use China as a production base from which to export. The foreign partner's intention to safeguard its proprietary technology, to control the management of its investment and to import components or materials could clearly conflict with Chinese interests. Access to the Chinese market can also be the cause of serious dispute when this threatens the position of Chinese producers.

Child (1994) indicates that foreign investing companies often wish to have access to China's domestic market and that the Chinese may desire joint ventures to facilitate the access of their Chinese parents to international markets. This has in practice been the most fundamental difference of interest between the partners participating in Sino-foreign joint ventures. Disputes are also endemic about the quality standards offered by local suppliers and achieved by the joint venture as a potential export producer, and about the foreign restriction of access to proprietary technology that had therefore to be imported or paid for through royalties. A major conflict of objectives occurs when a foreign investment company's striving for global integration of its business is at odds with the local Chinese enterprise's aim to maximise its profits or earn a target rate of return on their investments. Global integration means that foreign investing companies strive to integrate their joint venture within their systems of enterprises around the world in production, finance, marketing and management. Since joint ventures in China are generally a small part of the total international business of most foreign investment companies, the foreign parent company may not grant a high priority to them in resource allocation, management and technological support. A joint venture commonly represents a commitment of capital, management and ongoing support, and the Chinese side expects this commitment from the foreign partner in order to have a successful business. Serious conflicts can emerge when the Chinese partner finds that the foreign investment company does not grant the required high priority to the joint venture, and does not commit sufficient resources and effort.

Chinese Objectives

Contractor and Lorange (1988) point out that a joint venture may be used to bring together complementary skills and talents in high-technology industries. Most joint ventures in China are with state-owned enterprises (Beamish 1993), and the objectives of the Chinese authorities are likely to be achieved by the fusing of these complementary skills to foster economic development. The fundamental Chinese criteria for entering into foreign joint ventures are (1) to absorb foreign capital, advanced technology and management skills, and (2) to gain better access to export markets. The favourable terms granted to foreign-funded enterprises with advanced technology and a high export capability clearly reflect these objectives. Yan and Gray (1996), drawing on their case-studies as well as previous research on joint ventures, compiled a comprehensive list of objectives held by Chinese partners. These are to acquire advanced technology; earn a profit; acquire management expertise; earn foreign exchange through exporting; substitute local manufacturing for imports; pursue business growth; and develop technology for Chinese suppliers or users.

The objectives of Chinese partners with the very highest-priorities are to acquire or to learn advanced technology and to acquire management expertise. The acquisition of advanced technology and management expertise and the promotion of exports are particularly important when the Chinese partner is a state-owned enterprise. Chinese state enterprises tend to be active partners in joint ventures in highly capital-intensive industries that use complex technology such as electronics. State enterprises may have an ability to contribute local capital and raise funds from internal and international lending institutions. The general managerial responsibilities and the support of the government can be assumed. Foreign investment companies have provided primarily important technological know-how, engineering, technical training and specialised management. The results from Li and Shenkar's (1996) research indicated that state-owned local firms were more likely seek transfer of management skills from foreign partners than were non-state firms.

However, there were no significant differences between state and non-state enterprises in seeking the transfer of marketing skills and technology from foreign partners. The lack of differences in technology may be due to the fact that both state and non-state local firms are seeking technology, so that there is little variation in this dimension between the two organisational forms.

Technology transfer into China involves several major steps relating to content and time-scale: identifying barriers to technology transfer, establishing operational functions and identifying problem-solving tools (Guo and Akroyd 1996). Daniels *et al.* (1985) investigated eleven Sino-US joint ventures established between 1979 and 1983. They noted that in some cases foreign firms were unwilling to transfer technology to China without securing some control through an equity holding in the operation. From the Chinese point of view, technology transfer through a joint venture provides assistance and the prospect of learning. An advantage of technology transfer to China is that faster market entry is possible if the testing completed by the foreign investment companies is accepted by the other Chinese partner's territories. An important consideration with respect to technology transfer agreements is that they not only provide a right to a process but also allow the right to a territory. Contractor and Lorange (1988) stated that marketing or territorial rights are the dominant strategic issues behind the formation of joint ventures.

Chinese joint ventures partners that are collectively or privately owned tend to regard profitability as their most important goal. Most small and medium Chinese enterprises tend to regard joint ventures as a means of 'sharing risk' and 'enjoying a three-year tax holiday' (Child *et al.* 1997). Pearson (1991) noted that government officials have been keen to show quick results from joint ventures within their purview, since profitable projects bring in tax revenues and prestige to the municipality. Many state-owned enterprises, which became partners in foreign joint ventures, were not in sound financial health, and a speedy attainment of profitability was also welcomed by the Chinese authorities as means of underwriting such enterprises. Chinese managers have often been motivated to use a foreign joint venture to defend current positions against competition that is too strong for one firm to withstand. For example, the Beijing Yili biscuit-making factory set up a joint venture with the American Nabisco Company. Its main objective was to protect its product market in Beijing. Bei Bing Yang is a soft-drinks factory with a very good market reputation in Beijing. As many foreign beverages such as Pepsi-Cola, Coca-Cola and 7-Up are 'pouring' into Beijing's market, the only option for the Bei Bing Yang company was to form a joint venture to survive against this market competition.

IS CHINA DIFFERENT FROM THE WEST?

In 1979, the Chinese government began encouraging joint venture investment as part of its wider open-door policy. The joint venture is viewed as an important vehicle for integrating China into the world economy, securing a stable supply of raw materials, improving export opportunities, and strengthening economic relations with the world economy. China has provided a fascinating panorama of experiences in the treatment of joint venture investment as part of the expansion of its economy, technology and management, and government intervention has played a critical catalytic role in adjusting the relationships between ownership and control of joint ventures. The encouragement of foreign joint ventures is an integral part of Chinese industrial strategy, so the Chinese authorities intend to provide an attractive investment environment, and are developing the necessary institutional arrangements to meet the development of joint ventures in China. At the same time, the government has a number of concerns regarding capital and technology inflow, which it fears may direct resources at the expense of domestic national industrial development. It perceives that the development of joint ventures creates new competition for domestic Chinese enterprises. The government has gradually lost its control and influence in certain business sectors, even in some areas of national strategic importance. Difficulties in monitoring foreign equity investment in China have led to a loss of control over state property.

China remains officially a political and economic system based on socialist ownership. The institutional context of the management process in China is currently based on a mix of multi-tiered state governance structures and deep-rooted traditional Confucian ideology. There is a substantial difference between the Western concept of ownership and that conventionally implemented in China. Child (1994) stated that the Chinese concept of ownership is appreciably more ambiguous and is subject to political and ideological considerations rather than economic and legal ones. This implies that the overall system of governance is based on the ideological principles of socialism, articulated by the hierarchical structure of the party, while the Chinese notion of ownership signifies that state-owned industrial property is held by the ruling authority, so that a fundamental problem with the Chinese situation is that of identifying any specific owners to whom the managers of industrial assets should be accountable.

The relationship between ownership and control of joint ventures has taken on a new aspect in relation to their development. Joint venture ownership rights gain a new dimension in terms of inputs by the Chinese owning company itself and the regulatory framework governing relations between the Chinese companies and their higher authorities. The critical resources and competencies contributed by the Chinese side are established in a way, that reflects China's unique industrial governance system, namely the mix of state, collective and privately owned business. When joint ventures are formed, an individual Chinese parent company often faces problems that include (1) how to determine the use of its assets, (2) how to protect the use of the investment, and (3) how to benefit from the return. This contrasts with the ownership logic of Western business corporations.

Child (1994) argued that Western thinking offers concepts and theoretical perspectives that can be used to analyse Chinese management and organisation. With regard to the application to China of a

Western analytical framework of ownership and control, the studies conducted by Beamish (1993), Yan (1993) and Pan (1996) indicate that some new variables need to be incorporated. These include the level of state ownership of the Chinese partners, the variable characteristics of joint venture location in China, and the limited duration of joint venture contracts. Such characteristics are unique to joint venture investments in China.

The Chinese economic reform and the development of a business system have created an economy in transition from a central planning economy to a market economy. The restructuring of Chinese industrial governance during the economic reform provides a reasonable investment environment for foreign investment companies to gain foreign control in joint venture management. In order to differentiate China from the Western context with respect to the relationships between the objectives, ownership, control and performance of joint ventures, three main issues may be discussed, as follows.

First, as China is a state-dominated economy, government policies have played an important role in shaping the development of joint ventures. The Chinese government's laws, regulations and policies for joint ventures since 1978 have played a significant role, both towards increasing the basis of bargaining power for the local partner, particularly where this is a local state-owned company *and* for using joint ventures as a means of adjusting Chinese industrial structure and priorities. Chinese government influence in industrial governance is one of the country's unique historical characteristics. The government authorities continue to feel that they always have the right to intervene in business in order to meet their own requirements. The part the government plays over joint ventures in China places it at the boundary between intervention and market-forces. In theory, joint ventures are encouraged to exercise free choice over the establishment of a strategic market presence, over new market expansion and over the improvement of business performance in response to competition or market opportunities. However, the government retains the right of final approval of joint ventures in the light of the balance of its strategic priorities within national policy.

Second, management in Chinese state-owned enterprise can be regarded as typical of Chinese industrial management practices, because more than half of the Chinese enterprises are state-owned companies. This is viewed as another unique characteristic of managing joint ventures in the Chinese context. With regard to Chinese organisational structure, Child (1994:295) reported that the Chinese state-owned enterprise may be termed 'an implicitly structured organisation'. Its authority is highly concentrated through vertical dependency relations, while the structuring of its activities is limited and imprecise in terms of procedures and, definitions of responsibility. To operate a joint venture via a management system so 'implicit' and 'personalised' in nature will generate conflicts with Western foreign investing companies, which prefer to operate in a more formalised and systematic manner. As management and technology expertise are likely to be located primarily within the foreign companies, most foreign investment companies intend to contribute technology and management with both 'hard' and 'soft' packages. The foreign investment company's may intent to achieve control over IJV's management at operational and strategic level. It appears, therefore, that the realisation of foreign and Chinese strategic intentions may give rise to problems of joint venture management.

Third, Chinese state enterprise management still operates within an imperfect legal framework and an underdeveloped market information system. This will continue to generate some substantial difficulties in terms of market efficiency. The typical Chinese approach to dealing with such problems is to lay down a good network of relationships. Obviously, this is a different way of managing from that typical of Western countries, despite their use of some networking (Nohria and Eccles, 1992). Certain features of the Chinese context are regarded as providing the right environment for foreign investing companies. These include a positive attitude by local government to joint venture development, rapid economic growth, a large domestic market and infrastructural improvement. China can therefore be considered as an attractive, if challenging, opportunity for foreign investors.

Finally, because energy, telecommunications, water and transportation in China can be deemed 'bottleneck' industries, joint ventures there are still confronted with resource deficiencies. Most Chinese enterprises are highly dependent upon external resource suppliers. In this situation, actions taken by Chinese managers tend to aim at lobbying and soliciting government support to reduce their resource dependence. Central and local government may therefore be regarded as an important resource-enabling network for joint ventures located in China, and frustration has been expressed in many joint ventures at the control exercised by the external government bureaucracy, at regional resource regulation and at transactional inefficiencies.

SUMMARY

China is an investment environment in which joint ventures require compromises to be reached between the foreign and Chinese approaches to management. As the main Chinese objectives are the acquisition of foreign technology and management expertise, the Chinese authorities appear to be content to permit the introduction of Western management systems into joint ventures. The Chinese government favours the development of joint ventures with foreign investing companies, and indicates this preference with economic incentives and relevant FDI policies. The restructuring of Chinese economic reform provides an investment environment that can justify the relationship between the resources provided by foreign owners for forming a joint venture and the control that is derived from those inputs committed by foreign partners.

3 Theories Relevant to Ownership and Control

INTRODUCTION

The relationship between the ownership and control of firms has received attention for many years. Ownership is a combination of rights and responsibilities with respect to a specific asset. In some cases, those rights and responsibilities are more clearly defined than in others. Renner (1904) defines the institution of property as the set of legal imperatives relating to the power of possession of social objects. Scott (1979) states that ownership has a dual character, as both a legal relation and a social one. The legal relation of ownership comprises an owner's all-embracing legal power over a social object. The social relation of ownership refers to the actually effective power of possession, which may diverge from the legal relation of ownership. Renner argues that effective possession can be structured in a way that does not correspond to prevailing legal forms and that, in such a situation, rights over objects become relations of social power.

The argument can be extended to the study of joint ventures. The parent companies are legal owners of the means of production of a joint venture, but the actual power to determine the use of these means is derived from the joint venture board, which may act with some degree of independence. The social relations of the joint venture are established by the partners' provision of resources and competencies, but these can become dissociated from the partners' ownership rights to safeguard their respective interests. Berle and Means (1932) argue that the traditional logic of property involves two aspects: the right to determine the use of the asset and the right to benefit from its use.

> When the two aspects of property are dissociated it is possible to distinguish 'nominal ownership', which is the right to receive revenue as a return for risking one's wealth by investing in a company, from 'effective ownership', which is the ability to control the corporate assets. Thus, it is necessary to go beyond mere legal forms to the 'economic and social background of law'.
>
> (Berle and Means 1932:339)

Scott (1985) suggests that the link between legal owners and the locus of effective possession is no longer direct or straightforward. Legal ownership of company stock provides for 'economic ownership', the right to benefit from corporate activities, and this is gradually separated from 'technical ownership' which refers to actually using the means of production. The separation of ownership and control in the large modern corporation was first recognised by Marx (Bottomore and Rubel 1956). He noted a separation of management functions from ownership in mid-nineteenth century British joint-stock companies. Later writers have expressed special concern that the owners of business assets might lose control over their use to executive managers. They identified the amount of stock required to prevent this to be a minimum of 20 per cent. Larner (1970), Burch (1972) and Scott and Hughes (1976) have suggested that, with a highly dispersed shareholding in a unified firm, it is possible to exert control by owning 5 per cent or even less. The separation of ownership and control focused on the supposed weakness of ownership because of its increasingly scattered distribution (Child 1969, Scott 1985). The fear was that the interests of shareholders and managers might have diverged in terms of a company's strategic objectives. Owners seek growth of their investment, while managers may favour growth of the organisation (Marris 1964).

More recently, the relationship between ownership and control has taken on a new aspect, with the rapid growth in the number of joint ventures. The ownership of joint ventures is typically concentrated, whereby ownership is shared between two, or a few, partners, each of whom will, in most cases, be a legally constituted company rather than an individual. In the joint venture context the rights and responsibilities of ownership gain a new dimension, with reference to the different forms of resources made by the owning companies. The legal form of ownership in a joint venture provides the general framework within which the range of ownership resources are committed by the partners. Strategic control over the venture is mediated through local legal institutions and social relations. The effective possession of critical resources and expertise by the joint venture's parent companies may be constructed in a way that does not correspond to the prevailing legal form.

An owning company faces the problem of protecting the use and integrity of its investments when collaborating with a joint venture partner. It therefore has a strategic motive for seeking a certain level of control through legal rights and social relations. When the two aspects of property rights and social relations are not dissociated, it is possible to distinguish the range of ownership resourcing that provides the rights, allowing the owning company to achieve its strategic priorities from its joint venture. This may extend to the establishment of a strategic market position and the securing of economic development incentives as an additional return, contrasting with the traditional logic of 'nominal ownership', which focused on the right to receive revenue as a return for risking wealth by investing in a company.

In establishing joint ventures to exploit complementarities between themselves, the owning companies provide resources, skills and knowledge additional to their equity contribution. An equity joint venture is defined as a legal business organisation. Those assets that are within the possession of partner firms have an intrinsic value, and they amount to ownership resources with property rights. The range of ownership resources conveys control and influence over a joint venture, both through the formal terms of any contracts by which the resources are provided and through the less formal influence that derives from the partners' possession of resources and capabilities. The partners' objectives are more or less reflected in the management of the joint venture. The partners' capital, technological and management resources may be used by the management of the joint venture as a power base to support the pursuit of its objectives. These considerations suggest that the objective priorities of the partners when addressing equity joint ventures can be unlike those of a unitary corporate enterprise. Table 3.1 summarises the main features of the relationship between ownership and control in both conventional unitary corporate enterprises and joint ventures.

This chapter is divided into two sections. The first is concerned with the concepts of ownership and control; to the traditional view of ownership, the author makes certain refinements as it applies to joint ventures. The second section reviews seven generally accepted theories relevant to the relationship between ownership and control, namely ownership form: international business theories, agency theory: principal and agent relationship, ownership transactions: transaction cost economics, bargaining between owners: bargaining power theory, OLI Advantages: the ownership, location and internalisation model, resource-specific ownership advantages: resource dependence theory, and key, non-substitutable resources: strategic contingencies theory. Each of these theoretical contributions has some relevance to the search for insight into how the ownership and control of international joint ventures are configured.

Table 3.1 The main features of ownership and control in corporate enterprises and joint ventures

	Ownership context	*Control consequence*
Unitary corporate enterprise		
Organisation	Evolved largely according to task requirements	Identifiable single management hierarchy.
Objective	Objectives set up by the shareholders	Objectives implemented by agents, i.e. managers.
Equity	May be many shareholders, who do not necessarily provide non-equity capital and non-capital resources	Shareholders' control weakened if the equity is scattered and they do not provide other critical resources.
Resources	Secured mainly from the market	Control consequences may be limited if a wide range of substitute sources is available.
Revenue distribution	To shareholders	Wide range of distribution according to equity share.
Joint venture		
Organisation	Identified by the partners according to negotiated contract	Inter-organisational characteristics and often international management system, with some network characteristics.
Objective	Objectives established by partners	Controlled by partners via joint venture board and active involvement in joint venture management.
Equity	Divided into few shareholdings	Critical resources likely to be provided by partners.
Resource	Capital, and non-capital resources provided mainly by partners, at least in early years	Likely to be significant, owing to the small number of resource-providing owners.
Revenue distribution	To partners	Allocation according to equity share and, sometimes, according to contracts by which additional resources are provided.

JOINT VENTURES: A NEW CONTEXT FOR OWNERSHIP AND CONTROL

THE CONCEPT OF OWNERSHIP

Monks and Minow in *Corporate Governance* (1995) state that ownership has been an issue since the dawn of human history. Disputes over property appear throughout the Bible. In late eighteenth century, the Western notion of property involved a direct relationship between the owner and the object owned. The right of individual ownership of property was deemed important because it assured citizens protection in their independence from the centralised authority. In formal terms, ownership is the legal possession of assets. It is normally defined in terms of three fundamental rights which are (1) the right to possess an asset and/or its financial value, (2) the right, to exercise influence over the use of the asset, and (3) the right to information about the status of what is owned (Pierce *et al.* 1991:125). Other rights are those to transfer assets and to receive an income or return from them. Three categories of ownership rights are commonly illustrated in the literature. The first is the user right, defined in terms of the potential uses of an asset; this includes the right to transform or destroy an asset. Second the right to earn income from an asset and specific the contract over the terms from an asset with other individuals. Third is the right to transfer permanently to another party the ownership rights over an asset, or to sell an asset.

These three fundamental ownership rights apply to joint ventures in ways that are illustrated in Table 3.2. The dimensions of ownership rights in the context of joint ventures are constituted as follows. First are the rights associated with the range of resources valued as equity investments committed by the owning companies. Second is the structure of a contract for the range of resources provided by the partners on terms that usually depend on the local legal system, social customs and the technical attributes of the assets involved. Third is the configuration of a range of resources provided on a non-contractual basis, and which represent the level of commitment by the owning companies to their joint ventures. Partners in joint ventures provide resources, skills and knowledge additional to their equity contribution, which should, in turn, enhance the effectiveness of the control they possess as a formal right of ownership. The ownership of joint-stock companies is legally vested in their equity, with owners' rights being exercised through the appointment of directors. These points are now

Table 3.2 Control potential of equity, contractual and non-contractual ownership resourcing of joint ventures

Ownership resources	*Control potential*
Equity Capital	Right to representation on the board of directors. Occupancy of key managerial positions. Parent companies rely on equity share to gain voting control, in the expectation that they will thereby achieve effective control of joint venture activities as a whole. Equity ownership normally provides the right to exit from a joint venture, and equity commitment may be limited by a fixed-length joint venture contract.
Contractual resources	Control over designated areas of product and process technology, and over activities related to other contracted resources. A parent company might be able to rely on its technical superiority and other areas of competence, formally recognised in service and similar contracts, as a means of guaranteeing participation in the management of joint venture operations. However, laws governing foreign direct investment may be inadequate to regulate non-equity contractual forms of foreign involvement.
Non-contractual resources	A partner's possession of 'soft technologies', advanced management systems, training and HRM expertise, and strong organisational cultures provides a further basis for exercising control, through the shaping of employees' activities and values. It also supplies the legitimacy of 'superior expertise' for that partner's managerial authority. Acceptance of a partner's right to authority may further derive from the goodwill attaching to its willingness to invest in the host country and to demonstrate commitment to the joint venture. Trust placed in one partner by another, and/or by joint venture staff, may also lead them to accept control by the partner.

elaborated with reference to the relevant conclusions or observations of previous studies, which are summarised in Table 3.3.

Ownership Rights Associated with Equity-related Resources

Renner (1904:53, 73–4) states that

> the legal institution of ownership right is that set of legal imperatives which regulate the 'detention', or access to, social objects, and that a particularly important part of the law of property concerns the detention of the objects involved in the production of goods and services.

The essential feature of ownership rights in any joint venture is the set of laws and regulations that are set by the government of the locality where the joint venture is sited. These laws may cover ownership rights such as the total capital investment permitted, the proportion of the equity that can be held by partners, and the constitution of any joint venture's board. Although the allocation of the joint venture's dividend, net income and operation appear to be managed by the partners, government agencies can still play an important role in enforcing ownership rights by playing on the role of law and governing as guarantors and enforcers of formal ownership rights (Zeitlin 1974, Blodgett 1991). Obviously, the value of ownership equity rights also depends on the cost of enforcing those rights. Yan and Gray (1994b, 1996) regard equity as the provision of a 'capital resource' to a joint venture by its partner companies, typically finance and sometimes land and buildings. They distinguish between this type of resources and what they categorise as non-capital resources, including technology, management expertise, local knowledge, raw material procurement channels, product distribution and marketing channels, and global service support'. This distinction is important, because assets such as technology, market channels and management expertise have become increasingly recognised as ownership factors, especially in the formation of IJVs, where they may constitute more important complementary assets than purely financial contributions. The present author categorises the 'non-capital' resources as being either contractual or non-contractual in their basis, and as including the following items: product design, production technology, land, existing plant, new/existing equipment and facilities, brand names/trade marks, goodwill, and marketing support and distribution.

Table 3.3 Theoretical and empirical contributions to the study of ownership in joint ventures

Category of ownership resourcing	*Theoretical and empirical contribution*
1. Equity capital	1.1 Yan and Gray (1994a, 1996) regard equity as the provision of a 'capital resource' to a joint venture by its partner companies, typically finance and sometimes land and buildings. They categorise technology, management expertise, local knowledge, raw material procurement channels, and product distribution as 'non-capital resources. 1.2 The author points out that joint ventures may also value technology, land and plant as equity, which enables the partner providing these factors to have an advantage in its rights of control over joint venture management.
2. Contractual resources	2.1 Contracts expressing technological property rights include patents and licence agreements, and they are particularly important in the case of China (Guo and Ackroyd 1996). 2.2 Contractual control can avoid the costs of managerial supervision by (a) permitting the participation of local investors, who probably have an absolute advantage in the knowledge of local conditions and (b) leaving the foreign investing companies free to meet their own objectives through contract-based expansion (Dunning and McQueen 1981).
3. Non-contractual resources	3.1 Non-contractual ownership resources have assumed increasing importance, because an important key to success now lies in the knowledge and skill of managing complex interdependencies within and across joint venture boundaries and in the ability to manage multi-cultural units (Ohmae 1993; Nonaka and Takeuchi 1995). 3.2 The provision of non-contractual resources normally reflects a high level of commitment to an joint venture on the part of the parent company (Beamish 1988; Cullen *et al.* 1995)

Contractual Resources

'Non-capital resources' are those provided to a joint venture by its owners on the basis of formal contracts include technological know-how, management systems, management services and training. These may be termed 'contractual resources'. (Yan and Gray (1994a) make a distinction between 'capital and non-capital resources'. The present author makes a further distinction within the 'non-capital' category, between resourcing provided by owners on a contractual and on a non-contractual basis.) The structure of joint venture contracts depends on the legal system and the social customs, and on the technical attributes of the assets involved in the exchange by partners. The more detailed the legal framework, the more specific are the written contracts. The extent to which a joint venture contract stipulates the various dimensions depends on costs and benefits at the margin, when the rights to an asset by the partners are exchanged.

With a particular reference to the costs incurred in contractual equity joint ventures, Rugman (1982) mentioned that the negotiation of a contractual agreement for a non-standardised product is a very difficult task, but nevertheless found that 'these contractual arrangements are of increasing importance in international production and marketing'. Dunning and McQueen (1981) explain that contractual control can avoid these costs by enabling local investors who probably have an absolute advantage in the knowledge of local conditions to handle their product and service promotion. This leaves foreign investing companies free to meet their own objectives through contract-based expansion and control. Similarly, high external environmental uncertainty tends to make the writing and enforcement of equity contracts more expensive (Anderson and Weitz 1986). Citing the case of a joint venture in the airline industry, Hall and Eppink (1992) indicate that airlines combine through contractual resources to optimise the utilisation of available capacity. For example, when two passenger-carriers agree to merge their coverage to target a broader customer base, the blocked-space agreement enables them to remain as competitors when selling their seats. The agreement between the partners provides them with market coverage.

The distinction of input provision on a contractual basis has important theoretical implications for the bases on which resource providers may exercise control within joint ventures. The contracts made typically convey formalised rights to exclusive control over the use of, and/or benefit from, assets including technology and brands. Guo and

Ackroyd (1996) note that technological property contract includes patents and licence agreements. These are particularly important in the case of China. Such rights derive from the provision of resources to a joint venture by its owners, and hence they may be termed 'contractual resources'.

Non-contractual Resources

With the development of joint ventures in particular, and of globalisation in general, non-contractual ownership resources have assumed increasing importance as a key to success, which now lies in the knowledge and skill of managing complex interdependencies within and across joint venture boundaries, and in the ability to manage multicultural units (Ohmae 1993, Nonaka and Takeuchi 1995). The provision of non-contractual resourcing normally reflects a high level of commitment to a joint venture on the part of the parent company (Beamish 1988, Cullen *et al.* 1995). These resources are likely to give rise to *de facto* ownership rights, through claims to expertise and also through the goodwill and cultural capital they generate. The partner that is able to accrue goodwill, trust and the loyalty of joint venture personnel adds significant value to its original equity.

In joint ventures, organisational capability is enhanced by the replication of knowledge on an experiential basis with the partner – a process of learning-by-doing. Knowledge and skill transfer occur not so much at the top management level but rather as the result of daily interaction among employees at the operational level (Hamel *et al.* 1989). A joint venture is especially suited to knowledge transfer. This may provide scope for learning and the accumulation of capability (Hamel 1991). The partners in a joint venture can extend those limits outwards by learning and building up trust, and through providing non-contractual resourcing to the joint venture at its formation. From the organisational capability perspective, the logic for joint venture formation can be focused on knowledge flows within the partners' relationship. Joint ventures provide the structural mechanisms and the alignment of incentives for greater integration and sharing of knowledge (Davies 1977, Killing 1983, Osborn and Baughn 1990). Joint ventures generate exposure to different routines, through the exchange of personnel and other forms of interaction. This exposure to, and experience with, the routines of other organisations can facilitate a higher level of learning between the joint venture partners. The provision of non-contractual resourcing to joint ventures is one way to build up a partner's motivation and commitment. This is because it signifies goodwill.

The distinction between ownership resource provision on a contractual and on a non-contractual basis is important, because assets such as technology, market channels and management expertise have become increasingly recognised as ownership factors, especially in the formation of joint ventures, where they may constitute more important complementary assets than purely financial contributions (Yan 1994, Yan *et al.* 1995). Dunning (1993) points out that such factors amount to 'ownership-specific advantages' in the circumstances of forming a joint venture. Technological assets and brand names are sometimes valued as contributions to equity share, but not necessarily so. A comprehensive concept of ownership, applicable to joint ventures, would therefore incorporate equity and contractual and non-contractual resourcing. The distinction between these three categories is likely to be a significant one for the understanding of joint venture control, because of the different nature and scope of the power that stems from each of them.

In summary, equity share, and especially a majority share, confers certain legal rights to determine the overall direction of a joint venture. When non-capital resources are provided through contracts, these can specify rights as to the use and possibly the management of such resources. When non-capital resources are provided on a non-contractual basis, they may still confer powers to the providing company, because intrinsically they create a dependency on its expertise, and/or because they generate the moral authority that derives from the way they evidence commitment.

CONTROL

Control is multi-dimensional. It plays an important role in the capacity of a firm to achieve its goals. French and Raven (1959), Emerson (1962), Ouchi (1977) and Pfeffer and Salancik (1978) have undertaken path-breaking work in formulating the concept of control. This refers to the process by which one person or group influences to varying degrees, the behaviour of another through the use of power and authority. French and Raven (1959) define 'social power' in terms of influence by which they mean a change that party A can bring in party B. The definition of control and influence in terms of 'power' can be extended to the partners in the context of joint venture. In simple terms, the definition or expression of power can be stated in terms of the ability of a party to influence events or people's actions. The main purpose of control and influence in the context of joint ventures stems from the desire of each parent company to ensure that the benefits it seeks are actually realised.

Emerson (1962:32) specifies the equality or inequality in power in terms of the notion of reciprocity in power dependency relations. He argues that:

> two directional relationships are involved. First, the dependence of actor A upon actor B is directly proportional to A's motivational investment in goals mediated by B, and inversely proportional to the availability of those goals to A outside of the A–B relation.

The definition of 'goals' or objectives of the partners to a joint venture refers to their desired return on investment, and/or the market share, growth and other results consciously sought through the partnership. The availability of such goals, or objectives, outside the relationship refers to alternative avenues of goal achievement. The costs associated with such alternatives must be included in any assessment of dependency. As the joint venture is a cooperative organisation, the ability of an owner to exercise control will be a function not only of the power and influence it possesses over its managers, but also a function of the power and influence it enjoys in relation to the other owner or owners. All this contrasts with the classical debate on ownership and control, which focused mainly on the relationship between owners and their managers, but not on the relationship between the owners or that between owner and host governments.

Other considerations that discussion on control in joint ventures has identified are (1) its multi-dimensional nature, (2) the fact that it has a cost associated with it and (3) national differences in control preferences. Theoretical and empirical contributions to the study of control in joint ventures are summarised in Table 3.4.

Three Dimensions of Control Identified

Mechanisms

The mechanisms of control are those formal and informal organisational processes through which control over a joint venture is exercised by one or more of its parent companies. Friedman *et al.* (1971) suggest that control is not a strict and automatic consequence of ownership, but

Table 3.4 Theoretical and empirical contributions to the study of control in joint ventures

Control	*Theoretical and empirical contribution*
1. Mechanisms	1.1. Friedman and Beguin (1971) suggested that effective control such as right of veto, representation in management bodies and special agreements relate to either technology or management.
	1.2. Tomlinson (1970) indicated that firms could rely on majority voting rights to achieve management control of JV.
	1.3. Formalisation, targeting systems, cultural control, personal supervision Child (1984).
	1.4. Management accounting: Emmanuel and Otley (1985), Macintosh (1994).
	1.5. Organisational culture (Edstrom 1977, Ouchi, 1979)
2. Extent	2.1. The parent companies exercise control over the joint venture or permit general manager to enjoy autonomy (Lyles and Reger 1993).
	2.2. Killing (1983) studied control in 37 joint ventures from developed countries and concluded that they were easier to manage than others, if one parent was willing to play a passive role.
3. Focus	3.1. Schaan (1983) found that owning companies might choose to exercise control over a relatively wider or narrower scope of the joint venture's activities.
	3.2. Host government policies can reflect a focused approach to the control of joint ventures (Pearson 1991, Child 1994). In China, governmental control has concentrated on the maintenance of foreign exchange balances by joint ventures and personnel policies (Pearson 1991, Child 1994).

Table 3.4 (continued)

Control	*Theoretical and empirical contribution*
4. Control not costless	4.1. Bleek and Ernst (1993) reported that over-control by parent companies may inhibit the flexibility which their joint venture needs in order to develop within its own competitive environment.
	4.2. Ohmae (1993) stated managers must overcome the popular conception that total control increases the chances of success.
5. Cultural control preference	5.1. Multinational companies are interested in promoting corporate culture to improve control, co-ordination, and integration of their foreign subsidiaries (Schneider 1988).
	5.2. Child *et al.* (1994) stated that US, German and Japanese foreign owners prefer to introduce different managerial philosophies into their international joint venture, of which control is an important element.

that a variety of mechanisms are available to firms for exercising effective control, including the right of veto, representation in management bodies, and particular contracts that are related to either technology or management. A parent firm might be able to rely on its technical superiority, managerial skills and access to domestic or international distribution networks as means for guaranteeing participation in the management of the joint venture (Gullander 1976, Glaister 1995). This means of exercising managerial control can be found in the nomination of one of the parent firm's managers, either as the joint venture general manager or as a key functional manager. Tomlinson (1970) indicates that firms can rely on majority voting rights to achieve effective management control of joint venture activities. Yan (1994) states that implementation of government regulations on ownership structure in China usually enables local government authorities to gain some degree of control over joint ventures with foreign partners. Child (1984) classifies four mechanisms of control, including personal supervision, formalisation, targeting and creating positive attitudes. Emmanuel and Otley (1985) and Macintosh (1994) indicate that management accounting is used as one method of control in joint ventures. Similarly, organisational culture can be used as an 'indirect control mechanism' for joint ventures, as it encourages employees to share the values and behavioural norms advanced by one or more of the owning partners. Such control relies on informal communication, extensive training, socialisation and frequent personal visits between parent companies and joint ventures culture (Edstrom and Galbraith 1977, Ouchi 1979, Milliman *et al.* 1991).

Schaan (1983) classifies several control mechanisms over joint ventures: the joint venture board of directors, formal agreements, the appointment of key personnel, the joint venture planning process, and reporting relationships. He has made a significant contribution to the understanding of joint venture control by identifying two broad forms of control. Positive controls are mechanisms for parent companies to promote certain joint venture behaviours. Negative control mechanisms tend to be imposed by parent companies to stop or to prevent the joint venture from implementing certain activities or decisions. Schaan (1983) found that positive control was most often exercised through informal mechanisms such as staffing, participation in the planning process and reporting relationships. Negative control relies mainly on formal procedures, approval by parent companies and the use of the joint venture board of directors. Otterbeck (1981) has pointed out that administrative systems are introduced for coordination, performance evaluation and decision making. The desire for control leads owning companies to try to impose their own administrative procedures and policies upon a joint venture.

Some mechanisms of control may be specific to developing countries, such as China (Pearson 1991). First, restrictions on ownership equity structure can be enforced by host government policy. Implementation of favourable policies by government in certain regions or the specification of industrial priorities can lead to local partners gaining some bargaining advantage in negotiations to form a joint venture. Second, recruitment and social welfare policies that are introduced by the government usually have significant effects on coordination, integration and control within joint ventures. As those policies will provide some baseline for compensation and employment security, it should motivate Chinese managers and employees to integrate their existing systems with those of the foreign partner. Third, local partners seem to have opportunities to exercise a monopoly over non-transferrable resources, such as water, gas, and electricity supply and thus the potential to use these as bargaining factors.

Extent

The extent of control is, on the one hand, the degree to which a parent company exercises control over the joint venture at strategic and operational levels (Tomlinson 1970, Killing 1983). On the other hand, as Lyles and Reger (1993) suggest, the extent of control can be expressed in terms of the degree to which joint venture managers enjoy autonomy from the parent companies. Two aspects of the extent of control are (1) which partner exerts the greater control over the joint venture and (2) how much control in total is exerted by the parent companies over the management of the joint venture and how much autonomy the joint venture's managers retain. Killing (1982, 1983) studied control in 37 joint ventures from developed countries. He identified 9 types of decisions: pricing policy, product design, production scheduling, manufacturing process, quality control, replacement of managers, sales targets, cost budgeting and capital expenditures. Killing inquired whether each decision was made by the joint venture general manager alone, by the local parent alone, by the foreign parent alone, or by the joint venture general manager with input from the local parent or from the foreign parent, or from both parents. Converting this information into a scale of partner 'dominance', Killing concluded that dominant joint ventures were easier to manage than shared joint ventures, because one parent was willing to play a passive role. Killing measured the extent to which a venture was dominated by either of its parents by focusing on the way decisions were made or by determining how much influence each parent had on various types of decision.

Beamish (1984) applied Killing's scale analysis in an examination of joint ventures in developing countries. His results in that different context did not support Killing's findings. The main factors associated with the extent of control were: (1) the percentage of equity committed by the partners; (2) the joint venture general manager's autonomy, which tends to be controlled and influenced by the how much the joint venture fits into the parent company's organisational structure; and (3) the balance of technology, management expertise and distribution network contributed by the partner.

Focus

The focus of control suggests that partners tend to seek control over specific activities rather than over the whole joint venture. Schaan (1988) reported that owning companies might choose to exercise control over a relatively wider or narrower scope of the joint venture's activities. This was confirmed by Geringer's (1988) study of ninety developed country joint ventures. Geringer suggests that parent companies may emphasise selective control over those dimensions that they perceive as critical, rather than attempting to control the entire range of the joint venture's activities. This implies that joint venture owners may seek to concentrate on providing certain resources, and on controlling certain decision areas and activities. The approach of selective control may be informed by a cost–benefit perspective. The institutional context is also able to have a bearing on the focus of the control that parent companies can exercise. Host government policies can reflect a selective approach to the control of joint ventures. For example, government control may concentrate on the maintenance of foreign exchange, on ensuring local content targets and on personnel policies.

The Cost of Control

Control incurs costs, both direct and indirect. This is recognised in the economics of transaction costs, most of which are seen to be incurred in maintaining control so as to avoid opportunism, to protect use-specific assets with a high technological content and to avoid other risks. Transaction cost economics pays attention to the direct administrative costs that any control mechanism incurs, and leads to the expectation, for example, that contractual provisions to control the use of resources are likely to be favoured over more costly direct supervision in cases where those resources are sufficiently tangible to be definable in contracts. Moreover, there are also important indirect costs that arise from the detrimental effects that inappropriate control can have on motivation and the ability of subordinate units to behave flexibly. Several contributors to Bleeke and Ernst (1993) warn that over-control by parent companies may inhibit the flexibility that their joint venture needs in order to develop within its own competitive environment. Ohmae (1993:42) argues that: "Managers must overcome the popular conception that total control increases chances of success." Control is associated with cost. This means that the management of some areas of joint venture activity may be less appealing for one partner to undertake, because it has less competence and familiarity in so doing than does another partner.

National Differences in Control Preference

Control preferences might be expected to vary with the nationality of the foreign partner. Child *et al.* (1994) found that, for joint ventures in China and Hungary, it was the case that American, German and Japanese foreign owners prefer to introduce different managerial philosophies, of which control is an important element. Foreign partners of different nationalities tend to seek control over somewhat different areas of joint venture activity and development. For example, Chinese managers tend to set production targets as their management control. From a sample of UK joint ventures with partners from Western Europe, the USA and Japan, Glaister (1995) found that American parent companies tend to seek tighter control over joint ventures than do European or Japanese partners. There is a tendency to replicate the parent company's existing routines and standard operating procedures in foreign subsidiaries (March and Olsen 1976, DiMaggio and Powell 1983, Kilduff 1992, Brittain and Freeman 1980, Lincoln *et al.* 1978, Schneider 1988). This suggests that foreign investing companies try to replicate their successful domestic organisation in a foreign country and to safeguard the faithfulness of the duplication.

THEORETICAL CONTRIBUTIONS ON OWNERSHIP AND CONTROL

A basic assumption of this section is that the relationship between ownership and control of joint ventures can be explained more effectively by utilising a range of theories from the field of international business (Buckley and Casson 1988). The insights into the relationship between ownership and control revealed by these theories are summarised in Table 3.5. The author would argue that an account of the relationship between ownership and control of joint ventures must deal with the following questions:

1. Ownership form: why choose a joint venture as a market entry mode instead of other forms?
2. Principal–agent relationship: what enables 'principals' to ensure that their 'agents' fulfil their objectives?
3. Ownership transactions: how do the investing companies trade off benefits against the costs associated with their business transactions and the ownership structure they want?
4. Ownership bargaining: how do the investing companies retain ownership and control over the return of their investment, and what share of equity can they negotiate *vis-à-vis* their partners?
5. Ownership, localisation and internationalisation (OLI) model: what are the factors of ownership advantage that can ensure foreign investing companies compete successfully in the foreign market?
6. Resource-specific ownership advantages: possession of which key resources and competencies that are essential for joint venture gives the partner a control advantage?
7. Key, non-substitutable resources: how essential are resources provided by partners to the success or failure of a joint venture?

OWNERSHIP FORM: INTERNATIONAL BUSINESS THEORIES

International business theories are concerned with the ways firms can improve their ownership competitive advantages by achieving a good performance in foreign markets. These theories include what is often called 'strategic management theory'. Hymer (1960) was the first to distinguish between passive portfolio investment and foreign direct

Table 3.5 Theoretical and empirical contributions on the relationship between ownership and control in joint ventures

	In joint venture context
1. International business theory	Owners are concerned with maximising international efficiency by choosing a preferred ownership form.
2. Agency theory	Owners are concerned with their ability to ensure that their managers can fulfil their objectives.
3. Transaction cost theory	Studies taking a transaction costs economics perspective have analysed the benefits and costs of joint ventures *vis-à-vis* other investment modes. Owners are also assumed to prefer ownership configurations that minimise transaction costs.
4. Bargaining power theory	Owners are concerned with the effect of negotiation on what that they are actually able to obtain in terms of task-related or partner-related criteria. Equity ownership is seen as an outcome of negotiation, a representation of relative power between participating interests.
5. Ownership advantage theory model	Owners are concerned with the optimal ownership configuration of control relationships resulting from reporting and decision-making patterns.
6. Resource dependency theory	Owners are concerned with the key resources they contribute which may reduce dependency on other partners. Owners are also concerned with the level of control that prospective partners can obtain, given the assets that they command.
7. Strategic contingency theory	The centrality to any joint venture's task of the resources that owners commit to joint ventures, and whether they can substitute for key resources provided by their partners, give rise to the relative power of the partners.

investment. Focusing on the latter, he explained that multinational enterprises exist because such firms have unique sources of superiority over foreign firms in their own market. Hymer (1976), and also Caves (1971), argued that once multinational enterprises (MNEs) have superior attributes such as brand names, technology know-how, differentiated products and superior manufacturing processes, they can exploit these advantages overseas at virtually no additional cost over that of exploiting such an advantage in the home market. Caves (1982) stated that local companies have to pay the full cost of developing this knowledge; they are unable to compete with the foreign investing companies, despite their advantage in local market knowledge. Hymer suggests that an investing firm' equity portfolio can be identified by the levels of the internalisation of the firm's ownership advantages and the market entry modes chosen in the foreign countries.

Rugman (1980, 1981, 1982) has widened the theoretical scope of Hymer (1960) and Caves (1971) to suggest that the key characteristic of the MNE is that it has a firm specific advantage in knowledge. Johanson (1970) mentions that the MNE is a device for slowing the rate of diffusion of technical and marketing know-how. Two kinds of transferable property right are distinguished by Casson (1979). One is the right of access, the other that of exclusion. The important contribution here is that the market can improve allocation by separating knowledge producers from those best equipped to be knowledge users. The existence of firm-specific advantages (Buckley 1983) depends on the following: (1) the diffusion of technical and marketing know-how, (2) the comparative advantage of firms in particular locations, and (3) the existence of particular types of scale economy. The concept of a firm's ownership-specific advantage has become a unifying concept in the theory of multinational enterprises.

Competitive advantage theorists, such as Porter (1986), have argued that the strategy of gaining access to foreign markets tends to focus on maximising international efficiency by locating activities in low-cost countries. Buckley and Casson (1976) and Buckley (1985) confirmed that the possession of an internationally transferable advantage is a necessary condition for the foreign firm to be competitive. However, it does not guarantee that the firm itself finds it profitable to produce abroad. The explanation for the use of joint ventures stems from how these strategies influence the competitive positioning of the companies. Harrigan (1984, 1985) proposed three major categories for analysing how foreign investing companies use joint venture strategies: internal uses, competitive uses and strategic uses. The benefits of these three main uses can be gained if the firm takes partners in cooperative strategies. With regard to the strategies discussed above, the implications for ownership concern the relative ability of the companies investing in joint ventures to decide the strategies that are most viable and profitable for them.

Most international business theories have been based on Hymer's insights. The essence of international business theory is that MNCs are characterised by the ownership of firm-specific advantages, which are unique to the firm. These ownership advantages can be transferred in a manner that is relatively costless within the firm, but cannot be acquired easily by other firms. This allows the firm to exploit its advantages at home and in international markets. With reference to the relationships between ownership and control of joint ventures, international competitive theories give rise to two fundamental insights. The first is that an investing company's objectives are based on a firm's specific competitive advantages. Competitive advantage in the joint venture context may be defined as the ownership advantage of one firm relative to another firm over a fixed time period, and this can be developed through international scale economies, international scope economies, and organisational learning across different national markets (Ghoshal 1987). Competitive advantage can be taken a step further, to maximise joint venture efficiency as a whole, and not only that of the individual partners. Buckley (1990) indicates that the competitive strategies are there so as to derive maximum benefit from the net wealth gained by deploying them effectively. From the competitive strategy standpoint, strategic motives for forming joint ventures are to improve competitive positioning as driven by both cost-reduction and revenue-enhancing considerations. The second insight is that for investing companies to achieve their objectives, their activities across national boundaries must be actively managed.

The difficulty in explaining the relationship between ownership and control of joint ventures through Hymer is (1976) and Caves's (1971) internalisation theory lies in its assumptions regarding the rationality of foreign investment. These writers assume that firms with the same competitive advantages will act identically. Therefore, they regard internationalisation as simply an optimisation of cost and revenues across international borders. The author would put forward four arguments. First, companies that have developed and exploited their firm-specific advantage in the home country will not necessary engage in the same type of foreign direct investment. This is because some foreign environments may be perceived as riskier and presenting a greater need for prior learning than others. Second, the choice of foreign direct investment may be constrained by government industrial priorities in the foreign country. For example, the Chinese government does not allow foreign investing companies to have a majority equity share of joint ventures in certain strategically important projects or in certain industrial sectors. Third, internalisation theory does not explain the operation of joint ventures, because companies often make foreign investments before they have the knowledge to exploit a competitive advantage in the foreign market. It is therefore difficult to view this foreign investment as an extension of an existing competitive advantage, because the local knowledge, resource and distribution network of the joint venture partner does not necessarily fit with the type of foreign direct investment chosen by the foreign investing companies. Fourth, Buckley and Casson's (1976) comments on Hymer's theory indicate that it ignores the costs of acquisition. It is not always possible for the theory to explain or predict why firms invest in these ownership forms rather than in other types of asset.

On the whole, the major contribution of international business theories to an analysis of the relationship between ownership and control stems from their attention to the linkage between companies' strategies and market entry modes in foreign countries. This is of particular significance for the effects of strategies on the choices of preferred forms of ownership and the extent to which the level of control influences the choice of those specific forms of ownership.

AGENCY THEORY: PRINCIPAL–AGENT RELATIONSHIP

Agency theory is concerned with the control and influence that principals can maintain over their 'agents'. The rights and responsibilities of owner–principals are generally derived from the equity investments in a company. Berle and Means (1932) concentrated on the principal–agent relationship between the owners and managers of large public corporations. A number of studies have confirmed that most owners tend to use various control mechanisms and incentives to safeguard their equity investments (Jensen and Meckling 1976, Eisenhardt 1989). The purpose of the principal's control is to minimise the returns or benefits that go to the managers.

Agency theory connects to the relationship between ownership and control of a joint venture in two ways. First, the identification of the legal provisions of the contract between the owning companies and the managers of a joint venture lies at the heart of agency theory. Each partner in the joint venture is a principal in respect of contracts. As joint venture partners are assumed to have different self-interests and bounded rationales, and yet to some extent share the same interests, the control function of the principal–agent contract should avoid one of the partners being able to secure better information on the management progress of the joint venture than the other. More specifically, the principal–agent relationship draws attention to the consequence of the fact that the contract brings a range of rights and responsibilities to the owners of joint ventures. Therefore, it is absolutely vital that joint venture partners should use a joint venture contract, which frames the principal–agent relationship. One dishonest partner can bankrupt the others, and there have been countless cases where this has happened (Jensen and Meckling 1976, Fama and Jensen 1983).

Second, agency theory has re-examined the relationship between ownership and control in terms of joint venture organisational structure. A principal–agent relationship is most clearly established when joint ventures are formed such that their managers are accountable to owners. Agency theory would regard the relationship between joint venture owners and managers as a problematic one. The situation becomes more complicated if and when the partner companies themselves have different objectives. For example, one partner may seek profit over a longer term than the other. Most joint venture management comprises a mixture of agents: expatriate and local managers. This may result in some disagreements between parent companies that can impact on the joint venture. The agency cost will depend on the quality of collaboration between the partners. Implications of agency theory can also be drawn from the joint venture's operation. For example, each joint venture partner becomes an agent of resourcing for the other partner(s). In order to avoid or overcome a risk that one partner becomes a free-rider at the expense of the other, setting the contract over resources between the partners should play an important role in delineating the use of resources provided to the joint venture and the allocation of returns from that use. Therefore, the most useful contribution of agency theory lies in the identification of control mechanisms and the conditions (such as the ability of principals to understand the context in which agents operate) that bear upon the effectiveness of such mechanisms.

A limitation of using agency theory to explain the relationship between ownership and control lies in the difficulty in identifying the effectiveness from a control point of view of different combinations of incentives and monitoring mechanisms introduced by the partners. This makes it difficult for a joint venture's management to ensure that it can remain consistent with the principal's objectives.

OWNERSHIP TRANSACTIONS: TRANSACTION COSTS ECONOMICS

Transaction costs economics (TCE) is concerned with the cost-effectiveness of organising international economic activities. The transaction costs economics perspective endeavours to account for the choice between conducting international business transactions via market exchange and conducting it via the internalisation of production within a single hierarchically organised company. The attributes of the transaction are seen to determine this choice. Casson (1982) states that markets and hierarchies are alternative modes of governance, which have the transaction as the basic unit of analysis.

Williamson (1975) argues that firms choose how to manage their transactions according to the criterion of minimising the sum of production *and* transaction costs. Production costs may differ between firms, owing to the scale of operations, learning, and proprietary knowledge. Transaction costs refer to the expenses incurred in searching out new suppliers or customers, for writing, negotiating and enforcing contracts and for administering a transaction. Dunning (1989) recognised that transaction costs essentially comprise the costs of organisation and the cost of strategy. Williamson (1985) identifies the three key attributes of the transaction context as *asset specificity, uncertainty* and *transactional frequency*, which, 'when combined with small numbers bargaining and opportunism, creates contracting problems which increase the cost of transacting through the market'. It has been noted that the degree of market imperfection in the international context might be higher than in the domestic market, because the costs of resource mobilisation and managing contractual relationships are higher across national boundaries and where the risks of market failure are greater (Hennart 1988, Rugman and Verbeke 1992).

Transaction costs economics analysis has been used to address different aspects related to the relationship between ownership and control of joint ventures. With regard to the decision on a joint venture ownership, Hennart (1982, 1989), Kogut (1988) and Kogut and Zander (1993) suggest that a joint venture's investment can be considered as an extension of hierarchies across borders, reducing the cost of international coordination, facilitating knowledge transfer and increasing the efficiency of exchange. Anderson and Gatignon (1986), Gatignon and Anderson (1988), Buckley and Casson (1988), Contractor, (1989a, 1989b), Kim and Hwang (1992) and Woodcock *et al.* (1994) all attempt to integrate the literature on market entry mode decisions using long-term efficiency criteria within a transaction cost framework. They posit that the choice between full and shared ownership depends on the relative costs and benefits of the two alternative ownership structures. Hennart (1989, 1991) has also noted the importance of taking hierarchical costs into account in making a decision on the appropriate form of ownership.

Transaction costs economics links the cost of resources of a tacit kind that owners contribute to joint ventures and the cost of equity investment. Killing (1983) reported from his empirical studies that tacit knowledge transfer is often handled better through an equity relationship, owing to the greater incentive to transfer personnel and to take a more active interest in the operation. Technology transfer between partners in a joint venture includes tacit forms of knowledge, which require both a greater interaction of personnel and a greater willingness to learn. Equity relationships facilitate information sharing, because the transferrer is rewarded on more than the basis of the transfer. With reference to technology transfer in the context of joint ventures, Boisot and Child (1996) state that a more mature technology, where the know-how has been diffused over time and is more codified, will no longer attract substantial rents, because of its limited future market potential, the greater standardisation and diffusion of knowledge, and greater competition. At this stage, the transaction costs are lower and the expected value of the loss from opportunistic behaviour is also lower. Teece (1976) finds that technology transfer costs decline sharply for mature product categories. This was measured by the age of the technology and the number of competitors using similar or competing technology. Because the requisite knowledge is well codified and widely available for hire, the entrant does not need to supplement the control offered by the market mechanism.

However, there are several limitations to the explanation of the relationship between ownership and control of joint ventures primarily by reference to transaction costs economics. First, it ignores the strategic considerations that drive firms' ownership decision choices (Contractor 1990). This is one of its major shortcomings, since these may be strong driving forces behind such decisions. Transaction cost theory looks only at the minimisation of transaction costs, without addressing other benefits offered by a particular form of ownership. It does not take account of organisational capability as a competitive advantage and constraint. The choice of ownership form for any joint venture may be made with reference to improving the global competitive position of the company, even if the choice of joint venture may be more costly than alternative market entry modes. Competitive strategy is concerned more with the maximisation of profits or revenues with than the benefits from a particular ownership mode. Kogut (1988) emphasises the importance of separating a rent-maximising, competitive strategy logic from a cost-minimising, transaction cost one.

Second, transaction costs incurred in joint ventures include those of the search cost for suitable partners, monitoring the provision and use of capital and non-capital resourcing. Transaction cost theory fails to distinguish between the efficiency of an organisational form and its effectiveness in the light of overall corporate strategy. Dunning (1988b) and Ghoshal (1987) indicated that coordinative demands arising from the ownership form of a unit must match with coordinative abilities. Transaction costs economics is too narrow, as it focuses on the production- and marketing related aspects of internalisation at the expense of considering benefits from common governance, such as coordination efficiencies. This factor cannot be externalised to the market, because it has no value outside the firm. This element is in a sense recognised by transaction costs economics, in that it reflects market imperfections. In a perfect market, there would be no coordination costs or problems, because there would be perfect information and because resource allocation would be wholly responsive to clear economic signals.

Third, transaction costs economics inadequately addresses the forms of linkage between ownership and control that may derive from a partner's cultural preferences and national institutional setting. Lu and Lake (1997) suggest that economic systems in developing countries can take on forms other than markets and hierarchies. For instance, studies of Chinese economic institutions have noted that they have their own distinct logic, and these are very different from those in market economies (Boisot and Child 1996). As a result, joint ventures can be faced with contradictory forces that are rooted in the conflicts between the partners' task requirements and the country's unique institutions.

There are two contributions that transaction costs economics makes to understanding the relationship between ownership and control of joint ventures that are relevant to the present study. First, it provides insights into the concept of ownership, shedding light on the identification of owner resourcing to joint ventures and on how different forms of this may affect performance; further, it provides a wider cost–benefit analysis to specific individual forms of business, which offers greater understanding of the costs of business transactions. Second, it draws attention to the relative costs of managing different forms of resource provision to joint ventures by their owners, namely equity, contractual and non-contractual.

BARGAINING BETWEEN OWNERS: BARGAINING POWER THEORY

Bargaining power theory is concerned with the ways firms can convey their ownership advantages by securing control and influence over other investing companies and the host governments. Wright and Russels (1975), Fagre and Wells (1982), Lecraw (1984) and Gomes-Casseres (1987) all state that bargaining power accrues to those firms that enjoy ownership advantages. These are reflected in having sufficient capital, the capability of raising capital in the financial market, access to advanced technology, highly developed management, marketing skills, strong brand names and trademarks, risk reduction abilities and a global perspective. Traditionally, the study of bargaining power has three categories:

1. equity-driven: investing companies are characterised as having a strong preference for major ownership in their overseas subsidiaries, and their perceived 'relatively strong' bargaining positions allow them to realise those ownership options in most cases (Vernon and Wells 1991);
2. capability-driven: the study of bargaining power in organisations concentrates on the ability to affect outcomes or to get things done (Mintzberg 1983, Salancik and Pfeffer 1977);
3. resource-driven: power stems from control of critical resource (Robinson 1969, Vernon 1971, Pfeffer 1981a, Blodgett 1991).

The insight into ownership and control of joint ventures provided by bargaining power analysis is that investing companies will be satisfied only if their contributions and their expected control over their investments are kept in balance. The most significant contribution provided by bargaining power theory to the relationship between ownership and control of a joint venture is the linkage between a firm's ownership competitive advantages and its relations to partners and host governments. Blodgett (1991) identifies five elements in the bargaining that occurs between foreign investing partners and the host governments: technology, knowledge of the local environment, local marketing skills, and government persuasion. These are perceived as having a direct influence on the bargaining power of joint venture partners. Fagre and Wells (1982) have used a bargaining power framework to explore the relationship between, on the one hand, the characteristics of a foreign investing company such as its size, intrafirm transfers, R&D intensities and product diversity, and, on the other, the percentage equity ownership position that it achieves in the host country. Poynter (1982) has shown that a foreign investing company may find it more advantageous to bargain for control over the variables critical to the success of the subsidiary from the MNC's viewpoint rather than for increased equity ownership. Root (1988) and Blodgett (1991) both observed that foreign investing companies' bargaining power *vis-à-vis* host governments erodes over time, as the foreign investing companies invest critical resources into the joint venture and effectively become hostages.

The bargaining power of the *local firm* in developing countries has depended on knowledge of the local business environment, the supply of labour and raw materials, and connections with host governmental authorities and institutions (Lecraw 1984, Beamish 1987, Zurawicki 1975, Reynolds 1984). Local firms are more likely to get their way when they possess certain assets that are needed by foreign investing companies. Lecraw (1984) has attempted to articulate the relationship between the bargaining power of the partners and the level of control they exercise. He found that the three determinants of firm-specific advantages including technical leadership, advertising intensity and export capability, these could be used to gain bargaining power between partners.

The bargaining power of a host developing country's government derives from its control of the environment in which the joint venture will operate, especially its control of the scarce domestic resources and access to the domestic market. The desire of foreign and local partners to exploit their firm-specific advantages under the laws and regulations set by the host government may depend on the technical and managerial resources the partners have available to commit to the joint venture. Aswicahyono and Hill (1995) indicate that the host government policy regime is one of the most important determinants of foreign investment share. The intensity of implementation of law and regulations may vary over time and across government agencies. Lecraw (1984:31) suggests that

> if the host government controls access to its market through tariffs or non-tariff barriers to trade ... the host government can bargain access to its domestic market to gain equity participation for host-country nationals. Some foreign investing companies may increase their control of the joint venture by satisfying certain targets set by the local government such as increasing local content, export rate and employment.

Analyses of the linkages between explanatory variables and bargaining success have been presented by numerous writers, such as Bergsten *et al.* (1978), Kobrin (1982), Vernon (1977) and Vachani (1995). Vachani makes a distinction between the static and dynamic manifestations of bargaining success:

> Static bargaining success refers to the multinational's success in negotiations with the host government at a particular point in time, and is reflected in the level of foreign ownership at that time. Dynamic bargaining success refers to its success in preventing erosion of the terms of its deal with the host over time, and is manifest in the proportion of foreign ownership retained by the multinational over a period of time.
>
> Vachani. (1995:159)

He reports that bargaining success is affected by three moderating forces: (1) the political climate in the host country, (2) the host's perception of value associated with the multinational's operations and (3) the multinational's ownership preference. The contribution of his research is to examine carefully each attribute that is believed to affect bargaining success, in order to assess the durability of its effect over time. Vachani concludes that the influence of foreign ownership (static bargaining success) is found to be less important, or to have a different effect. Dynamic bargaining power can be affected by several factors, including size, nature of intangible assets, cultural and other historical ties between the host and home countries, export performance and the control preferences typical of managers in home country companies.

Yan and Gray (1994a, 1996) develop a model of joint venture bargaining power that incorporates components of two types: *context-*

based and *resource-based*. Context-based bargaining power can be derived from having alternative partners as substitutes. The components of resource-based bargaining power, on the other hand, are the resources and capabilities committed by the partners to a joint venture, which these authors assess in terms of the alternative partners available to negotiate the terms of the joint venture partnership, when the joint venture was being formed and the strategic importance of the joint venture to each partner, which presumably incorporates the possibility that another joint venture could serve as an alternative means to achieve real strategic objectives. Child *et al.* state that

> the problem with this approach to substitutability lies in its theoretical indeterminacy. First, if a partner negotiating to form a joint venture does not have alternatives, this could either indicate that it is in a weak bargaining position or that the negotiator does not need to take the trouble of seeking for an alternative. Secondly, it is questionable as to how much impact the initial negotiations will have on the on-going control over a joint venture that is up and running, particularly in a context like China which is rapidly changing and where much is re-negotiated over the course of time. Third, the strategic importance of a joint venture to a parent company may also be very relative to alternative ventures, and this would have to be taken into account.
>
> (Child *et al.* 1997:8)

Bargaining power theory also overlooks the case where a joint venture partner may wish to have only a minority interest, and is content to leave control to another partner, safeguarding its right to a return via its shareholding.

The bargaining power perspective offers several contributions to the analysis of relationships between ownership and control of joint ventures. First, the firm that possesses ownership advantages in technology, production, marketing, finance and management will tend to have greater bargaining power. Once the firm possesses a certain level of bargaining power, it will be able to exercise some control and influence on those particular areas. Investing companies may use proprietary technology and management expertise valued as equity, so increasing the bargaining position of an investing company over the host government, particularly if other companies cannot supply technology of the same type or level of development. However, once the investing companies have committed their assets to a joint venture then the cost of protecting those assets will also increase.

Second, an investing company will gain bargaining power if the resources it can provide to a joint venture are aligned with the needs of the other partners. Bargaining power may be reflected in and measured by how much the joint venture contract that is negotiated accords in fact with the foreign or local partner's objectives, when these are in conflict. For example, if capital is a scarce resource that can best be provided by one investing company then its bargaining power and its level of equity participation may increase with the size of the investment and the investment's capital intensity. This means that much of the bargaining power available to prospective partners is likely to arise from their command of significant resources. The foreign investing company's access to export markets may become an especially important source of bargaining power, if the host country is following a development strategy based on export-led growth.

Third, equity ownership is seen as an outcome of negotiation, which represents the relative bargaining power of participating interests (Fagre and Wells 1982). Here, it needs to be emphasised that the relationship cannot be a zero-sum game: the individual partners must expect to have some mutually desired outcomes from the partnership. On the whole, bargaining influence tends to be measured by percentage of equity. It may be argued that firms that have only minority equity, but have effective control through technology and other connections, ought also to be given greater consideration in the discussion of bargaining power. Then they normally resolve their differing goals according to the proportion of equity each partner holds. The alternative argument may suggest that when joint venture partners' interests coincide or are complementary, ownership will not be such an important (or necessary) factor for exercising influence over the joint venture. The bargaining process in joint ventures occurs only when companies experience a conflict of interest.

OLI ADVANTAGES: THE OWNERSHIP, LOCATION AND INTERNALISATION MODEL

A comprehensive framework proposed by Dunning (1977, 1993, 1995) has stipulated that the choice of a market entry mode is influenced by three types of factors: First, the concept of ownership-specific advantages (O) of firms is perceived to take explicit account of the costs and benefits derived from inter-firm relationships. Second, the concept of location advantages (L) of countries is perceived to give more weight to the following factors: geographical areas, changing economic activities and influence of national and regional authorities. Third is the idea that firms internalise (I) intermediate markets, primarily to reduce the transaction costs of using them. The patterns of investment are determined by the configuration of three sets of advantages as perceived by companies.

The ownership, location and internalisation (OLI) model has broadened understanding of the relationship between ownership and control of joint ventures in two main respects: the initial act of ownership contribution and achieving the growth of such investment. The relevance of each factor in determining the ownership advantage of firms will vary according to the initial ownership contributions to a joint venture. Agarwal and Ramaswami (1992) suggest that the ownership advantages of a firm are reflected by its size, its experience and its ability to develop differentiated products. Three types of ownership-specific advantages identified by Dunning:

> those that stem from the exclusive privileged possession of or access to particular income creating assets; those that are normally enjoyed by a branch plant compared with a de novo firm, and those that are a consequence of geographical diversification or multinationality per se.
>
> (Dunning 1988a:2)

With reference to the ownership advantage of joint ventures, it must be in the best interests of investing companies that possess ownership-specific advantages to transfer them across national boundaries.

The growth of ownership investment can be constrained by the attractiveness of a market, which is characterised in terms of its market potential and investment risk. Buckley (1988) suggests that the assessment of internalisation advantage is based on the relative costs or risks of sharing the assets and skills with a host country firm versus integrating them within the firm. Three main kinds of market failure are identified by Dunning:

> (1) those that arise from risk and uncertainty; (2) those that stem from the ability of firms to exploit the economics of large-scale production, but only in an imperfect market situation; (3) those that occur where the transaction of a particular good or service yields costs and benefits external to that transaction.
>
> (Dunning 1988a:3)

Dunning and Rugman (1985) make a distinction between structural and transactional market imperfections. They define structural market imperfections as those arising from some kinds of government intervention, which may encourage or discourage such investment. The transactional market imperfection is identified as country-specific and embedded in location factors.

The perspective on ownership and control of joint ventures offered by OLI analysis has received mixed support. The findings of Agarwall and Ramaswami's study (1992) provide broad support for the hypothesised effects of the interrelationships among ownership, location and internalisation advantages. The results of their study suggest that the long-term success of any foreign investment requires significant managerial and financial resources, even in markets that do not have high risks. Kogut and Singh (1988a, 1988b) found that the size of foreign subsidiaries was positively and significantly related to shared ownership of foreign affiliates. However, it was not significantly correlated to full ownership for foreign firms investing in the United States. Gomes-Casseres (1989a, 1990) and Hennart (1991) confirmed that familiarity with a host country was more likely to lead foreign investing companies to take on full ownership of their foreign subsidiaries. Stopford and Wells (1972) found that R&D-intensive American firms tended to fully own their foreign affiliates, indicating their desire to maximise the efficiency of transferring specialised competencies and to protect their own technologies.

The difficulty in explaining the relationship between ownership and control of joint ventures through OLI theory lies with its assumption that the interrelationships of the factors are based on wholly rational calculations. A number of empirical studies appear to contradict OLI analysis. Gomes-Casseres (1989b, 1990) found that restrictive host policies strongly encouraged US firms to establish joint ventures in countries where such policies were in practice. Kogut and Singh (1988b) found cultural similarity to be a significant factor increasing the probability for foreign firms choosing joint ventures over acquisitions for their operations in the US. Itaki (1991) criticised the OLI model and made a point of distinguishing between 'ownership advantage' and 'location advantage'.

The contribution that OLI analysis could make to the present study lies in the models and the concepts of ownership, localisation and internalisation provide an understanding of the link between the foreign partners, the local partners and government and the logic of partner's objectives, ownership and control. The partner's ownership advantages, derived from the initial investment and the growth of ownership investment constrained by the market attractiveness, are particularly significant contributions to the modification of the relationship between ownership and control of joint ventures.

RESOURCE-SPECIFIC OWNERSHIP ADVANTAGES: RESOURCE DEPENDENCE THEORY

Pfeffer and Salancik (1978) identify the command of critical resources as the basis for exercising power within and between organisations. Dependence on key resources gives rise to control of the focal organisation by external resource providers. External control over an organisation can arise from the power of external parties to command resources that are vital for the successful operation of the organisation. Internal control over, or access to, resources gives some organisational members more power over the organisation than others (Donaldson 1995).

Resource dependence analysis concentrates on resource scarcity. It illustrates a basic question as to why the resources provided by certain organisational members are more important than the resources provided by other members. The argument is that organisations are externally constrained and are not internally self-sufficient, because they require resources from the environment. In consequence, organisations become interdependent with elements of the environment within which they transact. Emerson (1962), in his article on power dependency relations, emphasises the critical role of dependence in creating power. He states that 'power resides implicitly in the other's dependency' (p. 32). Pfeffer (1981a) indicates that dependence is seen to be a function of the importance of what one actor gets from the other, and an inverse function of the availability of this outcome or performance in other places.

With regard to understanding the relationship between ownership and control of joint ventures, the empirical evidence on patterns of joint venture activity among industrial firms is consistent with the resource dependence perspective (Pfeffer and Nowak 1976, Pfeffer and Salancik 1978, Lorange and Roos 1992, Yan and Gray 1994a). Harrigan (1985) suggests that joint ventures can be resource-aggregating and resource-sharing mechanisms, which allow investing companies to concentrate resources in those areas where they possess the greatest respective strengths. Technology, management, distribution networks and other assets provided by the partners of joint ventures are means of coping with uncertainties and building competitive positions, because joint ventures can offer a means of leveraging synergy between the skills and resources of owning companies.

Resource dependence analysis has been used to account for the linkage between resource provision and control within a joint venture. The resource dependence perspective implies that a parent firm that contributes a resource necessary for the venture's success, and that the other parent cannot provide, will gain power relative to the latter partner and relatively greater control over the joint venture. In other words, the resource dependence view leads to an expectation that the ability of a parent company to exert control over a joint venture will be a function of the extent to which that joint venture depends on the parent for critical resources and also depends for the resources on that parent more than on the other.

Applying a resource dependence view, Bartlett (1986) and Lorange and Roos (1992) suggest that the vertical distribution of power within the parent–joint venture managerial network will depend on the density of the joint venture's transactional and information network within its own organisation set. The greater this density, suggesting that the joint venture has the ability to secure resources independently of its parents, the more restricted will be the hierarchical power of the parent company. Conversely, the greater the density of the network between the joint venture and a parent company, the more restricted will be the autonomy of the joint venture and also the power of the other partner.

It is recognised in the resource dependence literature that there are important strategic and competitive advantages that may be derived from resource-synergy joint ventures. An important advantage offered by joint ventures lies in the potential synergistic effects of combining the complementary assets of foreign and local partners. Foreign investing companies usually provide firm-specific knowledge regarding technology, management and capital markets. The local partner provides location-specific knowledge regarding host domestic markets, infrastructure and institutional matters.

Recently, several theorists have developed resource-based theories, which classify types of resource and emphasise that core resources or competencies are vital to long-term competitive advantage (Prahalad and Bettis 1986, Prahalad and Hamel 1990, Collis 1991). Core competencies are defined as the irreversible assets that the firm owns. In the case of joint ventures, the resource-based perspective addresses control symmetry or asymmetry, which derives from the partners' competence advantages. Resource-based theory can be used to illustrate ownership advantages and how the advantages are explored to control a joint venture.

Resource dependence theory provides a theoretical explanation for defining the relationship between ownership and control. In the case of an IJV, this means that a parent firm that contributes a resource necessary for the venture's success that the other parent cannot provide will gain power relative to the partner and relatively greater control over the IJV. It also implies that a parent's control will be focused on those activities of the IJV to which it contributes resources.

The significance of controlling resources can be well illustrated by the resource dependence theory. First, the core competencies and the resource committed by a joint venture partner will depend upon its perception of the risk of exposing its critical resource. The risk of such resource exposure can be judged by (1) the need for ongoing management, (2) the difficulties of transacting with the market in terms of tacit versus non-tacit technology and (3) inter-partner trust and perception of the importance of sharing those resources. Second, resources provided by the market tend to be constrained by the nature and type of resource requirements. Finally, resource dependence requires joint venture partners to adjust to new markets, new organisational processes and systems, or new competitive factors. Possession of a competence, such as technology or management expertise, that is essential for joint venture performance, gives the partner a control advantage. Resource-based theory also draws attention to 'soft' technologies and human competence, which are given less prominence in resource dependence theory.

KEY, NON-SUBSTITUTABLE RESOURCES: STRATEGIC CONTINGENCY THEORY

Strategic contingency theory is concerned with the relative power of different units within organisations, and postulates that the power of an intra-organizational unit will be a function of the extent to which it is difficult to substitute for its control over critical resources. The theory can, however, be extended to the case of joint ventures where parent companies and their appointees are intra-organisational as well as extra-organisational groups. The theory argues that individual organisations adapt to their environment. The environment is seen as posing requirements for efficiency, innovation or whatever, which the organisation must meet to survive (Hage and Aiken 1967). There is held to be a fit between the organisational structure and the contingency that affects organisational performance. Strategic contingency theory (Hickson *et al.* 1971) builds upon Crozier's (1964) insights to point out how power within an organisation can accrue from the ability of certain groups or units to cope with uncertain but key contingencies, owing to their central position within the network of the organisation's activities. This is particularly the case when it is difficult to substitute for, or routinise, their specialised knowledge. While resource dependence theory points to a command of external resources as the basis for exercising control, strategic contingency theory identifies a command of internal knowledge resources as a basis for control. Although this theory is concerned with the relative power of different units within organisations, it identifies factors that it is also helpful to incorporate into a theory of inter-organisational power, and hence to apply to the issue of ownership and control of IJVs.

The strategic contingency argument suggests that parent company control over a joint venture depends both on (1) the critical nature of the resources it provides, and (2) whether alternative sources of such resources are available to the venture, either from the other parent company or companies or externally. A command of knowledge resources necessary for a joint venture tends to enable one partner lay a good basis for control over the other partners. The implication that stems from both resource dependencies and strategic perspectives is that overall control over a joint venture can derive from commanding key resources such as technology know-how. An important corollary is that investments for which the other partner cannot find ready substitutes are likely to be highly effective bases for exercising control. This implication also means that joint venture owners may seek to control only certain resources, decision areas and activities, and not show so much concern to control others.

However, strategic contingency theory postulates that the power of an organisational unit is also a function of the extent to which it is difficult to find a substitute provider of its services. Lyles and Reger (1993) explore the relationships among influence, autonomy and control in a joint venture setting. They address the mechanisms available to joint venture managers to influence and gain compliance from parent firms. The results suggest that the use of upward influence to gain autonomy in a joint venture is different and more complex than in unified structures or among independent organisations. The strategic contingency perspective implies that control is focused on certain IJV activities according to the criticality and substitutability of its resourcing.

A FRAMEWORK OF OWNERSHIP, CONTROL AND PERFORMANCE IN IJVs

The Chinese have a saying that 'Stones from other hills may serve to polish the jade of this one.' The literature reviewed in this chapter contributes several theoretical perspectives relevant to the relationship between objectives, ownership, control and performance of Sino-foreign joint ventures. However, this literature is rather fragmented, and there is an absence of a comprehensive framework for the analysis of joint venture ownership and control (Newman 1992). Most studies of ownership and control have examined the context between dominant control by one partner versus shared control. This approach overlooks the possibility that joint venture parents may exert varying degrees of control over decision-making in different functional areas (Hill and Hellriegel 1994). Pierce *et al.* (1991) suggested that different types of ownership might serve to moderate the relationship between formal ownership and the degree to which the parent firm identifies with and internalises the joint venture as an organisation. This book proposes and tests a research framework of ownership and control in joint ventures that integrates the concepts of objectives, ownership, control and performance, and treats these concepts as interdependent factors that influence overall joint venture performance (see Table 3.6). The four key variables identified for examination are given prominence in the joint venture literature (Blodgett 1991, Geringer and Hebert 1989, 1991, Lecraw 1984, Yan and Gray 1994b, Woodcock *et al.* 1994).

As an attempt to move towards greater integration, Figure 3.1 postulates the main linkages, which can be drawn from the literature, and which are of particular relevance for the subject of the present study.

The framework presented in Figure 3.1 encompasses three research models that are believed to make distinctive contributions to an understanding of the relationships between objectives, ownership, control and performance. These models offer theoretical explanations for the postulated linkages contained within the research framework.

Table 3.6 Theoretical perspectives relevant to ownership and control in joint ventures

Perspective		*Factor considered*					
	Linkage between IJV ownership and control	*Objectives*	*Ownership*	*Control*			*Performance*
				Mechanism	*Extent*	*Focus*	
1. Legal	Formal ownership right		✓	✓	✓	✓	
2. International business theories	Preferred ownership form in foreign market	✓	✓	✓			✓
3. Agency theory	Relations between owners and controlling the joint ventures	✓	✓	✓	✓	✓	✓
4. Transaction cost theory	Preference of owners to control in manner that optimises cost—benefit balance	✓	✓	✓		✓	✓
5. Bargaining power theory	Influence of owners' resource-holding mediated by negotiating strength		✓		✓		
6. OLI model	Ownership, localisation and internalisation	✓	✓		✓		✓
7. Resource dependence theory	Provision of key resources	✓	✓		✓	✓	✓
8. Strategic contingency theory	Non-substitutable provision of key resources		✓	✓		✓	✓

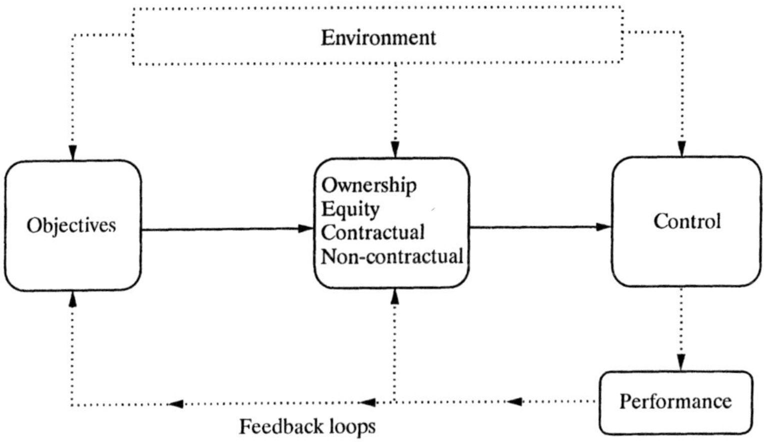

Figure 3.1 A Framework of objectives, ownership, control and performance in IJVs

A *formation model* is concerned with the link between objectives and ownership (see Figure 3.2). It explores how, at joint venture formation, the strategic and financial objectives of the investing companies are reflected in the preferred equity level and range of ownership resourcing that they have committed to the joint venture. *International business theory, strategic contingency, agency theory* and *transaction cost economics* are particularly relevant to the strategic choice of market entry mode, that is, the form of a joint venture. *International business theory, agency theory* and *transaction cost economics* also offer explanations for the levels of control that investing companies will seek when forming joint ventures.

A *universalistic model* is relevant to the links between ownership resourcing, control and performance (see Figure 3.3). It regards the level and range of ownership resourcing brought by each investing company to the partnership as enabling them to exercise the control they desire. The *resource dependency theory* offers a significant

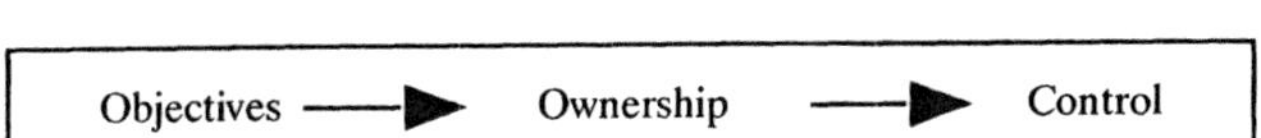

Figure 3.2 Formation model

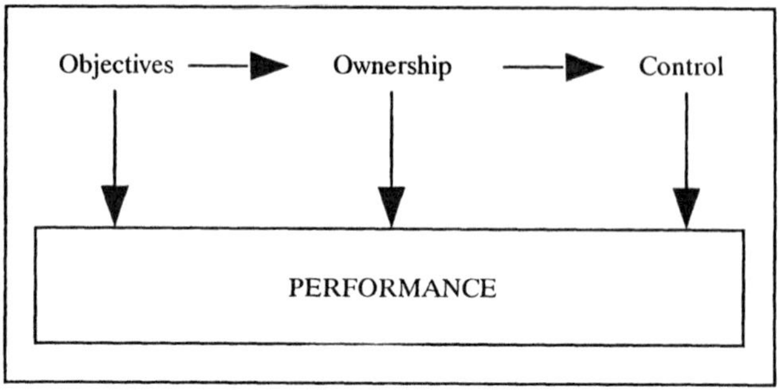

Figure 3.3 Universalistic model

contribution to this argument. Also, most arguments from economics refer to the contributions that factors of production make to the performance of firms.

A *contingency model* is concerned with the match between the variables and the implications of this match for joint venture performance. In particular, it identifies the 'fit' between the configurations of ownership resourcing and control, and regards this as a key influence on the level of joint venture performance (see Figure 3.4). *Resource dependence* and *strategic contingency theories* are particularly central for the analyses of the fit between the ownership, control and performance of joint ventures.

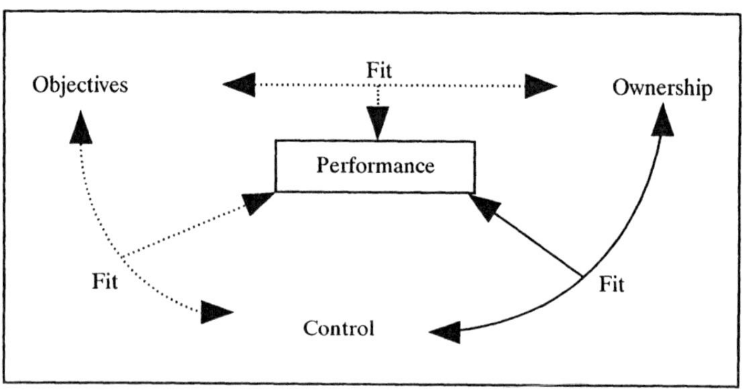

Figure 3.4 Contingency model

SUMMARY

In order to clarify the relationship between ownership and control of international joint ventures, the seven most relevant theories have been reviewed. *Resource dependency theory* and *strategic contingency theory* are central to the discussion, because the analyses of the relationship between ownership and control stem from their attention to the linkages between the range of a partner's ownership resourcing and the control mechanisms available in China. Other relevant theories, such as *international business theory, transaction cost economic theory* and *agency theory* also give some, but limited, attention to the relationship between joint venture objectives, ownership, control and performance. It has also been found in previous studies of IJVs that cultural factors have play important roles in IJV' management, because foreign or Chinese owners prefer to introduce different managerial philosophies. All these considerations imply that IJV owners may seek to concentrate on providing certain resources and on controlling certain decision areas and activities. Since three categories of ownership inputs have been identified, it is important to ascertain what level and form of control leverage attach to each, because some trade-offs may be possible between them.

4 Research Models for Exploring the Ownership, Control and Performance of IJVs

The research models allow for the incorporation of the various theoretical perspectives that are believed to make complementary contributions to the relationship between ownership and control in the Sino-foreign joint ventures being studied. Figure 3.1 identified objectives, ownership, control and performance as four conceptually distinctive sets of variables for describing the relationship between ownership and control in joint ventures. This chapter looks at the main linkages between the four sets of variables grouping them by reference to the formation, universalistic and contingency models. The three research models are shown from in Table 4.1.

THE FORMATION MODEL

This identifies objectives for joint venture formation as influences on the preferred joint venture equity level and on the range of ownership resourcing contributed by the parent companies. It is recognised that a wide variety of objectives are likely to be present at joint venture formation. Parent company objectives are seen to give rise to joint venture ownership configurations primarily through the expression of preferences at the time of formation. The ownership resources contributed by each parent company, to set up and control the joint venture, are likely to vary widely. The importance of examining the effects of the interrelationships between partners' objectives, and the ownership resourcing that they commit to joint ventures, derives from the fact that these relationships may explain joint venture behaviours that cannot be accounted for by the independent effects of the factors (Agarwal and Ramaswami 1992).

Objectives can be defined as the motivation to fulfil strategic aims set at the corporate level for the purpose of maximising overall corporate

Table 4.1 Research models in the postulated relationship of ownership, control and performance

	■ *Set of perspectives*	*Theoretical focus*
Formation model 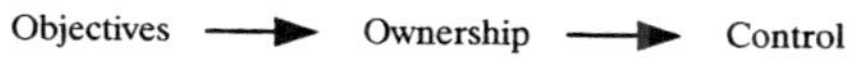	■ Objectives long-term: more likely to contribute (a) a wide range of ownership resources to the joint venture it undertakes and (b) a higher value of equity capital ■ Objectives short-term: more likely to contribute (a) only a limited range of ownership resources to the joint venture it undertakes and (b) a lower value of equity capital.	Strategic objectives and ownership
Universalistic model 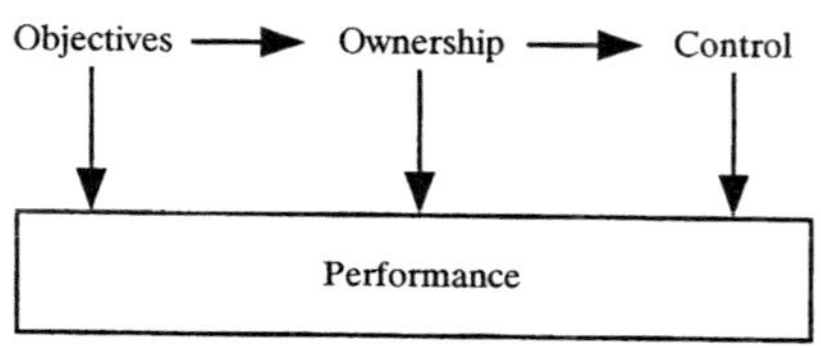	■ The greater the share of equity, the greater overall control. ■ The more resources are provided on a contractual basis, the greater will be control in the corresponding areas. ■ The more resources are provided on a non-contractual basis, the greater will be control in the corresponding areas. ■ The more comprehensive the range of ownership resources, the greater will be overall control. ■ The more comprehensive the range of ownership resources, the better will be the performance. ■ The higher the proportion of joint venture transactional resources supplied by partners, the better will be its performance. ■ The higher the level of control exercised by one partner, the better will be the performance. ■ The longer the length of time the joint venture has been in operation, the better will be the performance.	Ownership, control and performance

Table 4.1 (continued)

	▪ *Set of Perspectives*	*Theoretical focus*
Goodness of fit model 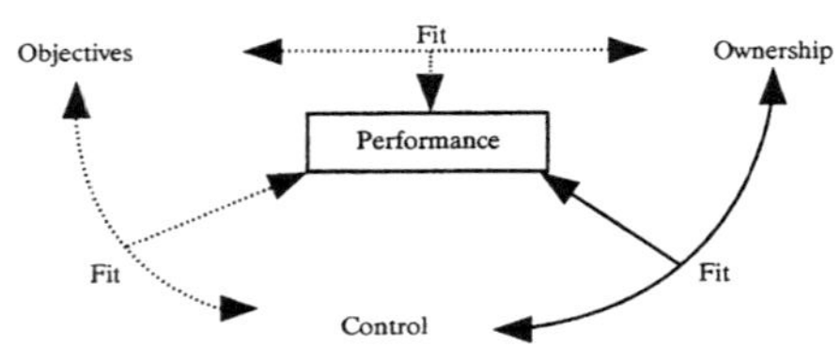	▪ The more the configuration of ownership resources matches that of control, the better will be performance. ▪ The more control matches the joint venture's transactional dependence on its parent companies, the better will be performance.	Performance in relation to the fit between ownership and control

efficiency. The objectives for joint venture formation are underpinned by: *strategic management theory* – strategic positioning; *institutional economics* – transaction costs theory, risk and cost minimisation; and *organisation theory* – learning theory. Kogut (1988) summarised the strategic management approach as focusing on competitive positioning and the impact of such positioning on profitability. Transaction costs arguments are driven by cost minimisation considerations. Organisation theory explains the choices available to joint ventures relative to other modes of cooperation and learning from partners as an objective for entering into strategic alliances. The transition from an overall theoretical perspective to the parent company's objectives is not straightforward, because the theoretical approaches do not map directly onto objectives. The formation model is used to examine the extent to which the partners' desired objectives based on the long or short term have been reflected with regard to their range of ownership resourcing and equity investments in joint ventures.

An explanation for the use of the joint venture form stems from theories on how strategic behaviour influences the competitive positioning of the firm (Kogut 1988). In the business strategy approach, the focus of attention is competition and corporate strategic needs. Hwang (1988) reviews the vertical integration and business strategy literature. He identifies several factors impacting on the firm's decision to commit resources abroad, including the stage of industrial evolution (market attractiveness), the degree of volatility of competition (market stability), the existence of synergistic considerations, the existence of exit barriers, host country risk and location familiarity. Mariti and Smiley (1983), from an early empirical study, identified a number of core objectives for joint venture formation. Porter and Fuller (1986) stress four classes of strategic benefits of joint venture formation in the context of the globalisation of firms and industries. Contractor and Lorange (1988), in addressing the conditions necessary for entering into a cooperative relationship, take the viewpoint of one partner and examine the contribution it makes to a given venture's strategy.

Strategic management theory focuses on the joint venture as a means to realise opportunities in the global business environment. It considers choice of ownership structure in relation to perceived opportunities and available competencies, and also the desired integration of joint venture operations with those of the parent company (Harrigan 1988, Lorange and Roos 1992). Strategic management theory advocates that parent company resource commitment in forming a joint venture will be influenced by its ownership advantages in relation to global and local sector conditions (Dunning 1995). The strategic positioning approach leads to the appreciation of the fact that firms may be driven by strategic objectives.

Erramilli states that

> ownership ... often represents the degree to which the parent multinational corporation exercises control over its subsidiary's activities. This in turn has strong implications for sourcing strategies, standardisation of corporate and marketing strategies, transfer pricing, integration of the MNC's world-wide activities and ultimately its performance'.
>
> Erramilli (1996:225)

Translation of a firm's objectives into an appropriate ownership position is contingent upon its ability to implement a strategy that exploits its distinctive competencies along one or several critical dimensions of a firm's activity.

The relationship between longer-term orientation in objectives for forming a joint venture and a greater owner resource commitment has received different degrees of support in terms of theoretical and empirical contributions. The purpose of profiling the following objectives is to see (1) in what way these objectives are long-term, and (2) why a longer-term orientation is hypothesised to encourage greater owner resource commitment. Partners that have a long-term perspective are considered likely to hold the following objectives:

- to gain a strategic position *vis-à-vis* competitors;
- to establish strong business presence/credibility;
- opportunity for good long-term profit;
- international expansion;
- access to foreign markets;
- diversification of products and services.

To gain a strategic position vis-à-vis competitors and to establish strong business presence/credibility Entering into a joint venture can influence which other companies a firm competes with and the basis of that competition (Porter and Fuller 1986). As was observed earlier, Buckley (1990) suggested that to gain a strategic position is to derive maximum benefit from a firm's net wealth by deploying it effectively. Hence there is a need to identify strengths and weaknesses relative to competitors and to seek to minimise threats and to take advantage of opportunities.

Joint ventures can defend current strategic positions against forces that are too strong for an individual firm to withstand. Through the combined internal resource of diverse firms, joint ventures can create more effective competitors (Harrigan 1984). Joint ventures may be used as a defensive ploy to reduce competition, for example by co-opting potential or existing competition into a joint venture. Alternatively, a joint venture may be used as an offensive strategy, for example by linking up with a rival in order to put pressure on the profits and market share of a common competitor (Contractor and Lorange 1988).

Long-term profit Long-term profit is the product of a successful strategic approach. Geringer and Hebert (1991) stated that profitability is classified as an objective performance measure. The achievement of long-term profit by joint venture partners provides information regarding the extent to which a joint venture has or perhaps will meet its objectives.

International expansion and access to foreign markets For small and medium-sized enterprises that lack international experience, initial overseas expansion is often likely to be via a joint venture. Contractor and Lorange (1988) indicate that the move to a new foreign market and the development of a global strategy can be facilitated by joint venture formation, even for firms with considerable overseas experience.

Ownership resources committed by investing companies Collis (1991) and Hamel *et al.* (1989) have suggested that core resources or competencies are vital to long-term competitive advantage. Lecraw (1984) indicated that desirable technology can command an unusually high degree of leverage and bargaining position, even in countries characterised by higher investment risks. A firm with high R&D intensity may prefer to have complete control over its proprietary know-how in order to preserve and/or best exploit that know-how, given imperfections in the external markets for technology (for example, Buckley and Casson 1976). Thus, the higher the parent R&D intensity, the greater the possibility that the foreign affiliate will be fully owned (Stopford and Wells 1972).

Equity capital to joint ventures An investing firm is more likely to possess the necessary financial resources for full ownership of its foreign operations. Vernon (1983) and Ting (1988) suggest that when the owning company possesses these skills then majority equity shares may be more efficient.

The relationship between a short-term orientation in objectives for forming a joint venture and a limited owner resource commitment has two aspects. The first is to consider what objectives are short-term. The second is to see whether a short term orientation in objectives tends to lead to a lower equity and a more limited range of ownership resources commitment. Partners that have a short-term perspective are considered likely to hold the following objectives:

- low-cost sourcing;
- low labour cost;
- benefit from advantageous transfer pricing;
- opportunity for quick profit;
- benefit from tax incentives.

Low-cost sourcing; low labour cost; benefit from advantageous transfer pricing Global sourcing involves setting up production operations in different countries to serve various markets, or buying and assembling components, parts or finished products worldwide (Davidson 1982). If the combination of complementary distinctive resources and competencies is a major objective for engaging in joint ventures then firms are more likely to insist on low-cost sourcing, low labour cost and the diversification of products and services to ensure the transfer of the distinctive resource and competencies to the joint venture. A joint venture may attempt to reduce costs by expanding output to achieve these benefits. By effectively coordinating sourcing activities, firms may secure lower cost structures and achieve higher-quality outputs. Moreover, by operating in several countries, multinational firms have the ability to coordinate manufacturing activities on a global scale, to exploit not only their competitive advantages but also the comparative advantages of different countries (Murray *et al.* 1995). Because of these advantages, the effective use of global sourcing should improve a firm's market performance such as market share, sales growth and profitability.

Opportunity for quick profit; benefit from tax incentives Preferences for a quick profit and gaining a benefit from tax incentives are by definition short-term objectives. This is likely to be associated with capital shortages and cash flow pressures such as are experienced by many developing country joint venture partners, especially state-owned enterprises in China (Child 1994, Warner 1996b). Contractor (1989b) indicates that technology can be used more quickly and market penetration achieved more easily through a joint venture. One of the partners may have an established distribution system or may have better access to local suppliers, either of which can create a greater volume of sales in a shorter period of time.

Equity capital Stopford and Wells (1972) and Hennart (1991) found that joint ventures that manufactured products different from those of the parent were more likely to have a minority equity share. A firm entering into a product area not produced by the parent may find that the necessary product-specific capability such as technology, manufacturing know-how, distribution and so on is possessed by another partner firm. Under such conditions, firms will be more likely to have a minority equity share.

Ownership resourcing to joint ventures Dunning (1980) and Contractor (1989a) suggest that the use of limited investment is needed to absorb the high costs of marketing, for enforcing patents and contracts and for achieving economies of scale. Therefore, a firm with these objectives will tend to favour a lower-scale investment, and minority equity shares may be more efficient. Generally speaking, investing firms may need complementary knowledge and experience to operate successfully in culturally dissimilar countries and may prefer minority equity share investment.

THE UNIVERSALISTIC MODEL

This identifies the extent to which joint venture partners bring distinctive resources and competencies to the partnership and the provision of resources that enable them to exercise control. The universalistic perspective applies to the relationship between ownership and control that contains attributes of ownership resourcing. The range of ownership resourcing influences the joint venture's control over strategic and operational matters. Control can be treated as a function of (1) equity capital resources, (2) ownership contractual resources and (3) ownership non-contractual resources. This will postulate how each category (1, 2, or 3) leads to an overall area of control or to a specific one. Alternatively, it measures how a combination of the categories 1, 2, and 3 provides control over strategic and operational areas.

Yan and Gray (1994a) suggest that equity structure is not equivalent to management control. Once equity structure is agreed, it delineates the relative positions of the partners, and sets a tone for the successive negotiations over management structure and control. Many researchers have suggested that equity carries with it a legal right to influence decisions (Contractor 1990, Blodgett 1991,

Gomes-Casseres 1989b, 1990). They noted that equity generally brings a number of formal means that generate owning company participation.

Geringer (1991) indicated that the ownership resources committed by an owning company could be tangible or intangible in nature. Examples include financial resources, patents or technical know-how, experienced managerial personnel, and access to markets and distribution systems. Valuation of technology investment as an equity share can easily lead to a dispute among parent companies if one side intends to undermine the exclusivity of the proprietary technology that leads to the other partner having a greater equity share. Technologies as equity investments include core competencies and value-creating disciplines that are precisely the kinds of firm-specific assets for which there are only imperfect external markets. Clearly, the value of technology is related directly to the relationship with its external environment – that is, demand for the products, competition, host government attitude and country risk (Harrigan 1987, 1988).

The equity position held by a parent company appears to be important, because it determines the mix of skills, resources, operating policies, procedures and overall competitive viability of a joint venture. The long-term strategic vision for the joint venture tends to be made and influenced by the board of directors and general managers. Therefore, the greater the share of equity held by a parent company, the greater will be its overall control and influence in an joint venture. Schaan (1983, 1988) found that nominations of members of a venture's board of directors and general manager were important control mechanisms. Yan and Gray (1994b) found in a sample of Sino-US joint ventures that the general manager had always been a board member and served as the executive officer, and they made important operating decisions for the joint venture. Yan and Gray found that the ownership split was consistent with only one dimension of control, namely board membership. With respect to the other dimensions, no consistent relationship was observed. Yan and Gray's findings provide additional evidence that equity structure is not equivalent to management control. Rather, as a type of resource committed by the partners, equity investment constitutes a source of bargaining power, which in turn contributes to management control. Once the equity structure is agreed on, it delineates the relative positions of the partners and sets a tone for the successive negotiations on control.

Boards of directors are likely to have overall control (Bjorkman 1995) and strategic influence. There is normally a correspondence between membership of the board and percentage of equity shareholding, although the chairman of the board and the appointment of general manager are not necessarily dependent on equity share. In the context of managing a joint venture's operations, boards of directors serve many specific purposes in deciding long-term strategic vision, profit allocation and reinvestment policy, and in providing strategic indicators for the parent companies that can lead to revisions in their control polices. A parent company may be able to influence the relative allocation of control over a joint venture by influencing staffing of the joint venture's top management positions. The joint venture general manager's position, in particular, can affect a joint venture's operation (Schaan and Beamish 1988), since the general manager is responsible for maintaining relationships with each of the parents, as well as running the venture. The means of selecting, training, evaluating and rewarding the performance of joint venture general managers can significantly affect not only the joint venture itself, but also its relationship with each parent (Geringer and Hebert 1989).

Ownership resources may have a contractual basis. Contractual ownership in business takes two forms: (1) equity and (2) formalised rights to exclude control over, and/or benefit from, assets including technology. Examples of technology ownership include patents, intellectual property rights and the contractual acknowledgement of proprietary technology.

It is expected that, as the perceived importance of product and process technology, marketing expertise to joint venture increases, the tendency for investing companies to define their responsibility on a contractual basis will increase also. Pierce *et al.* (1991) stated that the strength of this commitment should be positively associated with each of the design features of the formal ownership system. From a legal perspective, ownership and its implicit right to control, in turn, create responsibility. Critical resources committed by owning companies on a contractual basis may increase the probability of achieving a desired behaviour or outcome, efficiently utilising its resources, and effectively implementing its strategy. Critical resources are those few key areas of activity that must be performed particularly well in order for the organisation to outperform its competitors (Buchel *et al.* 1998). These key resources are determined by the underlying characteristics of the firm's industry (Porter 1980) and influenced by the perceptions of different parent companies. The more parent companies contribute their product and production technology through contracts, the more influence will they exert in most of the key joint venture functions.

Ownership resourcing on a contractual basis appears to be important in the formation and operation of the joint venture, since the contract can limit obligation and responsibility in terms of the realisation of ownership resources. Contractual after-sales service provides a strategic mechanism whereby companies can gain direct access to the local market. A contractual requirement for one party to provide management systems legitimises the power and rights they put into local management and technical training. These resource contributions are explicitly specified in joint venture agreements (contracts, memorandums and licences) or in other associated legal agreements.

The non-contractual bases of ownership in business can include 'soft' technology in the form of technological know-how, manager competencies, professional services and training. They also extend to the goodwill and cultural capital that may derive from the provision of such resources. Efforts to define non-contractual ownership resources continue. Madhok (1995) has reported how the trust-centred approach provides additional insight and enriches current understanding of multinational ownership preference and the tolerance for joint ventures. Beamish (1984) and Reichers (1985) recognise two components of commitment relevant to joint venture relationships. One is behavioural commitment, which focuses on the prime behaviours of continuing the relationship and compliance to organisational rules, largely in response to cost–benefit analyses. The other is attitudinal commitment, which focuses on acceptance of organisational goals and values, a willingness to exert effort for the organisation and a strong desire to be a part of the organisation. Non-contractual ownership resourcing demonstrates that commitment in the actions and values of key decision-makers regarding continuation of the relationship, acceptance of the joint goals and values of the partnership and a willingness to invest resources in the relationship (Beamish and Banks 1987).

As a parent firm's contribution of key resources on a non-contractual resourcing to joint venture increases, it is expected that the relative importance of the commitment, trust and goodwill will increase correspondingly. If the partners have distinctive competencies in technology and management then they tend to dominate in the corresponding functional areas. Over time, non-contractual resourcing provides trust, goodwill and learning. The more the local partners contribute knowledge and skills that are in the areas of marketing assets (brand names and distribution networks), the more they transfer from their own company where their knowledge is wholly owned to the joint venture where it is only partially owned. Contributing ownership resourcing on a non-contractual basis may be the way managers become more involved in the joint venture's decision process. One recent study, however, has provided evidence that cultural differences between partners affect how they define trust and its importance in structuring performance assessment (Parkhe 1993). Thorelli (1986) observed that in Asian cultures trust may supplant contractual arrangements.

The 'universalistic' model considers the implications of the combined ownership categories on overall control. Ownership configurations can be factored into equity, contractual and non-contractual investments in the joint venture. The idea that joint ventures pool partner ownership resources of expertise and other assets features prominently in the classical entry decision literature (Stopford and Wells 1972, Vernon and Wells 1991, Lecraw 1984, Contractor 1990, Contractor and Lorange 1988). The actualisation of ownership resources to the ongoing process of joint venture management has also received attention (Doz *et al.* 1986). The ownership resources provided and expected benefits accruing to the participating firm are continually adjusted to align with shifts in relative power between the partners (Robinson 1969).

Equity and contractual resources approximate to the 'task-related' complementarities identified by Geringer (1991), while non-contractual resources are likely to include to his 'partner-related' complementarities and competencies, as well as some task-related competencies. The utility of this three-fold distinction becomes apparent when one is considering the implications of each ownership component for control within joint ventures.

Lecraw (1984) and Killing (1983) report that a partner's ownership contributions to joint ventures provide a base for the partner to exercise control. Control exercised over strategic areas of joint venture activity is categorised into use of profit, reinvestment policy, setting strategic priorities, allocating senior managerial positions, and technological innovation. This *strategic control* relates to maximising an owning company's resources for success, which is based on strategic decision-making via the board of directors and the general manager of the joint venture. Initial studies showed that firms rely frequently on majority ownership or on voting control (largely determined by majority equity shareholdings) to achieve effective management control of a joint venture's activities (Tomlinson 1970, Friedman and Beguim 1971). An owning company may also require the participation of its corporate staff in the joint venture's strategic planning in order to safeguard its own interests.

Control exercised over *operational* areas by parent companies is focused on sales and distribution, product pricing, quality control, purchasing policies and production planning. Operational control relies partly on equity-based power, which arises from technology, management and marketing ownership resources to joint ventures. Child (1972) notes that it consists of the utilisation of a limited and explicit set of codified rules and regulations, which delineate desired performance in terms of output and/or behaviour. The control strategy set by owning companies is implemented by using specifications and evaluation against agreed targets in joint ventures. Power and authority have a rational-legal basis (Weber 1947). Foreign partners protect product and process technology, marketing and supplies through formal contracts, which can be used to ensure the potential ownership resources are realised. Most written standard procedures in joint venture are laid down and monitored by the joint venture board and general managers.

Very few studies of a joint ventures have directly addressed performance. This is due largely to the great variety of joint venture types, which makes comparability a problem (Edstrom and Galbraith 1977). Given the complexity of the problem, it is not surprising that there are many different theoretical propositions on the determinants of performance in joint venture. Child identified two main theoretical prospectives on the determinants of performance in companies; he indicated that

> universalistic theory comprises arguments that the presence of certain attributes will, of itself, be conductive to superior performance in most, if not all, circumstances ... Contingency theory contains propositions that the attributes favourable to higher performance will alter according to the circumstances under which a company is operating.
>
> Child (1974:175)

The universalistic perspective, as applied to such performance, hypothesises that certain attributes influence the level of such performance.

It holds that higher performance will be a function of (1) ownership resourcing, (2) transactional operational resources, (3) control and (4) duration of joint venture operation. The universalistic model examines how each factor (1, 2, 3, or 4) predicts performance variation. The universalistic perspective implies that a wider range of ownership resourcing will contribute positively to the fulfilment of a joint venture strategy. Joint venture transactional resources refer to the owning company's access to resources, and the proportion of input–output transactions supplied by the owning companies. Control might influence performance through the imposition of accountability for standards. The duration of the joint venture is assumed to promote collaboration and integration between the joint venture's owning companies.

With regard to the impact of ownership resources on joint venture performance, Lee and Beamish (1995) found that MNE executives from the low-performing joint ventures regarded their local partners' contribution as unimportant, while those from the high-performing ventures considered their partners' contributions important. Buckley and Casson (1988) indicate that committed partners have more efficient joint ventures. This implies that greater commitment of resources leads to higher performance. The work of Killing (1982, 1983), Schaan (1983) and Beamish (1985) suggests an ownership resources hypothesis, where the combined technological and managerial capability between the foreign and local partners affects the pattern of performance of the joint venture.

Barney (1991) suggests that resources and core competencies generate competitive advantage and superior performance. Pfeffer and Salancik (1978) and Murray *et al.* (1995) suggest that availability of alternative sources of supply is one factor that allows joint ventures to switch from one supplier to another, or to use substitute products, without incurring high switching costs. Agarwal and Ramaswami (1992) suggest that when a firm possesses superior assets and skill it may run the risk of loss of long-term revenues if it shares this knowledge with host country firms. Therefore, when the firm possesses these skills, their transfer to a joint venture should lead to higher performance.

Collis (1991) defines core competencies as irreversible assets by means of which the firm is uniquely advantaged. If a firm contributes more critical resources to an inter-organisational arrangement does its partner, it will gain power in the partnership. Put simply, critical resources such as cash capital, technology and marketing expertise constitute power in interorganisational relationships, its nature being determined by who brings what and how much to the joint venture. A partner will gain power if the resources provided are critical and difficult for the other partner to replace. Hamel (1991) has shown that a firm's competitive position is threatened by sharing or exposing core resources.

Whether joint ventures are performing well or badly may be expected to depend on the proportion of operational inputs supplied from the parent companies, and how much the parent companies provide outlets for the joint venture's products. Operational inputs are defined as the materials/components directly supplied by the parent companies. Hennart (1982) notes that on the supply side the exchange is costly because the buyer cannot know the characteristics of what he is buying without appropriating it. Therefore, performance may be influenced by the density of the distribution of transactional resources between the owning company and its subsidiaries. With regard to transactional resource dependence, the proportion of the resources supplied by parent companies is used to predict the level of protection and guarantees to which the partners are committed.

Most of the joint ventures in China had the proportions of their sourcing supplied from the foreign and Chinese parents roughly in balance (Zhou 1996). The judgement of whether a joint venture is performing well may be made in terms of the proportion of resources inputs supplied by the partners, or the resource outputs taken by them. Hickson *et al.* (1971) indicate that the degree of competition is taken as a measure of the extent to which alternatives are available from other organisations. This implies that one organisation can have power over others.

Killing's study (1983) indicated that dominant-partnered joint ventures are more likely to be successful, at least compared with shared management ventures. Killing measured performance via management's assessment of the joint venture's performance. To justify the use of such variables rather than financial indicators, he explained that the profitability of the joint venture for a parent firm is based not solely on the joint venture's profits but also on transfer prices, royalties and management fees not included in traditional financial performance measures. Killing suggested that a joint venture's autonomy was more a result than a cause of its performance.

One way to gain an insight into performance is to assess the extent to which control is obtained from holding equity. Most foreign investing companies tend to assess their satisfaction with the performance of joint ventures by reference to the extent of the critical managerial and technological resources they brought to them. However, a critical determinant of joint venture performance appears to be the control exercised by parents over a venture's activities (Janger 1980, Killing 1983, Geringer 1988). Blodgett (1991) and Lecraw (1984) suggest that a crucial factor determining the return that parent companies can expect to get from a joint venture is the amount of control the parent is able to levy on the joint venture. With a sample of 71 joint ventures in India and Pakistan, Tomlinson (1970) found that joint ventures evidenced higher levels of profitability when their UK parents assumed a more relaxed attitude toward control. Using a sample of 169 US MNCs involved in more than 1100 joint ventures, Franko examined how parents exercise control over joint ventures. Franko's main argument is that different strategies have different control requirements, and that these influence the stability of joint ventures (Franko 1976). Geringer and Hebert commented that

> Franko made a significant contribution by examining the joint venture control–performance link using the 'strategy–structure' conceptual framework. Within this perspective, the degree of parent control as well as the joint venture's performance is presumed to be contingent on the MNC's strategy and structure.
> (Geringer and Hebert 1989:243)

Buckley and Casson (1988) note that dominant control is a mechanism for reducing the risks associated with coordination, potential conflicts, disclosures and, consequently, for minimising transaction costs and stabilising the joint venture. Beamish and Banks (1987), Dunning (1977) and Hennart (1982) suggest that attention is given to how a parent can use its resources and its core competence to gain a higher level of overall control, which, in turn, may lead to a better performance. These arguments appear to support Killing's (1983) view that shared control constitutes the major source of management difficulties in joint ventures, while dominant-partnered joint ventures are easier to manage and consequently more successful.

The performance achieved by joint ventures seems to vary over time, though this has rarely been studied. Harrigan (1987) finds that the joint ventures of longer standing tend to achieve a more successful performance. The reason is that the gap between mutual foreign and local partners' knowledge of the economy, technology, politics and culture is reduced by the actual operating of the joint venture. Learning foreign business practices and experience is likely to reduce the totality of the cost of doing business in the foreign countries (Child and Faulkner, 1998).

THE CONTINGENCY (GOODNESS OF FIT) MODEL

This postulates that the more consistent are the configuration of parent ownership and control then the better will be the performance of the joint venture. In other words, performance is seen to be an outcome of the goodness of fit between these three sets of variables. The model is generally associated with the nature of fit or match between characteristics of joint ventures as an influence on their performance. Indeed, a parent firm may adopt very different ownership resourcing commitments to each of its subsidiaries, in order to establish an optimum strategic presence *vis-à-vis* competitors. It is important to consider the role of parent firm ownership resourcing in the influence and exercise of power over joint ventures, and how these can be attributed to the ownership positioning of the joint ventures. Full contingency fit is not tested in the present study, as it is very much involved with the external environment.

The empirical work conducted by Hill and Hellriegel (1994) suggested that complementarity actually has a negative impact on several dimensions of joint venture performance. Qualitative data suggest that joint venture partners with distinctive competencies in different operational areas may experience difficulties in implementing potential complementarities, owing to problems of integration and the danger of segmentation. On the other hand, Schaan (1983) stated that joint venture success, or the extent to which parent expectations for the joint venture were met, is a function of the fit with three variables: the parent's criteria for success, the activities or decisions it controls and the control mechanisms that are utilised. He concluded that joint ventures in which a parent achieved this fit will show better performance. Janger (1980) suggests that joint venture success should be enhanced when the joint venture's structure fits the owning company's strategy.

The performance of a joint venture will be satisfactory to the partners only if the contributions of the partners, and the expected benefits to them, are kept in balance. Robinson (1969) observed two things. First, the joint venture relationship cannot be a zero-sum game, or else the two partners would not commit ownership resources at all. Second, each of the partners must expect to gain from the partnership. Robinson concluded that the performance of a joint venture was dependent, to a certain degree, on the balance of benefits the partners achieve from the performance. If the joint venture is in a 'win–lose' situation then the likelihood of low performance is high.

Very few studies have focused on the relationship between parent–joint venture transactional links and market performance. Murray *et al.* (1995) is a recent exception. From an examination of prior literature, Murray and his colleagues identified two contingent factors as relevant to their study: the bargaining power of suppliers (Porter 1986), and transaction costs (Williamson 1979). For each of these factors, the ownership resources can be explained by evaluating the overall transactional control aspects and the nature of the joint venture structure. Murray *et al.* (1995) selected transactional resource inputs supplied or outputs taken by the partners as the indicators of performance.

The contingency perspective assumes that it is possible to identify a number of factors that will in combination determine levels of joint venture performance. In the present study, certain factors in this study can be regarded as dependent variables, for example the channels for technical and managerial support, the channels for useful information to the joint venture partners, the possibly advantageous terms for the joint venture's product pricing, a reduced uncertainty for a joint venture, and reduced transaction costs. These dependent factors are more likely to stimulate the partners to make adjustments in their strategies and in their control modes.

SUMMARY

In summary, the three models can be used synergistically to bring a multi-faceted understanding of IJV operation. The objectives identified for joint ventures in conjunction with the formation model can be used to explain a foreign investing firm's strategic behaviour with regard to international market presence, profit and cost considerations and equity preference. The universalistic model postulates the effects of the combination of ownership resourcing on the management of IJVs. The concept is based upon the supposition that the range of ownership resourcing inputs (including distinctive resources and competencies contributed by IJV partners) provides control leverage over strategic and operational matters. The contingency model argues that it is the goodness of fit between the distinctive resources brought by partners to the IJV, and the control leveraged from those resources and competencies, which determines the level of performance of the IJV.

Part II

The Field Study

5 Research Undertaken

INTRODUCTION

Most studies of the relationship between the ownership and control of IJVs have utilised a limited perspective on both of these factors, or have looked at only one of their dimensions (Yan and Gray 1994a). Parkhe (1993) has argued that the body of theory on IJVs as a whole is underdeveloped and 'messy' – the latter to the extent that there are many competing perspectives. On the other hand, these perspectives offer a range of insights that can be brought together sufficiently to distinguish key concepts and arguments from which a research model can be derived. This chapter discusses the other methodological steps that were taken prior to analysing the data.

EXPLAINING THE FIELD METHODOLOGY USED IN THE STUDY: CHOICE OF A SURVEY APPROACH

Yin (1994) suggests three criteria for choosing a research strategy: the type of research questions, the control an investigator has over actual behavioural events, and the focus on contemporary versus historical phenomena. The research behind his book can, to a large extent, be identified as of the survey type, in that (1) the data were collected at a single point in time, (2) there is a fixed set of checklists and (3) responses are systematically classified, so that quantitative comparisons can be made.

A survey approach involves the construction of a relatively comprehensive view from a large number of cases. The method used for the surveys include postal questionnaires, interviews and, where possible, the use of existing statistics. A survey strategy tends to favour describing the prevalence or frequency of a phenomenon. Compared with interview studies, a postal questionnaire survey has a number of advantages, including a substantial saving of time and money, greater assurance of anonymity, lack of interview bias, standardised wording and accessibility. Among its disadvantages are a low response rate, the capability of gathering information only on reported behaviour, lack of control over the research setting, lack of control over the order in which questions are answered and the impossibility of repeating or clarifying questions when necessary. These disadvantages can be overcome more readily using interviews.

The research design and method of fieldwork used in this study place it primarily within the comparative, survey category. This study was undertaken using a relatively quantitative approach, with a moderately large sample (Kerlinger 1979, Bryman 1989), in contrast to a small-scale, qualitative case-study research design.* Three considerations led to this decision.

First, the key concepts of objectives, ownership, control and performance can be defined and operationalized. It is therefore possible to apply such concepts across a sample. Second, there is evidence of the likelihood of resistance by joint venture managers to intensive studies, as these would take up a lot of their individual time. Third, by working in collaboration with a research project, it was possible to gain access to funds to visit a large number of joint ventures during the fieldwork phase.

The research was also carried out within a comparative design, and involved a structured checklist. Some of the questions on the checklist are closed-ended, and lend themselves readily to quantitative analysis, while others are open-ended and more exploratory in nature (Yin, 1994). Personal visits to each research site provided further insights of a qualitative nature, which have been used to assist the interpretation of results (Creswell 1994).

The author chose to use interviews in the research. Among the disadvantages of interviews are travel cost, time consumed and interview bias. However, the advantages of interviews over postal questionnaires include the generally higher response rate, flexibility, ability to observe non-verbal behaviour, control over the investigative environment and control over question order, as well as the ability to explore by follow-up probing and a greater chance to assess the validity of responses (via cross-checks, observation of non-verbal behaviour and

* A case-study research strategy is focused and holistic. Appropriate methodologies can be interactive, and objective. Case-studies are more likely to answer the 'how' and 'why' questions about a contemporary phenomenon. They are strongly contextual, and are able to gain insights from a sequence of events, and tease out the critical part from the specific contexts. The case-study method, however, can be costly in terms of time, money and energy. It relies on the collection of rich documentary information, and the extensive use of interviewers and/or observation. Parkhe (1993) has indicated that the limitations of the case-study method can lead to over-complex theories and the sacrifice of parsimony. Its ability to test hypotheses is limited to disconfirmation.

so forth). One advantage of using an interview study is the higher response rate. The participating companies knew the interviews would take only a maximum of one day of their time. For this reason, and also to improve the validity of recorded information through the use of tandem interviewing (two interviewers), this study was conducted as part of a wider team project, as described below.

PILOT STUDY

While the concepts of 'ownership' and 'control' need to be defined with reference to the specific context of international joint ventures, in order to enable measures to be constructed, this construction of measures and the formulation of questions associated with them can benefit from a pilot study when new ground is being covered. A pilot study was therefore conducted in September 1993. Five international joint ventures in China were chosen to test the appropriateness of draft questions and the tolerance of joint venture managers for the kind of research proposed, as well as to gain insights that would assist the formulation of research models. The one or two senior Chinese managers (general manager or deputy general manager) in each of the joint ventures were interviewed. A basic checklist was constructed to gain insight into joint venture management and also to try ways of gaining precise information on ownership. The resulting notes were examined and analysed for relevant insights in relation to the building of research models. These were based upon the data being collected, and, as a consequence, led to a redefinition of ownership resources to make them more applicable to the business reality of the joint ventures.

Given the current primitive stage of theory development, conducting some preliminary fieldwork to understand the parameters relevant to the relationship between ownership and control was very important. Obviously, the empirical research on the relationship might be constrained by methodological barriers. This in turn could limit the potential for theory advancement. Qualitative research such as case-studies, participant observation, interviews and content analysis permits a deeper understanding and sharper delineation of concept domains. Quantitative research such as analysis of existing data sets, surveys, structured questionnaires, observational measurements and modelling improves the reliability of data and can delineate relationships. Constructing an interview method is used to generate reasonably reliable data to permit the test of the research models, but which at the same time could offer some insight into the nature of the relationship between the variables. The five pilot studies indicated that if the author could conduct a sufficient number of joint venture interviews, then data relevant to the models could be obtained by using a quantitative method, supplemented by qualitative insights.

ACCESS AND INTERVIEW PROCEDURE

China as a joint venture context has some special features, requiring its own methods of approaching managers from joint ventures. Having regard to the regional context of foreign investment in China, it is important to identify research locations in which Sino-foreign joint ventures are most prevalent. These are the coastal regions of China. However, managers in joint ventures located in the north and south of the country may react differently in terms of access and interview. With regard to access, an approach to Chinese managers is facilitated by their flexibility of management style. Most Chinese managers tend to answer the telephone themselves instead of using a secretary, so the easiest way is to get access by phoning a Chinese manager directly. Foreign managers in Sino-foreign joint ventures are less flexible. They prefer to be approached on a more formal basis, and generally take a more rigid view of the time they will put aside for an interview.

Confidentiality is a particularly sensitive issue in Sino-foreign joint ventures. Difficulties of data access in the research project arose in two areas: operational records providing statistics on joint venture performance, and the perceptions that Chinese and foreign managers held of one another. Information on the company's operational performance record is not easy to obtain. Senior managers tended to feel that the release of confidential information could put them at a competitive disadvantage. Their willingness to assess joint venture performance along scales, and to articulate perceptions of the partner's managers in the joint venture, could be influenced by how open and assured their personalities were. A few respondents felt that the information would be used against them, and thought that this part of the interview was not legitimate.

The fieldwork was conducted in the period May 1994 to April 1995. The interview procedure was as follows. Interviews were normally conducted either with a colleague either from the State Council's International Technology and Economy Research Institute of the People's Republic of China or from the University of Cambridge. The author generally took fifteen minutes to provide a brief on the research, and gave a three-page, well-written introductory statement of the project, together with a one-page covering letter that covered concerns about anonymity. The letter, written in two versions (English and Chinese) was prepared and authorised by the State Council of China and Cambridge University. The author asked the more sensitive questions at the end of the interview after all the other questions had been answered and rapport had been built up. Most senior Chinese managers tended to be less cautious about the company's operational performance data than were their foreign partners. In some cases, the author was aware that some managers preferred to focus on a particular topic such as procurement, investment decisions, product pricing or marketing. It was important that the author allowed the managers in companies to express their own interest or enthusiasm and to feel that they had the opportunity to talk about this within the scope of the interview. The author also encouraged a positive attitude towards the interview by indicating the benefits of previous international joint venture research, together with the feedback report that the participating companies would receive.

Marked differences between foreign and Chinese managers over joint venture management were expected as they are reflected in their perceptions of management. Such differences between foreign and Chinese managers may have had an effect on the quality of the data received. In order to be able to present an overall perspective for each joint venture, the subject matter concerning the relative influence of Chinese and foreign joint venture partners was in many cases answered separately by foreign and Chinese managers in each venture. This permitted a check to be made for national bias, as is reported below.

Research on ownership and control in joint ventures is a hot topic in China. Some interviewees knew what the investigator wanted to hear, as they had had dealings with different investigators at various times. There was, therefore, a risk of bias, because respondents were likely to say what they thought the interviewers would like to hear, rather than to provide their own opinions. In such cases, it was always important to try to double check information with other interviewees. The author did experience respondents who said they could not answer because the question was too general and vague, or because they had never thought about the topic. In such circumstances, the author tended to use more specific, probing questions to guide the answers. The author also experienced some cases where respondents were afraid that their replies would reveal a lack of education. In such situations, it was important to emphasise that there were no right and wrong answers to the particular questions.

Each interview normally lasted at least an hour, and many were much longer. Maintaining the respondent's commitment through the interview could be difficult. Some respondents suggested that their time was too valuable to waste on the study, or that the study was not applicable to them. As the study progressed, the author found it was very important to emphasise the number of cases she had completed and the potential importance of improving understanding about the management of international joint ventures. In order to gain an insight into the mutual perceptions of Chinese and foreign managers, some open-ended questions were asked that often contributed to an overrun of the interview beyond its previously agreed length. With this possibility in mind, the author asked the open-ended questions in the last section of the interview. Given the scope of the questions on objectives, ownership resourcing, control and performance, the knowledge and interpretation of different managers tended to vary depending upon their different positions in the companies. The aim was therefore to interview several respondents from one company, as this was likely to strengthen the validity of the information provided. This was also to get both a Chinese and foreign perspective, especially on control and the subjective evaluation of performance. On average, three managers were interviewed in each joint venture, through the actual numbers ranged from just one to as many as five.

SAMPLING

The joint ventures in the sample varied in term of their size. Most of the ventures were set up after 1990. The author first designated a population of interest. The criteria for selection were that the joint venture should have a minimum of two years' operation, and that at least one expatriate manager should be working in it. To identify those joint ventures within the population chosen, a list of Sino-foreign joint ventures within the chosen sectors was established through reference to telephone directories, newspapers, journals, published sources such as the 40 000-entry Joint Ventures Directory published by the Chinese Ministry of Foreign Trade & Economic Cooperation (MOFTEC), chambers of commerce, embassies and government departments in China. A total of 500 international joint ventures were identified as a result of this analysis. The author then approached 311 of these companies to seek some details that would ascertain their suitability for inclusion in the sample. Some of the companies proved impossible to contact, because they either had been taken over and restructured or had gone out of business altogether.

In addition, some firms had moved location and could not be traced. In some cases, although the firm could be contacted there was no longer anyone in employment with sufficient knowledge to provide the depth of answers the study required. The author even found some firms that had been established as equity joint ventures, but did not have real foreign parties involved at all.

Originally, the author had intended to construct a sample of 30 joint ventures, since this was thought sufficient for testing her hypotheses. However, her associations with a University of Cambridge research project and with the University of Hong Kong provided fieldwork funding for this number to be more than doubled. Finally, 67 Sino-foreign joint ventures agreed to participate in the study. Within this sample, 212 respondents were interviewed personally (see Appendix I). Some foreign parent companies have several joint ventures located in China, often with different Chinese partners. In exploring the sampling frame, the author deliberately tried to avoid the replication of foreign firms in the sample. The most effective way of reaching the target of 67 joint ventures, which were spread in locations across China, was to contact firms by telephone. The method of contacting the joint ventures was approximately 95 per cent by telephone and 5 per cent by fax.

In order to increase the rate of success of access to the joint ventures, it proved very helpful to have some background knowledge of a firm before making the initial approach. Gaining access to an expatriate manager required telephoning him or her in English and then agreeing to send an information sheet on the study together with a covering letter.

The sample size of 67 international joint ventures was arrived at using the following criteria. The target was set at 64 such joint ventures, divided equally into two sectors and distributed among four different categories of foreign owner nationality. More joint ventures than the target number had to be contacted to secure sufficient access within the limited time-frame, and this in the event led to the slight overshoot. The stratification of the sample was not strictly necessary for the progress of the present study, although it enabled a check to be made on the generalisability of its findings *vis-à-vis* sector and foreign partner nationality. The reason for stratification lay in the intention of the wider project to examine sector and nationality (or cultural) factors in some detail. In the sample, approximately 60 per cent ($N = 40$) of the joint ventures have over 50 per cent of their equity held by foreign parents. Twelve have a 50:50 split, while in the remaining 15 the foreign parent(s) hold under 50 per cent of the equity. Foreign equity shares ranged from 25 per cent to 95 per cent (see Appendix II).

ELECTRONICS AND FMCG SECTORS

Thirty-three of the international joint ventures are located in the advanced non-domestic electronics sector (mostly microcircuits and telecommunications), while 34 are located in the fast-moving consumer goods sector. The choice of these two sectors took into account the following considerations.

First, the pattern of joint venture investment in China is influenced by the Chinese economic and political climate. Chinese policy has shifted from emphasising heavy industry to the development of light industry such as FMCG and electronic sectors. Choosing these two sectors would reflect the emphasis of Chinese government policy. Second, the fact that these two sectors contain quite large populations of foreign companies operating in China ensured a reasonable population from which to select the sample. Third, the contrasting primary business needs of the sectors were expected to generate different ownership configuration patterns and control priorities.

In advanced electronics, technology transfer and its management are a key factor, with product design being a focus of competence. In fast-moving consumer goods, brand management and marketing are particularly important, and technological competence is more likely to rest in the process rather than the product. It was expected that choosing two different business sectors would be more likely to show distinctly any different characteristics deriving from the joint ventures' task environments.

The sample was also stratified to provide equal numbers of foreign parent companies from world regions for which some of the literature postulates different approaches to management – the US and UK (Anglo-Saxon), Continental Europe, Japan, and Overseas Chinese

Table 5.1 Distribution of ownership (equity share) by nationality of foreign partner

	Ownership by foreign partner		
Nationality	*Majority*	*50:50*	*Minority*
Anglo-Saxon (N = 17)	12	2	3
Continental European (N = 17)	10	3	4
Japanese (N = 16)	7	5	4
Overseas Chinese (N = 17)	11	2	4

(Alston 1986, Hofstede 1991, Trompenears 1993, Hickson *et al.* 1995). Although the sample was not constructed with the intention of building in a systematic local regional variation within China, it happens that the joint ventures were located in three main areas of Chinese industrial development: Beijing–Tianjin, Shanghai–Hangzhou and Guangzhou–Shenzhen. Given the size and historical internal differentiation of China, regional location may be expected to impact on joint venture management (Child and Stewart 1997).

The dispersion of the sample across sector, foreign parent nationality and regional location in China would test the limits of the generalisability of the findings from the sample taken as a whole. It is beyond the scope of this book to explore sector, foreign nationality and regional variations in any detail, although the data do exist to perform this complex analysis.

CHECKLIST DEVELOPMENT

During the fieldwork, members of the China State Council provided valuable assistance in recording the content of the interview. This was particularly helpful when interviewing Chinese respondents, because most of them were unwilling to permit the use of tape-recording. Some existing scales for measuring ownership resources were modified for this research, and others (such as the measures of control) were newly constructed. The author was aware that the measures should not be bound to a Western approach, and they were modified to suit Chinese joint ventures as much as possible. The pilot studies were of considerable assistance in this respect – for example, in developing the measures of contractual and non-contractual resources, especially those that might be provided by the Chinese partner. A preliminary version of the checklist was then reviewed by a small group of colleagues, who were experts on international joint ventures. Next, the checklist was evaluated through the five pilot studies. The questionnaire was trailed with specific managers to establish appropriateness, so as ensure that the checklist did not sound naïve when used with the full sample.

DATA COLLECTION

The author gathered information from both foreign and Chinese senior managers of the international joint ventures. Mandarin Chinese was the language of interviews with local and Overseas Chinese respondents, while English was generally used with foreign respondents. An interpreter was required in the case of some Japanese managers. Senior managers from each side (usually the general manager and deputy general manager) were interviewed, together with the heads of CP's two or three functions – typically operations, HRM and technology or marketing, depending on the sector. Interviews with general managers and deputy general managers normally lasted two hours or more, while those with other managers usually took between one hour and 90 minutes. Whenever acceptable, the interviews were tape-recorded. The interviews were conducted with foreign and Chinese managers on their own.

Both quantitative and qualitative data were collected. Those reported in this book are primarily quantitative in nature. In collecting them, interviewees were either asked directly for figures, to be verified where necessary from documents – such as percentage shares of equity held by parent companies – or asked to complete perceptual scales for which preprinted cards were used to assist the process. Following the interviews, all data were transcribed onto separate schedules from the original notes and tapes.

The full checklists used in the research comprised twenty-one pages of questions, and covered the interviewee's details in terms of position, contact address, the length of interview and brief previous working experience. The checklist as a whole was divided into nine parts. The first part was used to establish what were the objectives of parent companies, how the foreign and Chinese partners were brought together, and their previous international venturing experience. The second part was designed to record specific ownership resources supplied from parent companies to joint ventures. The third part was used to establish operational profile of the joint ventures. The fourth part was designed to create an understanding of the parameters of top management. The fifth part was constructed to profile the strategic benefits which the major foreign and Chinese parent companies sought from the joint venture and their achievement. The sixth part was concerned with the degree of influence is exercised by the foreign and Chinese parties over 13 decision areas of the international venture. The seventh part was used to register commitment. The eighth part was intended to categorise mutual perceptions and working style between foreign and Chinese managers. The ninth part was concerned with international joint ventures' experience. As the project also had an exploratory aspect, and the sample population was only 67, both open- and closed-ended questions were designed into the checklist schedule. The checklist is produced in Appendix III, and the background information collected in this study is in Appendix IV.

It was important to manage the interviews to ensure that all of the questions could be answered in the time allocated for the interview. Obviously, the time allocated also varied depending on any senior manager's situation on the day, but in a fallback situation it was essential to make sure all the questions had been covered within the agreed time-frame.

About 40 per cent of interviews were tape-recorded. Those conducted in Chinese were fully translated, but all interviews were subsequently transcribed onto schedules. It was beneficial to record interviews, but this was particularly helpful when they were conducted in English and Japanese. In some Japanese interviews, the author had to stop the interpreter from time to time to ensure that he or she understood about what the author had said. The prospect of tape-recording seemed to horrify some Japanese and ethnic Chinese joint ventures managers. They did not like to have their voice recorded, in case they might have to take personal responsibility for what they said. The author found it was very important to write full notes as soon as she left the office. She would sit in a corner to record impressions of what the interviewees had said before the details had left her memory. The presence of a second interviewer was extremely helpful in cases where only hand-written notes could be taken, and where recall of further detail was required after the interview. The shortest interview lasted sixty minutes, while the longest lasted four and a half hours. Most of the interviews lasted about one and a half hours.

Telephone contact with joint ventures revealed a preference for making arrangements at short notice. Confirmation of interviews was not necessary in China, and sometimes it could give the firms an opportunity to cancel the appointment. Generally speaking, faxes and telephones from UK to Sino-foreign joint ventures were helpful, because international communication carried some weight in indicating the importance of the interviews. Some information was derived from relevant documents, especially on products and performance. Published company brochures were also consulted.

Economic data of a secondary nature were collected from local commercial bureaux and libraries. These were used to identify the context for the research. The author paid particular attention to relevant Chinese regulations and provisions on international joint ventures located in different locations and business sectors. She also collected some secondary data from the *China Statistical Year Book*, the Ministry of Foreign Trade and Economic Cooperation, the *Foreign Investment Journal*, the *People's Daily*, the *Economic Daily*, and *Beijing Review*. The following information was collected in the interviews.

Objective priorities of parent companies at joint venture formation The financial and strategic objectives priorities of both Chinese and foreign parent companies choosing and then rank-ordering the top five from longer lists.
Equity The shares of equity held by foreign and Chinese parent companies; the composition of equity, distinguishing between contributions in the form of cash, product and production technology, land, buildings and equipment, brand names and marketing/distribution support.
Contractual ownership resources Resources that parent companies have a contract to provide to the international joint venture in addition to their equity contributions – with particular reference to product design, production technology, management systems, management services and training. These resources excluded materials, components and basic services provided as part of the production process, since these are regarded as 'operational inputs'. Also noted were the provision within each category of contractual resources and also whether the contracts carried with them any explicit limits on the joint venture's use of the resources committed by the foreign and Chinese parent companies.
Non-contractual ownership resources Resources that parent companies have provided to the international joint venture on a non-contractual basis – covering the same items as contractual resources and any other non-contractual resources.
Degree of influence over specific areas and issues of international joint venture management Senior Chinese and foreign managers were asked for their evaluation on five-point scales of the degree of influence exercised respectively by the foreign and Chinese parent companies or their representatives over thirteen areas and issues. The items covered were:

use of profit,
reinvestment policy,
setting strategic priorities,
allocating senior managerial positions,
technological innovation,
financial control,

reward and incentive policies,
training and development policies,
sales and distribution,
product pricing,
quality control,
purchasing policies and
production planning.

The choice of these thirteen areas is guided by work on IJV control (Geringer and Hebert 1989) and on decision-making in China (Child and Lu 1996). When there was more than one Chinese or foreign parent company, the questions on control and influence we put with reference to the Chinese or foreign parent most involved in the joint venture's management. The data reported are the answers given by the most senior manager in each international joint venture (normally the general manager).

Overall control over the international joint venture Senior Chinese and foreign managers were asked for their evaluation on five-point scales of the overall extent of control exercised over the international joint venture respectively by the main foreign parent company and by the main Chinese parent company (there was rarely more than one foreign parent company). The data reported here are also the answers given by the most senior manager in each international joint venture.

Context-oriented control The level of context-oriented control was assessed in terms of symbols, slogans, rituals and incentive systems organised for the joint venture by one or other of the parent companies.

Process-oriented control The level of control was assessed in terms of the involvement of parent company managers in the process of joint venture activity.

Board ratio The ratio of directors appointed by the foreign parent company (or companies) to those appointed by the Chinese parent company or companies.

Occupancy of the position of chief executive officer Whether the chief executive officer (general manager) is a nominee of the Chinese or the foreign parent company or companies.

Performance Assessment by senior joint venture managers in terms of the profitability, growth, market share, technological development and development of local staff/managers; operational profile of the joint venture associated with percentage of inputs and outputs and historical operational trend of the joint venture (sales, profit, employment) over the last five years if applicable. Perceived level of achievement of the priority objectives for joint venture formation.

Figure 5.1 summarises the process of data collection just described.

Figure 5.1 Data collection

Ownership and control in IJV

	Respondents	**Means**
Objective	General manager Deputy general manager	Choose and place in order of importance a maximum of five items from the set of cards that he/she thinks best describe the major strategic motives of parent companies (structured questions). Assess extent to which these major objectives have been achieved (Performance)
Ownership	General manager Deputy general manager	Qualitative and quantitative data Structural questions
Control	Functional managers	Financial and sales; structured subjective evaluations
Performance	Functional managers	Qualitative and quantitative data Structured questions

Notes: general managers = 44; deputy general managers = 29; functional managers = 139.

CODING

The author grouped all data into four categories according to the research framework. The first concerned the *objectives* of the parent companies. Foreign and Chinese senior managers of the joint ventures indicated the five objectives for forming their joint venture to which they perceived that the respective parent companies attached most importance, and were then asked to place these five in priority order. This ordering was then coded as the rank. In addition, each of the full list of items was coded in a binary manner (0/1), depending on whether or not the respondent included it among the top five objective priorities.

The second category concerned *ownership*. This included the percentage of joint venture equity held by each parent company, as well as the resources that the parent companies provided to the joint ventures valued as equity share, or provided on a contractual and non-contractual basis. Provision and non-provision were scored in a binary manner: 1 = has been provided by a partner, 0 = has not been provided by a partner. Composite measures were constructed for contractual resources, based on the binary scores, which indicated the provision or not by either the foreign or Chinese parent companies of each of the five items mentioned above. Inputs supplied by, and outputs taken to, the joint venture as owner are scored in a binary manner: 1 = has been provided by partner, 0 = has not been provided by a partner.

The third category concerned *control*. The percentages of foreign and Chinese directors were calculated from respondent descriptions of each joint venture's management structure and its board of directors. Respondents from both sides also indicated their perceptions of the degree of Chinese and foreign influence in the thirteen areas of joint venture management. This measure of influence was coded for each area (item) from 1 to 5, with 1 = very little influence and 5 = dominant influence.

The fourth category covered *performance* variables, including the operational trend of the joint ventures (over the last five years, if applicable) in terms of employees, number of foreign staff, sales turnover, proportion of sales exported by value, localisation and operational profit before tax. The respondents were also asked to indicate on a five-point Likert-type scale the extent to which they were satisfied with the performance of their international joint venture in terms of profitability, growth, market share, technological development and the development of managers and staff (from 1 = not satisfied at all to 5 = very satisfied). In addition, the senior managers who had selected foreign and Chinese priority objectives for forming the joint venture were asked to indicate how far they thought these objectives had been achieved along five-point scales, ranging from 1 = not achieved at all to 5 = fully achieved. The questions requesting subjective evaluation of each joint venture's operational performance profile were thus structured and closed-ended.

The author collected data from multiple sources. If the data were inconsistent, she tried to reconcile the differences either through checking with the original respondents or through looking to additional sources of secondary data. During the data coding, the writer did find that some data were missing and some illegible, and that there were simple coding errors. This obviously affected the results. The transfer of data from the interviewing notes and tape recordings to coding sheets could lead to small clerical errors such as reading a number incorrectly and then mistakenly loading such data into an SPSS computer file. These errors included uncontrolled extraneous factors in the environment such as personal factors (too tired to concentrate) or equipment failure (faulty tapes). It was possible that the author could misunderstand a respondent's answer or write so illegibly that the coding transposed the answers. It became important to identify data items with large 'outlier' values to ensure that such variances were not due to researcher error.

The national mix of senior managers introduces the possibility of bias in answers on control, because the subject matter concerns the sensitive topic of the relative influence of Chinese and joint venture partners. It was possible to make some assessment of the problem of potential bias due to interviewee nationality in the joint ventures where in the event two different respondents, one expatriate and one Chinese, answered the same questions. The author could assess this in 21 of the joint ventures where an additional manager, of the opposite nationality, also answered the questions on influence. Comparison of the two response sets reveals no significant differences for the assessment of control, though there was a consistent tendency for managers to attribute greater influence to the parent company to which they were affiliated. The correlations between the aggregated assessments of foreign and Chinese influence by each set of respondents were respectively $r = 0.78$ and $r = 0.75$. In this sample study, foreign managers tended to score higher levels of foreign influence in the joint ventures than did Chinese managers. Generally speaking, however, judging by the responses, it does not appear that a significant bias has been introduced that would seriously vitiate the findings reported in this book, especially those based on tests of association between variables. Tests of association constitute the greater part of the analysis to be presented here.

DATA ANALYSIS

Once the three main data bases were created, the variables in each group were tested and the strength of the hypothesised relationships assessed. Tabulations, Pearson correlations, Spearman rank-order correlations and analyses of variance were performed, as appropriate. The purpose of choosing tabulations is for descriptive profiling. Pearson correlations are used for testing the strength and direction of relationships between parametric or quasi-parametric scaled data – for example, equity share and extent of control. Spearman's rank-order correlation is used for testing relationships between ranked data, – for example, rankings of the importance of partner objectives for the formation of joint ventures. The analysis of variance (especially the *t*-test) is for testing for the relative convergence and dispersion of values between groups – for example, higher versus lower investing partners.

SUMMARY

This chapter provides an overview of the research design and methodology employed. Although the process of conducting business research in China is often difficult, it can be very exciting in terms of exploring an area of investigation that is at an early stage of development. The key stages in developing the research methodology for this study were: choosing the problem; constructing a research model; establishing research hypotheses; constructing measures; designing a sample; deciding on fieldwork methods; gathering the data; coding and analysing the data; and finally reaching conclusions. In the event, most of the data on objectives, ownership, control and performance were secured from the sixty-seven joint ventures. These are profiled in the following chapter.

6 Profiling of Objectives, Ownership and Control

INTRODUCTION

This chapter examines three of the four main categories of variables incorporated into the research framework: the objectives for entering into a joint venture, ownership resourcing contributed by partners and control. The purpose is to look at the distribution of these variables among the sample of sixty-seven joint ventures.

FOREIGN OBJECTIVES OF A LONG-TERM NATURE

Twelve potential foreign partner objectives were identified, as described in Chapter 4. Respondents were asked to identify what they perceived as the top five among these objectives for the foreign partner. Foreign partners are reported as giving priority to long-term objectives for forming joint ventures in China; in particular, these were: gaining a strategic position *vis-à-vis* competitors, the attraction of the Chinese market, the opportunity for good long-term profit, facilitating international expansion, establishing a strong business presence and achieving diversification of products and services.

Table 6.1 shows that the most frequently mentioned foreign objectives for joint ventures are gaining a strategic position (mentioned among the top five objectives in 79 per cent of cases), long-term profits (78 per cent), the attraction of the Chinese market (76 per cent) and establishing a strong business presence/credibility in China (55 per cent). The prospect of gaining access to what foreign investors perceive as the huge Chinese domestic market is clearly a dominant consideration for most foreign partners in the joint ventures sampled. Most of them also take a long-term view of the return they will receive. Gaining access to cheap labour is one of the most common priority objectives for foreign partners. Forty-one of the sample included this among the top five foreign partner objectives.

Table 6.1 Objectives in forming joint ventures reported to be pursued by foreign partners ($N = 67$ joint ventures)

Respondents were allowed to select up to five strategic objectives as objectives from the following list of twelve.

	% of cases
Objectives mentioned among the top five by 75% and more of the sample	
1. Gain a strategic position in China	79
2. Opportunity for good long-term profit	77
3. Attraction of the Chinese market	76
Objectives mentioned among the top five by between 25 and 74%	
4. Establish strong business presence /credibility in China	55
5. Low labour cost	41
6. Facilitation of international expansion	38
Objectives mentioned among the top five by 24% or less of the sample	
7. Learning how to do business in China	25
8. Benefit from tax incentives	25
9. Low-cost sourcing	22
10. Opportunity for quick profit	16
11. Benefit from advantageous transfer pricing	14
12. Diversification of products and services	9

The attraction of the Chinese market can be explained by how much the foreign parent companies value gaining a strategic position *vis-à-vis* competitors in terms of facilitating international expansion. Where expansion is critically important, foreign parent companies tend to regard China as one of the major global strategic markets. A German general manager expressed this long-term type of orientation by his company:

> The joint venture in China plays an important part in our firm's global business portfolio. Business developments in China have strengthened our confidence and the European position indirectly. Our business has covered at least some parts of one-fourth of the world population. This gives our business great potential.

FOREIGN OBJECTIVES OF A SHORT-TERM NATURE

A minority of foreign partners are reported as giving priority to short-term objectives, in particular learning how to do business in China, opportunities for quick profit, benefit from tax incentives and benefit from advantageous transfer pricing.

Most foreign investing companies do not attach the highest objective priority to short-term objectives, namely low labour cost (41 per cent), benefits from tax incentives (25 per cent), learning how to do business in China (25 per cent), or the opportunity for quick profit (16 per cent). Even less emphasis is placed on the benefits of advantageous transfer pricing (15 per cent). It is also the case that foreign companies do not attach the greatest priority to objectives of a financial nature when investing in Chinese joint ventures. Rather, the importance of access to the Chinese market is rated far more highly.

Figure 6.1 classifies the objectives emphasised by foreign partners according to the two dimensions of strategic versus financial and long-term versus short-term. Short-term objectives are consistent with using the joint venture as a platform for exploitation (Aiello 1991). For this reason, objectives of a short-term nature are based upon low-cost sourcing, low labour cost, the opportunity for quick profit and the benefits from tax incentives. A Japanese joint venture illustrates this short-term orientation. Its Japanese deputy general manager said:

> The most important reason to establish a joint venture in China was to use local sources, labour and service, which cost less than in

Figure 6.1 Classification of foreign objectives

	Strategic criteria	Financial criteria
Short-term	Learning how to do business in China Low labour cost Low-cost sourcing	Opportunity for quick profit Benefit from tax incentives Benefit from advantageous transfer pricing
Long-term	Gain a strategic position in China Establish strong business credibility in China Facilitate international expansion Attraction of the Chinese market Diversification of products and service	Opportunity for good long-term profit

Japan. If business is good, we will stay. If business is bad, we will leave. As our company is small, we cannot place ourselves at risk by committing major investment.

There are, however, some special cases. Some foreign partners that are R&D-intensive are anxious about both technology leakage within joint ventures and the Chinese government's attitude towards import and export controls. They may try to safeguard their proprietary technology by actively controlling the management of their investment, and by investing a small amount of resources in order to try the market and to evaluate the profitability of the situation. The results of foreign partners' objectives for joint ventures of a short- and long-term nature are summarised in Figure 6.1.

RANKING OF OBJECTIVES BY FOREIGN PARTNERS OF DIFFERENT NATIONALITY

An analysis of the average ranking given to the top five objectives selected overall by foreign owning companies of different nationality is undertaken, to examine whether these contextual factors give rise to any variation. The average rankings of objectives – out of twelve choice – for joint venture formation by foreign partners are shown in Table 6.2 for the four nationality groups.

Table 6.2 Average ranking of objectives by foreign partners of different nationality

Objective held by foreign partner	*Foreign partner*			
	Anglo-Saxon	*Continental Europe*	*Japan*	*Overseas Chinese*
Gain a strategic position in China	1st	2nd =	2nd	1st
Attraction of the Chinese market	3rd	1st	3rd	2nd
Opportunity for long-term profit	2nd	2nd =	1st	4th
Establish credibility in China	4th	4th	n.a.	n.a.
Low labour costs	n.a.	n.a.	4th	3rd

n.a. = not applicable.

Although there are some differences in ranking between these groups, all placed gaining a strategic position in China *vis-à-vis* competitors, the attraction of the Chinese market and the opportunity for good long-term profit among the first three strategic and financial objectives. The one exception was that long-term profit is on average ranked fourth for Overseas Chinese partners. This was due to a lower priority being given to long-term profit by partners from Hong Kong.

There are some specific differences in ranking typifying the national groups of foreign partners. Opportunity for good long-term profit tends to be more important for Japanese joint venture partners than the others, especially the Overseas Chinese. Low labour cost appears to be a more important motivating force for China joint ventures formed by Japanese and Overseas Chinese partners than for partners from the Anglo-Saxon countries and Continental Europe. Although not shown, Overseas Chinese companies also tend to value the availability of low-cost sourcing and tax incentives.

RANKING FOREIGN OBJECTIVES IN THE ELECTRONICS AND FMCG SECTORS

Table 6.3 shows that the ranking of key objectives by foreign partners in the electronics and fast-moving consumer goods sectors displays only a slightly different pattern. The ranking of objectives by foreign partners in the two sectors suggests a high degree of consistency.

Table 6.3 Average ranking of objectives by business sector

Objective held by foreign partners	*Electronics*[a]	*FMCG*[b]
Gain a strategic position in China	1st	1st
Opportunity for long-term profit	1st =	2nd
Attraction of the Chinese market	2nd	2nd =
Establish credibility in China	5th	4th
Low labour costs	4th	5th

Notes:
[a]Computers, telecommunications, electronic components manufacturing.
[b]Fast-moving consumer goods, such as branded foods, drinks, cosmetics, tobacco.

Gaining a strategic position in China, the attraction of the Chinese market, the opportunity for long-term profit, establishing credibility in China and acquiring low labour costs tend to be the most important forces motivating foreign partners in joint venture formation. The evidence indicates, therefore, that the underlying objectives for joint venture formation and the relative importance of these objectives for the foreign partners are not fundamentally related to the business sectors in which they are located.

CHINESE OBJECTIVES OF A LONG-TERM NATURE

Seventeen potential objectives of Chinese parent companies were investigated. Chapter 4 suggests that there might be a wider range of objectives for joint venture formation held by Chinese partners, because of variations in formal ownership, region and size. Moreover, there could be some contrast between objectives expressed in official policy, such as technology transfer, and those given priority by the immediate partner, such as the injection of foreign cash. These seventeen objectives do not divide as clearly as the foreign list into long-term and short-term categories; the reason may be that the longer list for Chinese objectives might have the effect of spreading out the scores somewhat.

The five objectives given most frequently as of high priority are relatively long-term in nature, with the exception of obtaining foreign cash investment. In reality, it depends on whether the Chinese objective is to get cash or to make a real investment. More than 60 per cent of Chinese parent companies mentioned learning management expertise, acquisition of technology and obtaining foreign cash investment among their top five main objectives for forming a joint venture. The single factor most frequently identified by the Chinese parent companies is learning management expertise (77 per cent). This objective is supported by the Chinese government, and it grants favourable terms to encourage joint ventures to realise them. A Chinese general manager in the FMCG sector gave the following rationale for the emphasis on learning management expertise and acquiring technology:

> The joint venture provides opportunities to acquire advanced technology and management expertise, which will enable us to establish a strong business presence and position *vis-à-vis* competitors.

It brings increases in our local employment, and guarantees a tax holiday for three years, but the most important factor is that the venture is physically operated in China.

Chinese companies have difficulties in accessing advanced technology from international companies, except through the medium of joint ventures. It is obvious to them that they can improve their current strategic positions by combining their internal resources with technology, management expertise and capital from their foreign partners, so creating a stronger competitive position in the Chinese market. Acquisition of advanced technology from the foreign partners is likely to increase the competitive leverage that Chinese parent companies can exercise. Table 6.4 indicates that other Chinese priorities for forming joint ventures with foreign companies are spread across a

Table 6.4 Objectives for forming joint ventures reported to be held by Chinese partners

Respondents were allowed to select up to five objectives from the following list of seventeen.

Items	%
Objectives mentioned among the top five by 60 per cent and more	
1. Learning management expertise	77
2. Technology transfer	61
3. Obtain foreign cash investment	61
Objectives mentioned among the top five by between 59 and 25 per cent	
4. Opportunity for good long-term profit	41
5. Gain strategic position	40
Objectives mentioned among the top five by 24 per cent and less	
6. Develop export opportunities	25
7. Help expand in China market	22
8. Opportunity to train Chinese staff	22
9. Establish strong business presence in China	20
10. Assist diversification of product and service	20
11. Benefit from tax incentives	19
12. Help upgrade Chinese suppliers' technology	14
13. Opportunities for quick profit	13
14. Acquire ability to import superior goods and components	13
15. Import substitution	12
16. Foreign exchange generation	10
17. Employment creation	7

Figure 6.2 Classification of Chinese objectives

	Strategic criteria	Financial criteria
Short-term	Learning how to export	Foreign cash investment Benefit from tax incentives Opportunity for quick profit
Long-term	Learning management expertise Technology transfer Gain strategic position Develop export opportunities Help with expansion in Chinese market Opportunity to train Chinese staff Establish strong business presence Employment creation	Long-term profit Assistance in diversification of products and service Foreign exchange generation Acquire ability to import superior goods and components

wide range of less frequently mentioned items. This suggests that, overall, the important objectives for Chinese firms are based mainly upon resource considerations, especially the improvement of competence.

Figure 6.2 applies the same classification as Figure 6.1 and on the whole indicates that the objectives of Chinese parent companies are spread evenly among the four categories, given that one would not expect to find many strategic priorities of a short-term nature.

The chance to obtain foreign cash investment, the ability to import superior goods and components, and gaining export opportunities are identified as basic needs for the Chinese partner for joint ventures. One of the Chinese personnel managers explained the reasons for this in the case of his joint venture:

> We only had buildings, old machines and people before we set up the joint venture. Our company is a state-owned enterprise. We are used to receiving instructions and 'planned targets' from the Ministry. We cannot face the competition as China changes from central planning to 'socialist marketism'. Our future is either as a joint venture or bankruptcy.

The objectives for setting up a joint venture are often intimately bound up with the interests of the local and central Chinese government. Because of the overlap of authority structures where there is sharing of resources, such as financial and human, between enterprises and higher authorities in China, it may not be easy to distinguish between objectives for a joint venture of the enterprise and the higher authority. This may help to account for the lack of clear patterns of objectives on the Chinese side. Also, the objectives are more likely to be driven by the Chinese firm's need to acquire resources, such as capital, technology and management expertise, and to gain exporting opportunities. The degree of involvement in these areas associated with acquiring resources can be used to judge the status of the Chinese parent firm in the context of its Chinese authority's evaluation. The type of Chinese ownership – state-owned, collective-owned or individual business – can be used to distinguish whether managers from the three types of organisation have the opportunity to take an active or a passive involvement in strategic decisions. The long-term objectives of a joint venture are more likely to be constrained by the Chinese organisational system. One Chinese manager in an FMCG joint venture commented on this constraint with reference to the question of whether the Chinese parent company would have the use of resources acquired through its joint venture:

> Before setting up the joint venture, we received some support from the local government, but not so much. At least, we knew it would be possible to get something from them through bargaining. The major problem at that time was the difficulty in guaranteeing whether the resource acquired by us could really be used in our enterprise. It was up to the bureau's decision. At present, we hardly get any help from the Chinese government. The reason is related to the ownership of the joint venture ... we are entitled to get involved in acquiring resources, but we have to be professional. We find our foreign partners always have full backing from their regional and corporate levels, but we do not get the same backing in terms of acquiring resources.

RANKING OF OBJECTIVES BY CHINESE HAVING PARTNERS WITH DIFFERENT NATIONALITIES

The ranking of the Chinese objectives, which over the whole sample were given the highest priority for joint venture formation, is shown in

Table 6.5 Average ranking of objectives by Chinese partners with different nationalities of foreign partners (N = 67 joint ventures)

Objective of Chinese partners	*Nationality of foreign partner*			
	Anglo-Saxon	*Continental European*	*Japanese*	*Overseas Chinese*
Management expertise	2nd	1st	1st	2nd
Technology transfer	1st	2nd	3rd	n.a.
Foreign cash investment	3rd	3rd =	2nd	1st
Long-term profit	n.a.	3rd=	n.a.	3rd =
Gain a strategic position in China	n.a.	3rd =	4th	3rd =

n.a. = not applicable.

Table 6.5. There are some differences in the order of average ranks between Chinese enterprises having foreign partners of different nationalities. The overwhelming goal in cooperating with non-Overseas-Chinese foreign firms is to acquire advanced technology and to obtain management expertise. These are ranked as the top two leading objectives for joint ventures with Anglo-Saxon and Continental European partners. Management expertise is ranked first on average by Chinese firms in joint ventures with Japanese partners.

Technology transfer is reported to be a very high priority for Chinese firms in joint ventures with Anglo-Saxon and Continental European partners, but a low priority by Chinese firms in joint ventures with Overseas Chinese partners. Chinese firms with Overseas Chinese partners tended to prioritise such objectives as improvement in their competitive position, securing export opportunities and obtaining cash. Another contrast of objectives among the Chinese partners is evident in that the importance of obtaining foreign cash investment is greater in the case of joint ventures formed with Overseas Chinese and Japanese partners than it is when joint ventures have Continental European and Anglo-Saxon partners. These findings suggest that there is an element of selection by Chinese partners among different categories of foreign investor, according to their priorities.

Table 6.6 Average ranking of objectives by business sector

Objective of Chinese partners	*Electronics*[a]	*FMCG*[b]
Management expertise	1st	2nd
Technology transfer	2nd	3rd
Foreign cash investment	3rd	1st
Opportunity for long-term profit	4th	5th
Gain a strategic position in China	5th	4th

Notes:
[a]Computers, telecommunications, electronic components manufacturing.
[b]Fast-moving consumer goods, such as branded foods, drinks, cosmetics, tobacco.

RANKING OF CHINESE OBJECTIVES BY BUSINESS SECTOR

Table 6.6 shows that the ranking of key objectives by Chinese and foreign partners in the electronics and fast-moving consumer goods sectors displays only a slightly different pattern. Although there is some small difference in average ranking between the industry groups, learning management expertise, technology transfer, obtaining foreign cash investment, opportunity for long-term profit, and establishing a strategic position in the domestic market are the five most important forces motivating Chinese partners to form joint ventures in both the electronics and the fast-moving consumer goods sectors. The results indicate that objectives held by Chinese partners are relatively independent from which business sectors they are in.

PROFILING OF OWNERSHIP: CONTRIBUTION TO EQUITY

Table 6.7 shows that almost twice as many foreign parent companies ($N = 41$) contribute to joint venture equity wholly in the form of cash as do Chinese parent companies ($N = 23$). Their greater access to cash is likely to increase the relative leverage from their equity investment. Foreign parent companies can exercise control from their equity share because of the crucial nature of cash as a resource. Chinese companies have difficulties in contributing equity through cash payments, because they have very little chance to raise bank loans from a Chinese bank, and almost no chance at all to get a loan from an international bank.

Table 6.7 Contributions to equity

Item	*Foreign parent(s)* %	*Chinese parent(s)* %
Cash only	61	34
Product design	16	1
Production technology	16	3
Buildings, plant and equipment	27	54
Land	0	54
Brand names and trade marks	6	6
Marketing and distribution support	1	9

One of the major objectives for joint venture creation by Chinese partners is to obtain foreign cash investment. It can be seen from the Table 6.7 that Chinese partners often build up their equity stake by having other resources valued as equity.

In over half the joint ventures, a major Chinese contribution to equity takes the form of land and/or buildings, plant and equipment. Out of 67 cases, 9 Chinese companies have marketing and distribution support and 6 have brand names and trade marks that are valued as equity. The Chinese partner tends to value existing plant and equipment by reference to original cost and subsequent depreciation, and to use Chinese price directories as references. The foreign partner tends to value Chinese existing plant and equipment in terms of its performance compared with world-class standards. The Chinese and foreign partners have difficulties in coming to agreement on the 'valuation' of the Chinese existing plant and equipment, because there is no definite standard acceptable to both sides. Although some Chinese partners were contributing access to external networks, especially to government agencies, this contribution was not valued as equity in any of the joint ventures. The distribution of contributions to IJV equity was as shown in Table 6.7.

In 16 cases, the foreign partner's contribution to equity included the valuation of product design, and/or production technology. In 27 cases, plant and equipment was valued as equity. In 6 cases brand names and trade marks were owned that were valued as equity. The foreign partners tend to use cash as equity investment, because capital can be easily identified and thus arguments between foreign and Chinese over the valuation of non-cash provision can be avoided. Very

Table 6.8 Provision of contractual resources (N = 67 joint ventures)

Item	*Foreign parent(s)* %	*Chinese Parent (s)* %
Product design	85	6
Production technology	84	6
Training	66	1
Management services	55	18
Management systems	34	13

often the foreign contribution is used to buy equipment, sometimes from the same partners.

PROVISION OF CONTRACTUAL RESOURCES

The provision of resources on a contractual basis includes control. This is particularly relevant to the product design, production technology, training, management services and management systems of the joint ventures. Table 6.8 shows the number of joint ventures in which some limitations on joint venture discretion was incorporated into contracts under which foreign owners' resources were provided. In the majority of sample firms where the provision of product design and production technology is on a contractual basis, the provider is the foreign parent company. More than 60 of sample firms had foreign partners supplying product design and/or production technology that is legitimised by contracts. The high incidence of technology provision on a contractual basis may reflect the ability to lower transaction costs in this way, given the relatively tangible nature of the resources being provided. This is in clear contrast to the Chinese partners, who provide on average only 4.1 per cent of the contractual resources to the joint ventures.

Table 6.8 shows that the most common form of foreign contractual ownership resource is the provision of product design and production technology, often supplied together as a technology transfer package (r = 0.83 between the two). This compares with 66 per cent for training, 55 per cent for management services and 34 per cent for management systems from foreign partners. Much of the training provided contractually by the foreign partners is related to technology transfer. The management services provided by foreign parent companies are primarily marketing and distribution support.

It is clear that contracts can give legitimacy to the foreign partner's authority to monitor the joint venture's decisions on matters that are governed by contracts, such as product design, suppliers and training. Indeed, the joint venture contract may also establish that certain activities and appointments are the prerogative of one partner rather than the other. Contracts therefore give the foreign partner the flexibility to take action, in the knowledge that it can always fall back on the position of its ultimate rights as specified in the contracts.

The picture that emerges from the evidence presented so far is one in which foreign rather than Chinese ownership resources are of a kind likely to provide leverage for control. Foreign parent companies are far more likely to hold a majority joint venture equity share and foreign companies are providing contractual and non-contractual resources far more often than are their Chinese counterparts.

The foreign partners tend to provide resources on a contractual basis at the formation of the joint ventures. The provision of these resources has the following implications. First, it provides an opportunity to define the use of resources, such as product design, production technology, and management systems. Second, it creates a link between the technical specification applied to resources and the definition of a specific person's responsibility for monitoring the resources. Specifications for product design, production technology, training, management service and management systems on a contractual basis confer a legitimacy on those providing them. This in turn gives the foreign partners the flexibility to take action, in the knowledge that they can always fall back on a position of claiming to be controller and authority. Finally, legal contracts are intended primarily to provide security for foreign technology, to guard against leakage, to guarantee standards and to secure an income stream from royalties. They are also used to protect brands.

There are relatively few cases where a Chinese parent company provides resources on a contractual basis. Only 18 per cent of Chinese partners provided management services on such a basis. Chinese parent companies are primarily concerned with legal matters and relations with governmental agencies and they tend to avoid providing resources on the contractual basis because (1) very few Chinese companies have actually provided product design, production technology and professional services; (2) Chinese companies find it is difficult to establish particular intellectual property standards and

Table 6.9 Provision of non-contractual resources

Item	*Foreign parent(s)* %	*Chinese parent(s)* %
Product design	69	12
Production technology	60	7
Training	60	12
Management services	48	22
Management systems	61	31

rights in China, which will help to define the intangible resources to the joint venture; (3) emphasising the resource inputs on a legal basis may not necessarily be the best alternative, because as it limits the rights of use.

PROVISION OF NON-CONTRACTUAL RESOURCES

Table 6.9 shows the most common forms of foreign non-contractual ownership resources. The provision of product design input is again highly correlated with that of production technology (r = 0.82). The profile of management systems in non-contractual resources features more prominently than in the contractual resources category. Although less than the incidence of technology contracts, it is perhaps surprising that there are so many cases of technical resources being provided by foreign companies on a non-contractual basis. This indicates the considerable commitment that some foreign partners are giving to their Chinese joint ventures.

The foreign partners tend to invest heavily in joint ventures on a non-contractual basis. This implies that non-contractual support can enhance the control available to the parent company. Non-contractual resources can be a way to transfer power and authority from the parent company to a joint venture. Product design, production technology, training, professional services and management systems can be provided free of charge. This provision is easily accepted by the Chinese side, and it generates goodwill. It also provides a basis for the acceptance of foreign 'expert power' (French and Raven 1959). Foreign managerial and technical assistance tends to be on an ongoing routine and incremental basis to a joint venture, when it is on a non-contractual basis.

Taking all ownership resources together,* an outstanding feature is that there is a heavy foreign provision of core and active resources, concerned with product, the technology of producing it, management systems and training/professional consultancy to back up the implementation of these provisions. It is notable that almost all foreign parent companies provide both contractual and non-contractual resources, whereas large numbers of Chinese parent companies do not.

In considering the contractual and non-contractual categories, there is a clear contrast between foreign and Chinese partners' ownership resources. The major Chinese contributions are rather passive, and impact less on the ongoing process of developing and managing a joint venture. They consist primarily of the provision of land, buildings and old equipment. The twenty-three cases where the Chinese parents provided management systems, largely in the personnel and production areas, constitute a limited exception. Management services provided were mostly advice on external relations and the institutional context, which can be critical in the Chinese environment and are likely to affect the more strategic issues of IJV management.

From the evidence available, it appears that non-contractual resources provide a more important basis for the integration of joint ventures into their parents' long-term strategic plans. 60 per cent of foreign partners provide non-contractual resources, in clear contrast to the mere 17 per cent of Chinese partners that do. The extent of the foreign parents' equity shareholding appears to make relatively little difference to provision of non-contractual resources.

COMMITMENT OF STAFF RESOURCES

Staff commitment is indicated by how many senior managers are occupied in the joint venture. Table 6.10 shows that the position of general manager of the joint venture is in most cases occupied by the foreign

* It should be noted that correlations between the three categories of ownership resourcing are positive but not particularly high, in the case of either Chinese or foreign partners. The correlations are:

Foreign ownership resourcing	2	3	*Chinese ownership resourcing*	2	3
1. Foreign equity share	.16	.27	1. Chinese equity share	15	.36
2. Foreign contractual		.39	2. Chinese contractual		.23
3. Foreign non-contractual		–	3. Chinese non-contractual		–

Table 6.10 Occupancy of key managerial positions (N = 67 joint ventures)

	Chinese managers		*Foreign managers*	
	No. of cases	*%*	*No. of cases*	*%*
General manager	14	21	53	79
Deputy GM	48	72	12	18
Production	33	49	34	51
Marketing	37	55	30	45
R&D/technical	24	47	27	53
Finance	42	63	25	37
Personnel	60	92	5	8

partner. In 53 out of the 67 sample firms, the general manager role is occupied by an expatriate and in only 14 cases is the general manager a Chinese. The occupancy of the general manager's position, and the headship of certain functions, are likely to increase a foreign parent's control over a wider range of joint venture decisions. These appointments are by no means wholly determined by equity share, and can therefore be negotiated separately. The right to appoint to given management posts can be specified in the joint venture contract.

The headships of certain managerial functions appear to be occupied by the general managers, which in most of these sample firms are from the foreign partner. The frequency of the occupancy of the headship of key managerial functions such as finance, production and personnel by staff recruited externally tends to be slightly higher. Foreign managers in China are likely to introduce their managerial approaches and methods into a joint venture.

Table 6.10 shows the foreign and Chinese companies from which the general managers of the joint ventures were originally appointed, and the occupancy of the main functional headships in the management teams of the joint ventures. The proportion of Chinese and foreign directors on the joint venture boards quite closely reflects the percentage of the partners' equity shareholdings (r = 0.76). The ability to dominate the board of directors is likely to be a powerful level of control, even though most decisions may be made by consensus. Within the sample of 67 joint ventures, in 47 cases the chairman of the board is provided by the Chinese partners and in 20 cases the chairman comes from the foreign partners. There is more of an even distribution in the appointment of board members than in equity share, thus favouring the Chinese side. 20 of the joint ventures have a majority of Chinese directors, 25 have a foreign majority on the board and 22 have equal numbers, which are reflected from proportion of equity shares held by foreign and Chinese partners.

Majority equity share bolsters a parent company's influence over managerial occupancies in a joint venture, namely its general manager and the heads of major functions. The composition of the joint venture board is obviously an issue of vital importance. A majority on the joint venture board secures this general policy control. Majority equity share usually provides a right to control key policy decisions, including reinvestment policy and profit distribution.

One issue here concerns the balance between managerial members working in joint ventures and those working outside it. 70 per cent of foreign partners' members of boards come from the regional or corporate levels of those partners' organisations. Such members often bring some fresh and challenging thinking to joint venture policy, as they are in a better position to understand the full situation of any joint venture and its management perspectives, having as they usually do a clearer view of the joint venture from the foreign parent company's perspective.

In no joint venture where the Chinese partner is the minority shareholder did the general manager originate from the Chinese parent company. The general manager is appointed from the foreign parents three times as often as from the Chinese parents. As a mechanism of control, therefore, the foreign parents appear to act aggressively in terms of providing the general manager of the joint venture.

The contrast between the board of directors and the percentage of general managerships held by the foreign parents should be borne in mind in considering the relationship between ownership and control in later chapters. The influence of the chief executive is likely to be relatively persuasive. Moreover, over four out five of the joint ventures are led by a chief executive occupied by the foreign parent company. Joint ventures in this study are mostly small to medium companies, only four of them with more than a thousand employees.

Among the 67 joint ventures as a whole, in 25 per cent of them the management team is sourced equally from both partners. There are also as many joint ventures where the source of the management team is mainly from the Chinese parent. Where the total capital investment is small, it is too expensive to employ expatriate managers, and joint venture managers are recruited mainly from the local environment.

The impression that foreign partners tend to dominate joint venture management is strengthened by assessing the total proportion of foreign key management positions.

There was also an imbalance in the percentages of inputs and outputs transacted with the owning companies. Of the joint ventures, 38 were receiving some operational inputs from their foreign parent companies, which averaged 27 per cent of the total by value. Only 21 joint ventures were receiving such inputs from their Chinese parent companies, averaging 18 per cent by value. 34 joint ventures were supplying some outputs directly to the foreign parent companies, averaging 24 per cent of their total output value. Only 18 joint ventures were supplying outputs directly to their Chinese parent companies, averaging 19 per cent of their greater transactional dependency on their foreign owning companies than on their Chinese ones.

CONTROL

Table 6.11 shows the overall extent of control over the joint venture exercised by the foreign and Chinese parent companies, with the mean scores in assessment, made against a 5-point scale (1 = low control, 5 = high control). With regard to understanding overall control patterns in joint ventures exercised by foreign and Chinese parent companies, it is important to distinguish that control in joint ventures differs from that in unified structures from at least three perspectives: (1) owner objectives, (2) the hybrid structure of joint ventures, (3) the legal status of joint ventures (Lyles and Reger, 1993).

As shown in Table 6.11, in the 67 joint ventures the overall control exercised by foreign parent companies appears to be higher than that by Chinese parent companies. The interpretation of the results can be as

Table 6.11 Overall control exercised by parent companies

Differences in means between 1 and 2: $t = 3.98, p = .000$

1. Control exercised by foreign parent company	3.33
2. Control exercised by Chinese parent company	2.61

follows: First, the greater foreign international venturing experience suggests that conflicts inherent in joint ventures can be a threat to their viability, but that foreign managers may be able to capitalise on the ambiguity and manage the conflict (Shenkar and Zeira 1992). Second, information on joint venture formation in this study implies that the foreign parent firms may rationalise their control in the areas of a joint venture where they have strength or expertise, and may not attempt to control those local public relationships with the joint venture where they have no expertise. Finally, most foreign parent companies contribute their product and production technology to the joint venture, and this provides their leverage for control over joint ventures.

Table 6.12 sets out the overall control and influence that the foreign and Chinese parent companies are perceived to exercise over strategic and operational decisions within the joint ventures.

Table 6.12 Control reported to be exercised by foreign and Chinese partners over 13 areas (N = 67 joint ventures)

1 = no influence at all, 5 = very considerable influence (2-tail test).

Decision areas/issues	*Mean scores*		*Paired sample t-test*	
	Foreign partner	*Chinese partner*	*Value of t*	*Value of p*
Gap between foreign and Chinese means scores > 1.0				
1. Technological innovation	3.9	2.2	6.1	0.000
2. Quality control	3.9	2.3	5.9	0.000
3. Product pricing	3.7	2.4	4.6	0.000
4. Setting strategic objectives	3.7	2.6	4.2	0.000
5. Sales and distribution	3.6	2.5	3.3	0.001
Gap between 1.0 and 0.80				
1. Training and development policies	3.6	2.7	3.4	0.001
2. Production planning	3.5	2.6	3.0	0.004
3. Financial control	3.5	2.6	3.4	0.001
4. Reinvestment policy	3.5	2.7	3.8	0.000
Gap 0.80 and less				
1. Purchasing policies	3.5	2.7	2.8	0.007
2. Allocating senior managerial positions	3.4	2.6	2.8	0.006
3. Allocation of profit	3.4	2.8	2.5	0.013
4. Reward and incentive policies	3.2	2.8	1.4	0.166

(In 8 joint ventures, the decision on the use of profit had not yet arisen, because they had yet to declare a profit. In 6, there had not yet been a discussion or decision on reinvestment policy. As a result, the measure of overall influence based on all 13 items applies to only 56 joint ventures in the sample.)

The foreign side as a whole is perceived to have greater influence in every area or issue. Even allowing for the possibility of some bias in the pattern of responses, the disparity between the two sets of scores is considerable, and is consistent with the trend that has been noted among foreign companies of seeking managerial control over their joint ventures in China (Meier *et al.* 1995). Foreign partners benefit by achieving the full potential of their strategies from the exercise of extensive control within the joint ventures. The exercise of this degree of control can generate overhead costs. The differences in influence scores are lowest for reward and incentive policies (mean difference = 0.38). The Chinese side is also often able to retain a significant measure of influence over staff training, particularly in running training programmes in China. Training and development policies tend to be designed according to the requirements of the product and production technology development of the joint venture. Training is emphasised by the Chinese, and is consistent with the objectives of acquiring the foreign technology and managerial skills. The influence that Chinese parent companies retained over the use of profit suggests that they had a somewhat greater say in board-level matters than in executive management decisions. Indeed, the distribution of IJV board members tended to favour Chinese partners when compared with their share of equity. The relatively narrow difference in influence over the use of profit and allocating managerial position suggests that Chinese parent companies tend to have a somewhat greater say in board-level matters than in executive management decisions.

The largest differences in foreign and Chinese influence tend to arise in the areas of technological development: technological innovation (1.7), quality control (1.6), reinvestment (1.3), setting strategic objectives (1.1) and sales and distribution (1.1). While the foreign partners are seen to exercise the greater influence across the whole range of issues investigated, the gap tends to be rather more marked in technology and marketing-related areas. The technological resources and marketing assistance that many foreign parent companies are providing to the joint ventures thus appears to have some impact on their degree of control over related areas of management.

Table 6.13 Context-oriented control

	Foreign partner		*Chinese partner*	
	Frequency	*%*	*Frequency*	*%*
Symbols, slogans, rituals	24	36	8	12
Reward and incentive system	22	33	5	8
Job rotation	4	6	3	4

However, the expectation of differences between the two sectors, with foreign influence over technology stronger in electronics joint ventures, and foreign influence over marketing stronger in fast-moving consumer goods joint ventures, was not found to be entirely warranted.

CONTEXT-ORIENTED CONTROL

Table 6.13 shows that in about a third of the joint ventures' symbols, slogans, rituals, reward and incentive systems were provided by the foreign partners. This contrasts with the very low number of joint ventures where symbols, slogans, rituals, reward and incentive systems were provided by the Chinese partners. Foreign partners tend to contribute more heavily to these elements of the context-oriented control of joint ventures than do their Chinese partners.

Symbols, slogans and rituals are designed to reinforce disciplines delivered by the foreign partners to joint ventures, which also directly enhance foreign influence in the core joint venture management process, itself an important level for control.

The control leverage for Chinese parent companies of context-oriented support tends to be different from that for foreign ones. The context-oriented control by Chinese partners is enhanced by the traditions of Chinese society, which (as mentioned earlier) favour trust-based and long-term business relationships. The significance of context-oriented resources derives, at least in part, from the way they demonstrate the parent company's commitment to this kind of continuing relationship in the joint venture. Context-oriented resources are seen by joint venture staff to be provided freely by either partner and on a flexible, continuing basis. In the Chinese context, these characteristics generate a greater acceptance of the parent company's role and its influence in joint venture management. The areas of management over which Chinese influence tends to be highest is reward and incentive policies and the use of joint venture profits. The Chinese side is often able to retain a significant measure of influence over staff motivation and commitment, which are regarded as extremely important issues in Chinese industry (Child 1994).

PROCESS-ORIENTED CONTROL

The incidence of process-oriented control within the joint ventures exercised by its parent companies is examined in Table 6.14. This shows the summarized frequency of direct reporting across levels to respectively the parent companies, the board of directors and the general manager. Foreign parent companies (94 per cent of the sample firms – 4 cases are missing data) appear to formally review joint ventures at least once a year. This contrasts with the Chinese parent companies, among which only 50 per cent formally review their joint ventures at least once a year. The regional and corporate offices of the foreign partners tend to review general strategic issues such as dividend policies, reinvestment and the allocation of senior managers on a regular basis. The Chinese industrial bureau or department-in-chief tends to review only the major financial areas of the joint ventures.

Table 6.14 Process-oriented control via the reporting system (N = 67 joint ventures)

Formal reporting of frequency	*To chinese parent*	*To foreign parent ($N = 63$)*	*To the board of directors*	*To GM/ CEO ($N = 65$)*
Weekly	1	1	0	15
Monthly	10	29	0	43
Quarterly	1	14	12	2
Half-yearly	12	12	31	4
Annually	10	7	24	1
Not at all	33	0	0	0

Foreign parent companies are quite willing to regularly visit and offer assistance to the joint venture. They try to ensure information acquisition through regular meetings and thus know what to expect from the joint ventures. Foreign partners can take advantage of the centrality of power within the reporting system for their business proposes. Business development reports are also likely to be discussed at the board of directors level. Operational reports tend to go to the general managers.

SUMMARY

This chapter has profiled parent company objectives, ownership and control in the sixty-seven joint ventures. Gaining a strategic position *vis-à-vis* competitors is the objective mentioned most frequently by foreign partners. Learning management and technology expertise are among the top two mentioned by the Chinese partners. Foreign partners of joint ventures tend to commit to a range of product and production technology on contractual and non-contractual bases, but they do tend not to value their brand name or trade mark as equity share. Chinese partners tend to value their land and existing equipment as equity share, but they rarely commit their technology to a joint venture on a contractual basis. Foreign partners tend to exercise their control in the areas of technological development. Chinese partners usually retain some control in operational areas such as personnel management.

7 Relationships Between Objectives, Ownership and Control

INTRODUCTION

This chapter examines the postulated relationships between a joint venture partner's objectives, ownership and control. One particular issue that has received little attention in the literature is the possible link between the partners' objectives in forming joint ventures and the range of ownership resourcing they provide. The resources contributed are expected to reflect the owning companies' objectives for those joint ventures, in particular whether these are long-term or short-term in nature. Ownership resourcing from the partners will be influenced by the trade-offs they make between long- and short-term objectives.

The configuration of ownership resourcing encompasses the items valued as equity, as well as the provision of other resources by the same parent company. Both foreign and Chinese companies expressed great concern regarding the issue of the relationship between ownership and control of joint ventures in terms of its implications for attaining their objectives. The reasons for this were expressed by a foreign general manager in the electronics sector:

> It takes much longer than we expected to transfer technology and management to the Chinese ... Chinese labour and sourcing are never cheap and acquiring quality sourcing is another big issue ... As these are important in terms of running a joint venture, having a majority equity share will certainly give us the power to deal with such issues.

The question therefore arises as to whether the potential influence of the transfer of contractual and non-contractual resources to a joint venture's management is independent of the effects of equity share.

THE RELATIONSHIP BETWEEN OBJECTIVES AND OWNERSHIP

A reasonably clear distinction between long-term and short-term objectives could be drawn for the objectives given priority by foreign companies, but it was difficult to sustain when considering the objectives given priority by Chinese parent companies. The profiling of objectives in Chapter 6 suggests that gaining a strategic position in China *vis-à-vis* competitors, the opportunity for good long-term profit, gaining access to the Chinese market and the establishment of a strong business presence in China all tend to be foreign objectives of a long-term nature, which are frequently given priority. The objective of gaining low labour cost was also mentioned as a priority in 41 per cent of the cases. It is not, however, necessarily long-term in nature, because labour cost can change fairly quickly and is subject to inflationary and exchange rate influences, so far as the foreign investor is concerned. Taking advantage of tax incentives, low-cost sourcing and learning how to do business in China were the foreign objectives of a short-term nature, more frequently given priority, although only by a quarter or less of the joint ventures.

A Pearson correlation analysis of the relationships between parent company objectives and three subcategories of ownership resourcing was performed, with the results shown in Table 7.1.

Table 7.2 refers to composite measures of non-capital resourcing, the derivation of which requires an explanation at this point. In instances where the provision of specific categories of owner resourcing are sufficiently correlated, these are aggregated to form a single composite measure. Tests of internal reliability were conducted on the multi-item categories of ownership resourcing, namely those valued as equity, contractual and non-contractual resources. Table 7.2 indicates that aggregation into composite measures is acceptable for the indicators of contractual and non-contractual ownership resourcing. The composite measures for contractual and non-contractual resourcing are aggregates of the binary scores for the sub-items of each category, scored as 0 = the resource has not been provided, and 1 = the resource has been provided. It was not acceptable to aggregate the non-cash contributions made to equity by foreign parent companies (alpha coefficient = .57) or by Chinese parent companies (alpha coefficient = .53). Equity share will therefore be used as the indicator of ownership contribution in this category. The normal minimum acceptable value of the alpha coefficient is 0.70.

Table 7.1 Relationship of objectives and the range of ownership resources ($N = 67$ joint ventures)

Correlations are respectively for foreign objectives with foreign ownership resourcing, and Chinese objectives with Chinese ownership resourcing. Pearson correlations between (1) objectives (2) ownership resourcing.

	Foreign owner: resource provision range		
Long-term objective attributed to foreign partner	*Equity share*	*Contractual resources*	*Non-contractual resources*
1. Gain a strategic position in China	0.30*	0.18*	0.03
2. Attraction of the Chinese market	0.20*	0.21*	0.28*
3. Establish strong credibility in China	0.02	0.00	0.28*
4. Opportunity for good long-term profit	0.00	0.05	–0.05
	Chinese owner: resource provision range		
Long-term objective attributed to Chinese partner	*Equity share*	*Contractual resources*	*Non-contractual resources*
1. Gain a strategic position	0.07	–0.12	–0.12
2. Opportunity for good long-term profit	–0.04	0.07	0.00
3. Technology transfer	0.34*	0.07	0.34*
4. Learning management expertise	0.04	0.20*	0.20*

*$p < 0.05$; 1-tail significance.

Table 7.2 Alpha coefficients for the aggregation of ownership indicators into composite scales ($N = 67$ joint ventures)

Aggregation	*Alpha coefficient*
Ownership resources	
Equity resources from foreign parent companies	0.57
Equity resources from Chinese parent companies	0.53
Contractual resources from foreign parent companies	0.71
Contractual resources from foreign parent companies	0.72
Non-contractual resources from foreign parent companies	0.74
Non-contractual resources from Chinese parent companies	0.67

An association is suggested in the study between the objectives of the parent companies and the range of ownership resourcing they provide, including equity and contractual and non-contractual resources. Table 7.1 lists correlations between (1) the priority objectives of foreign partners and Chinese partners that could be considered long-term in nature, and (2) the resourcing provisions of foreign and Chinese owners. The hypothesis states that a partner with long-term objectives will be more likely to contribute a wider range of ownership resourcing to the joint ventures it undertakes. To avoid rejecting support for this hypothesis, the coefficient for the relationships between the three categories of ownership resourcing and the long-term objectives should be significant and positive.

The statistical analyses in Table 7.1 reveal some modest bivariate associations between the objectives and the ownership resourcing provided by the parent companies. There are low but positive correlations between the foreign partner's long-term objectives and the three subcategories of ownership resourcing contributed to the joint venture. It has been noted that correlations are present for market-related long-term objectives, but not for long-term profit opportunity. The correlations between the technology transfer objectives of the Chinese partners and their equity, non-contractual resources are positive. There is a weak positive correlation between the long-term Chinese objective of acquiring management expertise and the Chinese provision of both contractual and non-contractual resources. The following interpretation is offered for these results.

First, gaining a strategic position and the attraction of the Chinese market are seen to be supported by equity investment. Gaining a strategic position and the attraction of the Chinese market are also associated with ownership resources that are provided on a contractual basis. Foreign firms are more likely to contribute their technology, brand name or trademark on a contractual basis in order to gain a strategic position. The objective of establishing a strong business presence in China is associated with the provision of a wider range of non-contractual resources by foreign parent companies, but not with either equity or contractual provision.

Second, the acquisition of technology through the transfer mechanism is seen to be positively correlated with the range of Chinese ownership resourcing in terms of both equity and non-contractual resourcing investment. In other words, the Chinese can achieve their technology transfer objective by investment of equity and non-contractual resources. The result is consistent with the local

Chinese government objective priority, which encourages using joint ventures to acquire technological expertise from foreign partners.

In this study, long-term objectives are used to correlate with the higher value of equity capital. A higher value of equity capital is expected to be used when a joint venture parent gives high priority to strategic and market position objectives. Variance analysis is used to compare the objectives desired by both the foreign and Chinese parent companies against different capital investment levels. The t-test for independent samples has been selected to test the significance level of the difference between the observed frequencies of the objectives and the capital investment indicator.

Table 7.3 shows the frequency with which certain objectives are included among the top five priorities by foreign and Chinese partners, cross-tabulated individually against capital investment. Capital is the value of the equity that foreign and Chinese firms invested in each joint venture at its formation. The t-test for independent samples is used to measure significant differences in the frequency distributions for the two levels of investment groups. In this study, one group is those companies with less than US$ 5 million initial equity invested, the other those with more than US$ 5 million.

Chinese parent companies oriented toward longer-term profit objectives appear prepared to accept the foreign equity share being the larger one. The frequency distribution analysis of the Chinese objectives shows that the objectives of the Chinese partners are largely independent of the level of capital commitment they make. Objectives, such as learning management expertise, are associated with the lower level of Chinese capital resource commitment. The objective of acquiring foreign technology has no correlation with the value of capital commitment. The Chinese government is more concerned with the acquisition of foreign advanced technology, managerial expertise and cash. These objectives are representative of 'typical needs' for most Chinese firms. The objectives of Chinese firms are much more influenced by government policy than is apparent in the objectives of the foreign firms. According to joint venture law, there is no upper limit to foreign investment in a joint venture, but the laws set a minimum of 25 per cent for investment by foreign parties. This reflects the objectives set by the Chinese government for the investment of foreign capital. The long-term objectives of Chinese partners are unrelated to capital investment to joint ventures, because almost all the Chinese firms require the resources of foreign partners to include financial resources, technological know-how and management expertise.

Table 7.3 Analysis of variance comparing the objectives by partners with respect to their level of capital investment (N = 67 joint ventures)

Analysis of distributions is respectively for foreign top-five objectives with foreign capital investment, and Chinese top-five objectives with Chinese capital investment.

Area/issue	*% mentioning among top-five priorities*		*t-test for independent samples*	
	Less than US$ 5 million	*More than US$ 5 million*	*t-value*	*Significance (p) value*
Foreign capital investment				
Top-five objective of a long-term nature held by foreign partner	*(N = 39)*	*(N = 28)*		
Strategic position	42	58	–1.02	0.04
Chinese market	47	53	0.66	0.18
Long-term profit	45	55	–0.16	0.74
Credibility in China	38	62	–1.26	0.02
Chinese capital investment				
Top-five objectives of a long-term nature held by Chinese partner	*(N = 49)*	*(N = 18)*		
Management expertise	54	46	–1.35	0.00
Strategic position	56	44	–0.36	0.50
Long-term profit	57	43	–0.15	0.77
Technology transfer	49	51	–1.99	0.00

The results reveal a tendency for any foreign partner with the objectives of establishing a strong business presence and credibility in China to make a larger capital investment. The findings show that these two objectives held by foreign partners are positive and statistically significant. In order to achieve an objective such as gaining a strategic position in China *vis-à-vis* competitors, foreign firms tend to pay attention to putting a higher value of equity capital into their joint ventures.

In contrast with the results just discussed is the association between partners with short-term objectives and the limited range of ownership resourcing to the joint ventures that partners are likely to contribute. Partners who have short-term objectives usually minimise the capital and contractual resources committed to the joint venture, because as a strategy this is usually both risk-averse and cost-effective. As shown in Table 7.4, there is a fairly consistent tendency for negative correlations between ownership resourcing and giving prior-

Table 7.4 Relationship of objectives of a short-term nature and the limited range of ownership resources ($N = 67$ joint ventures)

Correlation is respectively for foreign objective with foreign ownership resourcing, and Chinese objectives with Chinese ownership resourcing. Pearson correlations are between (1) ownership resources and (2) objectives.

Area/issue	*Equity*	*Contractual resources*	*Non-contractual resources*
Foreign range of ownership resources			
Objective of a short-term nature attributed to foreign partners			
1. Low-cost sourcing	–0.16	0.28*	0.00
2. Benefit from transfer pricing	–0.24*	–0.09	–0.07
3. Low labour cost	–0.13	–0.18	0.12
4. Opportunity for quick profit	–0.14	–0.07	–0.21*
Chinese range of ownership resources			
Objective of a short-term nature attributed to Chinese partners			
1. Obtain foreign cash investment	–0.11	0.09	0.30*
2. Benefit from tax incentives	0.18*	0.18	0.31*
3. Opportunity for quick profit	–0.47**	0.00	–0.13
4. Diversification of products and services	–0.22*	–0.05	–0.12

*$p < 0.05$; **$p < 0.01$; one-tailed significance.

ity to foreign short-term objectives. An exception to this trend is the positive relation between practising low-cost sourcing and providing resources on a contractual basis.

Overall, the findings indicate that the foreign objectives of low-cost sourcing, low labour cost and the opportunity for quick profit are relatively independent of the ownership resourcing they commit to the joint ventures. There is a negative correlation between the importance ascribed to Chinese parent companies of 'opportunity for quick profit' and their share of equity. This suggests that some Chinese parent companies pursue a policy of committing little to joint ventures and getting profits out as soon as possible. The Chinese objectives of obtaining foreign cash investment and seeking to benefit from tax incentives indicate modest positive and moderately strong correlations with non-contractual ownership resource commitment.

Taking the most frequently mentioned short-term objectives of foreign and Chinese partners, the results reveal a similar pattern of capital investment between foreign and Chinese partners. *T*-tests applied to the foreign and Chinese partners grouped by level of capital investment in their joint ventures show that the foreign partner objectives are not independent of their level of capital commitment to joint ventures. (see Table 7.5)

Those joint ventures where low labour cost is given priority tend be associated with having less than US$ 5 million of foreign investment. The foreign desire to set up a joint venture in order to benefit from low labour cost appears to be relevant to the level of capital investment in the joint venture at its formation. With respect to the Chinese objective of obtaining foreign cash investment, however, the results show no support for the relationship hypothesised.

THE RELATIONSHIP BETWEEN OWNERSHIP AND CONTROL

In order to gain a better understanding of the relationship between ownership and control in Sino-foreign joint ventures, the association between the partner's equity share and its control over joint venture strategic and operational areas can be tested. The Pearson correlation coefficient is used to examine the postulated relationships between equity and control in joint ventures.

Table 7.5 Analysis of variance comparing the objectives held by partners with respect to their level of capital investment ($N = 67$ joint ventures)

Analysis of distributions is respectively for foreign top-five objectives with foreign capital investment, and Chinese top-five objectives with Chinese capital investment.

Area/issue	*% mentioning among top five priorities*		*t-test for independent samples*	
Top-five objective held by partners	*Less than US$ 5 million*	*More than US$ 5 million*	*t-values*	*Significance p-value*
Foreign capital investment				
Objective of a short-term nature held by foreign partner	*($N = 39$)*	*($N = 28$)*		
Low labour costs	57	43	1.74	0.05
Chinese capital investment				
Objective of a short-term nature held *by Chinese partner*	*($N = 49$)*	*($N = 18$)*		
Foreign cash investment	56	44	–0.43	0.38

Table 7.6 Alpha coefficients for the aggregation of control indicators into composite scales (N = 67 joint ventures)

Aggregation	*Alpha coefficient*
Control	
Overall foreign influence	0.93
Overall Chinese influence	0.94
Foreign influence over strategic issues	0.78
Chinese influence over strategic issues	0.81
Foreign influence over operational issues	0.86
Chinese influence over operational issues	0.88

When the specific variables of control are strongly intercorrelated, they are aggregated to form a single composite measure. As shown in Table 7.6, tests of internal reliability are conducted on the categories of control, namely items valued as strategic issues, and operational issues. Table 7.6 indicates that aggregation into composite measures is very acceptable for the indicators of both overall foreign and Chinese influence over strategic issues and foreign and Chinese influence over operational issues. The multi-item control indicators are expressed in terms of the thirteen items of influence over strategic and operational areas. Internal consistency among the items is further assessed by estimating coefficient alpha.

Equity share is more strongly associated with a joint venture parent company's influence over strategic issues than it is with influence over operational matters. If higher equity share confers a greater right to manage the JV, than in practice this right appears to be exercised primarily at the policy level. The share of IJV equity consistently predicts the levels of influence ascribed to the relevant parent company and its representatives. As shown in Table 7.7, Chinese equity share and Chinese influence are more closely associated than foreign equity share and foreign influence. The correlations between Chinese equity share and control over strategic (r = .64) and operational areas (r = .52) are strong and positive. Chinese equity share and its overall control are closely associated. Equity share also appears to provide a consistent basis for the perceived level of Chinese control and influence over each of the thirteen specific strategic and operational areas.

Chinese control is more likely to be derived from local knowledge, which is primarily associated with domestic marketing, sales and

Table 7.7 Correlations between partners equity share and their influences (N = 67 JVs)

Indicator of control	*Ownership equity resources*[a] *Foreign equity share*	*Chinese equity share*	*Differences in equity share*
Overall control (N = 56)[a]	0.59***	0.67***	0.66**
Control by parent (single 5-point scale)	0.21*	0.42***	0.51**
Strategic control	0.59***	0.64***	0.67***
Use of profit (N = 59)[a]	0.42**	0.40**	0.48**
Reinvestment policy (N = 61)[a]	0.41**	0.52***	0.52**
Setting strategic objectives	0.43***	0.48***	0.49**
Allocating senior managerial positions	0.40***	0.36**	0.42**
Operational control	0.49***	0.52***	0.53***
Technological innovation	0.42***	0.44***	0.46**
Financial control	0.32**	0.46***	0.42**
Reward and incentive policies	0.40***	0.43***	0.45**
Training and development polices	0.38**	0.50***	0.49**
Sales and distribution	0.43***	0.41***	0.43**
Product pricing	0.33**	0.39**	0.39**
Quality control	0.41***	0.46***	0.47**
Purchasing policies	0.41***	0.49***	0.47**
Production planning	0.39**	0.41***	0.43**

Notes:
[a]Correlation is respectively for foreign equity share and foreign control, and Chinese equity share with Chinese control.
One-tail probabilities: *$p < 0.05$; **$p < 0.01$; ***$p < 0.001$.

sources of supply. With most Chinese firms being only suppliers of limited non-equity joint venture resourcing, they are often unable to gain control of international competencies in technology, marketing, management and management services, which are supplied on both contractual and non-contractual bases. This is probably why the correlation between Chinese equity and control is so high.

The share that foreign parent companies have in Sino-foreign joint venture equity is positively and consistently related to the level of overall foreign control, and to control over both strategic and operational areas. As is also shown in Table 7.7, the relationship between foreign equity share and control over strategic (r = .59) and operational areas (r = .49) is a consistent and strong one. The foreign influence is derived mostly from the strategic areas of decision-making in joint ventures, such as use of profit, reinvestment policy, setting strategic objectives and allocating senior managerial positions. If a high foreign equity share conveys the 'right to manage' a joint venture then in reality this right appears to be exercised primarily at the strategic level.

The operational control is mostly derived from the areas of decision-making, such as technological innovation, financial control, reward and incentive policies, training, quality control, sales and distribution, product pricing, purchasing planning and production planning. The technology supplied by foreign partners appears to be a dominant additional factor influencing the management of joint ventures, particularly where foreign partners can also provide management services, marketing and sales channels associated with the international market. In this study, 55 per cent of foreign firms contributed cash capital to their joint ventures, and 16 per cent of foreign parent companies also committed product and production technology as part of their equity share. This in turn generates some degree of control in relation to product and production technology.

As is shown in Table 7.8, the hypothesised relationship between occupancy of key managerial positions and control over strategic and operational areas also receives very strong support. Strategic control is found to be closely related to the occupancy of general management and key functional positions. Strategic control tends to be concentrated into the positions of general manager, marketing manager and finance manager for the purposes of setting strategic objectives and gaining sales and distribution in the international and Chinese markets. Findings indicate that 80 per cent of the joint ventures were led by a chief executive nominated by the foreign parent company – 53 were so nominated, as opposed to only 14 who had been nominated by a Chinese parent company.

Joint venture control is usually exercised through the right to representation on the board of directors and the occupancy of key management positions. Chinese joint venture law and implementation regulations stipulate that the board of directors must be the highest body of authority for a joint venture. The boards in the study have varying degrees of responsibilities, such as evaluating and approving annual financial plans, production plans, expenditure plans, and distribution of dividends. They meet usually twice a year.

Table 7.8 Correlations between foreign occupancy of key management positions and foreign control (N = 67 joint ventures)

Measure of control	*Occupancy of key managerial positions by expatriates*					
	CEO	*Marketing*	*Finance*	*Production*	*HRM (N = 65)*	*Technical (N = 51)*
Strategic area						
Use of profit (N = 59)	0.17	0.07	0.28*	0.05	0.26*	0.14
Reinvestment policy	0.29*	0.04	0.16	–0.02	0.05	0.02
Setting strategic objectives	0.43***	0.35**	0.28**	0.24*	0.17	0.27*
Managerial positions	0.43***	0.22*	0.29*	0.16	0.26*	0.20
Operational area						
Technological innovation	0.32*	0.34**	0.26*	0.23*	0.13	0.08
Financial control	0.21*	0.23*	0.16	0.01	–0.03	0.04
Reward and incentive policies	0.14	0.29*	0.29*	0.16	0.24*	0.25*
Training and development polices	0.26*	0.09	0.23*	0.05	0.03	0.00
Sales and distribution	0.38**	0.36**	0.20*	0.25*	0.19*	0.31*
Product pricing	0.26*	0.31**	0.23*	0.18	0.26*	0.19*
Quality control	0.33*	0.16	0.23*	0.19*	0.04	–0.02
Purchasing policies	0.29*	0.22*	0.18	0.14	0.15	0.22*
Production planning	0.28*	0.19*	0.23*	0.23*	0.33*	0.34*

One-tail probabilities: $^{*}p < 0.05$; $^{**}p < 0.001$; $^{***}p < 0.00$.

Most appointments of a Chinese board chairman appear to be of merely symbolic value. Very often, the appointee is not empowered with special authority such as having a casting vote. There are some complaints about the choice of personnel chosen by the Chinese side as the chairman. Some of them are likely to be heads of administrative departments from local government, who are responsible for these ventures. They therefore have a conflict of interest, as well as being too busy to lead the board effectively.

In one case, the Chinese vice-chairman of the joint venture board actually had three different positions on the board of the joint venture, as he also worked in the local industry bureau. At times, this chairman from the Chinese side had no business experience or specific knowledge of the venture, and as nominated as a member of the board as a reward for their position. Similar circumstances could also create a conflict of interest, where directors coming from the Chinese side represented a large number of interests, such as those of the local region. Often they had very little actual knowledge of the industry involved, and were unable to make a realistic input. Because the joint venture board is a specific channel for control, deriving from parent company equity share, the above suggests the possibility that the board plays a limited role in the control of any Sino-foreign joint venture.

The choice of personnel by the foreign side tends to be made by the joint venture's board: CEO of joint ventures and staff from regional office and headquarters. Only a very small percentage of nonexecutives are nominated externally; such board members usually have rich international venturing experience and specific knowledge of running subsidiary or joint venture. When the foreign firms have a minority equity share in joint ventures, the foreign control and influence consequently appear to flow through the normal channels of multinational enterprise networking, rather than through joint venture boards. The joint venture tends to be run with a sleeping board.

Expatriate managers exert higher control and influence over strategic and operational areas than the balance of equity share between foreign and Chinese would predict. Partial correlation analysis confirms that once the effects of equity share are taken into account, the relationship between the key managerial positions occupied by the foreign partners and the measures of control tends to remain.

Operational control is strongly impacted by general managers and production and technical managers on operational areas such as technological innovation, sales and distribution, and quality control. The results shown in Table 7.8 indicate that foreign managerial appointments are likely to provide leverage for control. These results support to some degree the findings of Lecraw (1984) and Killing (1983), who suggest that equity control and management control should be differentiated in studies of joint ventures.

The ongoing management relationships between the key functional managers and the areas of control have taken place through regular reporting procedures and personal visits. The control that foreign partners consistently exercise appears to flow through the design of the vertical structures of joint ventures. These frequently encompass corporate, regional and joint venture levels. The occupation of key managerial positions in joint ventures by foreign partners tends to be a way of controlling the formal reporting system and aligning it strictly with the partner's management system. This enables the managers in regional and headquarters to get information from the expatriate managers in the joint venture. The ongoing management relationships between joint ventures and foreign parent companies take place through regular reporting procedures and personal visits, which are much more frequent than meetings of the board. Communication takes place through the frequent use of fax, telephone and email.

The Chinese side most commonly negotiates a contract where the management structure divides the responsibilities evenly between partners. They typically negotiate a shadow management system – that is, one where the head of a department appointed by a representative of one side would be matched by a deputy from the other side. This shadow system is designed to allow foreign managers to teach Chinese managers their management skills as well as to maintain some Chinese influence within the joint venture. Despite this arrangement, over the years there has been no noticeable decline in the proportion of foreign top managers. Also, in the joint ventures studied, there did not appear to be that many shadow management structures.

The relationship of joint venture management both with the board and with parent companies is indicated by looking at the pattern of reporting by managers from the various areas and also the reporting required from the general manager of the joint venture. Management of technology, finance and marketing is clearly dominated by the foreign partners, who tend to have operational control. Most of the technological expertise is introduced by the foreign partners, as they have the knowledge and desire to manage it. The area of finance is definitely dominated by foreign managers. Internationally accepted financial practice is an area the Chinese wish to learn, and the use of a foreign manager to teach their managers may be the reason behind this arrangement. International sales is naturally an area where the foreign partner dominates, since it is generally the foreign partner that has access to the foreign market.

The results from the study indicate that the foreign partner dominates most key managerial positions in any joint venture, even if it does not have majority equity share. The reasons are more likely to lie in the specialised product and production technology that is introduced by the foreign partner, and which is generally protected from acquisition by the local Chinese partner. Marketing and, to a lesser extent, sales are also areas of expertise contributed by the foreign partner. Most Chinese managers lack marketing skills, because they have grown up in a planned economy. If the products were destined for markets outside China then only the foreign partner would initially have the knowledge or ability to manage the sales. As in most cases the foreign partner has knowledge and experience in technology, marketing and management, this enables it to have a greater influence in designing the structure of the joint venture as well as setting informal control over it. Keeping Chinese managers away from key management positions of the joint venture is another mechanism for controlling a joint venture.

Control is studied in terms of exercising through (1) holding a high equity share and (2) the right to representation on the board of directors and occupancy of key management positions. The significant and positive correlations between partners' equity share and occupancy of key positions on one hand and the control indicators on the other lend support to this result.

The formal aspects of management control in joint ventures are established by committing product and production technology and management systems on a contractual basis. The survey examined the postulated relationship between the contractual resources and the control over designated areas of product and process technology that was presumed to derive from contracted ownership resources.

Table 7.9 presents the correlations between contractual ownership resources and the measures of control. The contractual resources in this study predict differences in influence in a limited number of areas, such as technological innovation, quality control, reinvestment policy and purchasing policies.

Findings relating to the contractual resourcing suggest that foreign partners tend to strengthen their positions at the strategic level, and quality control at the operational level, by legitimising resourcing on contractual basis. From the standpoint of foreign ownership contractual resources, the key to whether a foreign parent company must

Table 7.9 Correlations between levels of partners' ownership contractual resources and their operational control (N = 67 joint ventures)

Correlations are respectively for foreign contractual resources and foreign control, and Chinese contractual resources with Chinese control.

	Ownership contractual resources		
Indicator of foreign control	*Foreign resources resources*	*Chinese contractual resources*	*Differences between foreign and Chinese contractual resources*
Overall control (N = 56)[1]	0.27*	0.52***	0.31**
Control by parent (single 5-point scale)	0.10	0.33***	30**
Strategic control	0.21	0.11	0.19
Use of profit (N = 59)	0.07	0.11	0.12
Reinvestment policy (N = 61)	0.30**	0.21*	0.35*
Setting strategic objectives	0.26*	0.12	0.24*
Allocating senior managerial positions	0.16	0.07	–0.03
Operational control	0.25*	0.22*	0.29*
Technological innovation	0.44***	0.27*	0.42*
Financial control	0.15	0.12	0.15
Reward and incentive policies	0.13	0.09	0.14
Training and development polices	0.30**	0.25*	0.25
Sales and distribution	0.26*	0.27*	0.15
Product pricing	0.24*	0.14	0.17
Quality control	0.13	0.26*	0.30*
Purchasing policies	0.44**	0.31**	0.35*
Production planning	0.19	0.33**	0.23

One-tail probabilities: $*p < 0.05$; $**p < 0.01$; $***p < 0.001$.

exert control and influence in a joint venture's activities will lie in how much interaction is needed between the parent company and its joint venture in China, in order to achieve its strategic purpose of keeping its standard in terms of product design and production technology in certain Chinese regions.

Contractual inputs do not, however, appear to be strongly or consistently related to influence, even when account is taken of the differences between Chinese and foreign joint venture parent companies. Examination of the relationship between foreign contractual resourcing and the areas of control reveals only a limited number of significant correlations, such as in the areas of technological innovation, reinvestment policy, the setting of strategic objectives, quality control, training and development policies, purchasing planning and production planning. The most significant contractual resources are technological ones. The provision of contractual resources appears to have be a lever for control over operational areas of product and production technology.

A greater provision of contractual resources does lead to a correspondingly greater foreign influence in running the joint venture at the operational level. While such contracts often lay down service specifications for products, it is apparent that the importance of the control function of contracts lies in the attempt to keep quality control standards, and to avoid the misuse of brand names, trade marks and other proprietary assets by other Chinese companies outside the joint venture. This appears to set boundary conditions to joint venture management rather than to encourage managers in the joint venture's day-to-day ongoing business processes.

The provision of resources by foreign parent companies via the forms of formal contracts has a very defined boundary impact on control and influence within the joint ventures. A Chinese manager from the electronics sector commented that the effects of foreign contractual resources are as follows:

> When foreign partners lay down product and production technology specifications, it is apparent they are very sensitive about those areas. It is obvious that the contract sets a boundary in order to avoid 'technology leakage', but it also brings some side effects such as less flexibility, greater costs of marketing in different areas and creates a lower trust level between the foreign and Chinese sides.

Contractual resources provided through formal contracts normally specify payments and lay down conditions, time limits and other constraints. Contractual resources are not necessarily directed primarily at internal management control and influence. They may be at least as much concerned with establishing the boundary conditions within which joint venture management can proceed. It also appears that another important motivation for foreign parent companies to supply resources on a contractual basis is to secure a guaranteed income stream through the royalties the joint venture is then committed to pay.

Contracts expressing technological property rights include patents and licence agreements, and they are particularly important in the case of China (Guo and Ackroyd 1996). Results relating to the measures of contractual resourcing suggest that very few Chinese partners contribute resources on a contractual basis. This is normally a way to strengthen their position at the operational level of joint venture management. But provision of resource could be a way to set the boundaries in technology and management, which will in turn impinge on the operationalisation of the joint venture management.

Examining the relationship between Chinese contractual resources and areas of control identifies a limited number of associations, such as production planning, purchasing policies, quality control, technological innovation, and training and development policies. The relative predictive power of the contractual resources from Chinese partners lies in the general management areas of joint ventures, such as production planning. The level of contractual resources provided by the Chinese companies has relatively strong predictive effects, particularly on the control over purchasing and production. The study suggests that the better result can be achieved in terms of the shaping of employee's activities, training and HRM expertise provided on a non-contractual basis.

In general, the results suggest that the more a parent company contributes key resources on a contractual basis, the greater will be its overall control and influence in the corresponding functional areas of the joint venture. A greater provision of contractual inputs by either parent does not lead to correspondingly greater influence over IJV operation in general. The difference of input provision on a contractual basis between Chinese and foreign parent companies does, however, predict differences in their influence over a limited number of areas, namely technological innovation, quality control, reinvestment policy and purchasing polices. These connections reflect the fact that the most significant contractual inputs are technological ones. The restrictions on the use of technological inputs that were contained in or accompany the majority of technology contracts were not associated with the influence attributed to the parent company in corresponding areas of management.

There is no clear-cut picture in the case of non-contractual inputs invested in Sino-foreign joint ventures. As shown in Table 7.10, a

Table 7.10 Correlations between levels of partners' non-contractual resources and their operational control (N = 67 joint ventures)

Correlations are respectively for foreign non-contractual resources and foreign control, and Chinese non-contractual resources with Chinese control.

	Ownership non-contractual resources		
Indicator of foreign control	*Foreign non-contractual resources*	*Chinese non-contractual resources*	*Differences in foreign and Chinese non-contractual resources*
Overall control (N = 56)	0.42**	0.33**	0.59***
Control by parent (single 5-point scale)	0.26*	0.33*	0.43***
Strategic control	0.33*	0.46***	0.52***
Use of profit (N = 59)	0.29*	0.39**	0.46**
Reinvestment policy (N = 61)	0.24*	0.36**	0.41**
Setting strategic objectives	0.38**	0.35**	0.48**
Allocating senior managerial positions	0.20*	0.25*	0.34*
Operational control	0.46**	0.44***	0.61***
Technological innovation	0.36**	0.45***	0.52**
Financial control	0.18	0.39**	0.36*
Reward and incentive policies	0.21*	0.36**	0.36*
Training and development polices	0.14	0.33**	0.36*
Sales and distribution	0.44***	0.29**	0.50*
Product pricing	0.38**	0.35**	0.47**
Quality control	0.32**	0.42***	0.57**
Purchasing policies	0.30**	0.41***	0.47**
Production planning	0.41***	0.37**	0.55**

One-tail probabilities: *$p < 0.05$; **$p < 0.01$; ***$p < 0.001$.

greater provision by the foreign parent of non-contractual resources is a consistent predictor of foreign context control. The results suggest that non-contractual resource provision has independent effects over all of the operational areas of management. It also has an independent effect on defining which party exercises the greater influence over setting strategic objectives, sales and distribution, product pricing and production planning. The non-contractual inputs invested by foreign parent companies in technology, training and management are linked with their level of operational influence, especially in sales and distribution product pricing, and production planning. When foreign non-contractual resource provision is more extensive than Chinese, the foreign parent company is seen to exert greater influence over technology and quality control as well. A Japanese general manager from the electronics sector made the following comment on the effects of foreign non-contractual resources:

> In order to build up a corporate culture in the joint venture, we insist on having a ten-minute meeting before we start work every day. All staff come together to sing the company song and read the corporate ten-point slogan. We have to put an enormous effort into establishing a positive attitude towards work. We run seminars, together with technical and managerial training from time to time. Our colleagues are happy with the way we are organised [in] the company. Our business is developing well and this means that our methods work.

Moderate to high correlations are obtained between items of foreign non-contractual resources and most areas of control. The correlations are in fact significant and positive between foreign non-contractual resourcing and all the measures of control in Table 7.10, except for training policies and financial control. In the picture that emerges, resources provided contractually on a non-contractual basis are more likely than those provided contractually to serve as a lever for control. Most foreign firms tend to provide non-contractual resources more often do than their Chinese counterparts (see Table 6.9). In any joint venture, these resources appear to have significant influence and control in a number of areas, such as sales and distribution, production planning, product pricing, quality control and purchasing by the joint venture. When foreign non-contractual resource provision is more extensive within the joint venture, the foreign parent company is also seen to exert greater influence over technological innovation.

Many of these non-contractual resources are of management systems, 'soft' technology and training that would by their nature enhance the influence of the parent company over the conduct of joint venture operations. Foreign non-contractual resources provided to joint ventures in China facilitate managerial control by establishing a reciprocal Chinese obligation to accept the authority of the resource provider. This means that in the Chinese context a non-contractual provision of resources further enhances the provider's control through the goodwill, and indeed obligation, it engenders. The provision of non-contractual resources fits in with these normal channels of foreign company international management. Support in areas that include technology, marketing and management systems is provided on this basis through the process of visits, development projects and training that is part of the normal internal functioning of a multinational corporation. Many of the non-contractual resources from foreign partners are in the form of management systems, technology and service training, which would, by their nature, enhance the control and influence of the foreign company over the conduct of joint venture operations.

With the development of joint ventures in China, and of globalisation in general, non-contractual ownership resources have assumed increasing importance as a key to success. Success now lies in the knowledge and skill of managing complex interdependencies within and across joint venture boundaries and in the ability to manage multi-cultural units (Ohmae 1993, Nonaka and Takeuchi 1995). The findings of the present study suggest that the provision of non-contractual resources normally reflects a high level of commitment to joint ventures on the part of the parent company. These resourcing inputs are likely to give rise to *de facto* ownership rights through claims to the expertise, goodwill and cultural capital they generate. The partner that is able to accrue goodwill, trust and the loyalty of joint venture personnel adds significant value to its original equity. In establishing joint ventures to exploit complementarities between partners, non-contractual resourcing can be a way to provide resources, skills and knowledge additional to their equity contribution. Such assets, which are within the possession of partner firms, have an intrinsic value, and amount to ownership resources with property rights.

There are significant and positive correlations between the measures of Chinese non-contractual resourcing and all but one of the indicators of control shown in Table 7.10. When Chinese parent companies provide non-contractual resources, the respective relationships between this resourcing and their strategic and operational controls are almost equal (r = 0.46 and 0.44). Non-contractual resources committed by Chinese parent companies are associated mainly with external institutional relations, and understanding local government rules and regulations. Such topics are more likely to be discussed in board meetings, which in turn enhances Chinese control and influence in strategic matters. Non-contractual resourcing committed by the Chinese partners could be a way of showing their willingness to learn and accept training. This would enhance their influence over technology and management in the daily business operational activities. As mentioned earlier, high value is attached in China to trust-based relationships and to commitment, both personal and institutional (Child 1994). The significance of non-contractual resources as levers for control and influence, in the joint ventures studied, derives from the way they are perceived to assert the commitment to a continuing relationship in a society, which retains its traditional norms and values.

The picture emerges that the resourcing that the Chinese partner commits on a non-contractual basis is related to the power of control. As shown in Table 7.10, Chinese non-contractual resources appear to gain relative influence in a number of areas, such as use of profit, reinvestment policy, allocating senior managerial positions, technological innovation, financial control, quality control and purchasing policies. The categories of non-contractual ownership resourcing account for between 11 and 20 per cent of the variance for influence over more specific strategic and operational issues. The provision of non-contractual resources has a somewhat stronger impact, because of its significance for operational issues.

Non-contractual resources therefore represent a more ongoing relationship between parent company and joint venture than either equity or contractual resourcing. To support the result, the correlations between owning companies and the resources should be significant and positive. The results reveal that there are significant and positive relationships between owning companies and the resources they contribute on a non-contractual basis.

A postulated relationship between the configuration of ownership resourcing provided by the parent companies – namely equity, contractual, and non-contractual resources – and the indicators of control by those parents is verified here. This was tested by means of multiple regression analysis, and the results are shown in Table 7.11.

Partners' equity shares appear to provide a foundation for the overall control they are perceived to exercise over their joint ventures. Partners' non-contractual resourcing also predicts their level of overall control. Both foreign and Chinese ownership resourcing are thus strongly reflected in the respective partners' overall control of their joint ventures. The power to predict joint venture control is derived from both the percentage of equity and the range of noncontractual resourcing investment. Contractual resourcing does not contribute significantly to the prediction of overall control when considered alongside equity share and non-contractual resources.

Table 7.11 Multiple regression of foreign and Chinese overall control, and the difference in their control, on the configuration of ownership resources (N = 67 joint ventures)

Predictor variables for Chinese overall control are Chinese equity share, Chinese provision of contractual and non-contractual resourcing. For foreign overall control, predictor variables are foreign equity share, foreign contractual resource and foreign non-contractual resourcing. In the case of the difference in overall control (that is, foreign minus Chinese overall control), predictor variables are the difference between foreign and Chinese equity shares, and differences between foreign and Chinese contractual and non-contractual resourcing.

	Predictor variable						
	% Equity share		*Contractual resources provided by partner(s)*		*Non-contractual resources provided by partner(s)*		
	beta	*p*	*beta*	*p*	*beta*	*p*	*Multiple* R^2
Overall Chinese control	0.41	0.000	–0.01	n.s.	0.29	0.02	0.57
Overall foreign control	0.46	0.000	–0.19	n.s.	0.29	0.01	0.59
Difference in overall control (N = 56)	0.49	0.000	–0.05	n.s.	0.38	0.002	0.53

In order to test the postulated association further, Table 7.12 presents a multiple regression analysis of the ownership predictors of strategic and operational control. Table 7.12 indicates that the level of strategic control is more strongly predicted by percentage of equity share than by the other aspects of ownership resourcing. The relative contribution of equity share and non-contractual resourcing to operational control is somewhat variable. In all the analyses, non-contractual resourcing contributes to the prediction of operational control. However, in the Chinese case, non-contractual resourcing does not contribute to operational control more than it does to strategic control. In the foreign case, it has slightly less predictive power than equity share, and the if difference in ownership resourcing and operational

Table 7.12 Multiple regression of foreign and Chinese strategic and operational control, and differences in their control, on the configuration of ownership resourcing ($N = 67$ joint ventures)

The choice of variables entered into these regressions follows the same principles described in the headnote to Table 7.11.

	Predictor variables						
	% Equity share		*Levels of contractual resources*		*Levels of non-contractual resources*		
	beta	*p*	*beta*	*p*	*beta*	*p*	*Multiple* R^2
Chinese strategic control	0.55	0.000	0.23	0.05	0.37	0.004	0.50
Foreign strategic control	0.55	0.000	–0.05	n.a.	0.15	n.a.	0.36
Difference in strategic control ($N = 56$)	0.56	0.000	–0.12	n.a.	0.31	0.01	0.51
Chinese operational control	0.42	0.000	–0.05	n.a.	0.32	0.01	0.35
Foreign operational control	0.39	0.001	–0.03	n.a.	0.35	0.002	0.35
Difference in operational control	0.35	0.002	–0.05	n.a.	0.49	0.000	0.47

n.a. = not available.

control is examined, non-contractual resourcing is found have a stronger predictive power than equity share.

A more comprehensive range of ownership resourcing by parent companies is thus reflected in a correspondingly enhanced degree of control over strategic and operational areas. The prediction of control by equity share is consistent with conventional Western ownership theory, but non-contractual ownership resourcing seems to have its own, different impact on joint venture control. A Chinese deputy general manager from an FMCG company commented as follows on the control implications of active non-contractual resourcing by the foreign owner:

> Our partner is an America multinational corporation. When we set up this joint venture, they invested in product technology and management systems for the venture ... Some technology has been contributed to the joint venture for free ... the managers from the regional office or headquarters of the US company visit the joint venture at least once a month, but our Chinese parent rarely visits us and has not invested anything since the joint venture was started. With regard to international venturing experience, our partner knows how to run the joint venture. You can tell this simply from how they invest in the joint venture.

Foreign parent companies tend to enjoy greater influence across the whole range of management areas, when they provide a greater spread of non-contractual resources than do their Chinese counterparts. The impact of differential foreign non-contractual resource provision is also greater than that of holding a larger equity share, in some operational areas. This tends to be the case in the areas of sales and distribution, product pricing, quality control, production planning and technological innovation. It was also evident that there was a close association between foreign non-contractual provision of HRM input and foreign influences over the kind of reward and incentive scheme operated by the joint ventures. This suggests that non-contractual resourcing may be a particularly important source of parent company influence in the field of joint venture culture building.

The configuration of ownership resources is reflected in the pattern of their overall control and influence in a joint venture. To support these results, the coefficient of the three variables of ownership resources and the overall control variables should be significant and positive. As was shown in Tables 7.11 and 7.12, the results are statistically significant and in line with the results for two of the ownership variables (equity share and non-contractual resourcing).

SUMMARY

This chapter has discussed to the postulated relationships between objectives, ownership and control reported for foreign and Chinese partners of joint ventures. The findings show that the top five objectives of Chinese partners are in line with an organisational learning view of joint ventures, particularly when it is recognised that the joint venture is formed because the Chinese partner lacks the necessary management and technical expertise to undertake the venture alone. Hamel (1991) mentions that joint ventures provide the opportunity for one partner to internalise the capabilities of the other, and thereby improve its competitive position both inside and outside the joint venture. It is apparent that for the study's sample firms, the main objectives of Chinese partners are driven by the needs of national economic development.

There is a pattern of comprehensive foreign influence across both the strategic and operational areas of joint venture. The results further indicate that the provision of additional resources on a contractual and, particularly, a non-contractual basis adds significantly to the influence that partners can exercise over many areas of joint venture management, especially in the basic operational areas. The provision of resources on a contractual basis has generated rights such as those to defend brand names and trade marks, to the use of technology, to guarantee the quality-control led professional services. As contracts usually provide specifications for product and production technology, they assist owners to specify the management positions they wish to hold in return for the technology they provide.

The control and influence derived from non-contractual resources tend to be greatest in the areas of operational activities. This is particularly critical for raising the performance of joint ventures in China up to internationally competitive standards, and for extending their market penetration. At the same time, equity share and provision of resources on a contractual and non-contractual basis are significant predictors of higher foreign influence relative to that of their Chinese partners, over a broad range of joint venture management activities. The findings in this study provide confirmatory evidence that ownership commitment from foreign partners to joint ventures has a significant impact on the control they are able to exercise.

The pervasive association of expatriate control and influence within joint venture management is clearly apparent over strategic and operational matters. The foreign partners are perceived to have greater control and influence over strategic and operational decision-making activities. The areas where foreign partners have most control and influence are technology, marketing and setting strategic objectives. The senior positions in these areas are often held by expatriates or persons nominated by the foreign partner. The position of CEO is predominantly occupied by expatriates. The pattern of managerial appointments is consistent with the foreign partner exerting the greatest influence in all the aspects of joint venture control. Generally speaking, the relationships between ownership resourcing from foreign partners and the overall control produce a clear-cut picture. Nomination of key managers from foreign partners is not only legitimised from the impact of equity, but also derived from the influence of contracts, especially the joint venture contract itself.

8 Sino-Foreign Joint Venture Performance

INTRODUCTION

Evaluating the performance of a joint venture is an important challenge. No consensus on the appropriate measure of performance has yet emerged. Relatively little of the research relating to performance has directly examined joint ventures between firms from advanced market economies and those from China (Glaister and Buckley 1994, Yan and Gray 1994b, Osland and Cavusgil 1996). Janger (1980), Lecraw (1984) and Schaan (1983) indicate that it is more difficult to achieve satisfactory joint venture performance in developing countries than in developed ones. Lee and Beamish (1995) point out that performance problems are costly not only to the parent companies, but also to the host country itself, owing to the social costs and economic disturbances associated with such problems. Performance requirements that are applied to joint ventures by developing countries often include local content and a stimulus to local employment. Government may present special conditions – through legal provisions, taxation structuring, and approval of expansion plans – that highlight the significance of joint venture performance criteria from the local perspective.

During the last twenty years, more foreign direct investment has flowed into China than into any other emerging economy, and it ranks second only to the United States as a host country for such investment (UNCTAD 1997). The evidence from recent surveys suggests that some foreign firms are disappointed with the performance achieved by their Chinese investments, owing to factors such as the cost of relying on expensive expatriate managers, and the imposition by the Chinese authorities of new taxes on such items as imported capital goods and the cost of training those managers (Vanhonacker 1997).

A major controversy over the measurement of joint venture performance appears to be in finding an appropriate yardstick (Doyle 1994). The debate revolves around whether to use financial criteria such as return on capital investment, profitability, and growth of sales, or whether other economic development criteria, like technology transfer and the learning of managerial expertise, are more appropriate. Obviously, an inadequate performance evaluation of joint ventures may affect the efficiency of their resource acquisition and utilisation, and it could eventually lead to stress or demotivation among joint venture managers, simply because the investing companies are applying inadequate performance criteria (Scott 1973, Shapiro 1982, Emmanuel and Otley 1985, Demirag 1988, Anderson 1990, Glaister and Buckley 1994). This debate hinges on the objectives in forming joint ventures, and it therefore permits the assessment of the relevance of joint venture performance in terms of the extent to which the partners' objectives have been met.

Seashore and Yuchtman (1967) argue that the conventional concepts of goals and goal attainment are not wholly appropriate to the assessment of organisational performance, and that this can instead be assessed and described in terms of generalised resource-getting capabilities under conditions of competition for scarce and valued resources. They state that it is too simplistic to assume that organisations have goals that can be identified and become the yardstick for assessing organisational effectiveness. The factors of performance that emerged from their study did not represent the stable goals of the organisation, namely low production costs. They therefore proposed a 'system' approach as an alternative basis for performance assessment. According to this perspective, performance may vary according to how successfully organisations secure new resources through the ongoing processes of exchange with their external environment. A joint venture is set up specifically to achieve certain objectives. Having only two or a few owners, it is therefore easier to identify goals, while those goals are likely to have more impact and meaning for the joint venture. The system approach is oriented towards the assessment of organisations' performance in terms of how successfully they operate as systems and enhance their future capabilities.

With regard to the ways of measuring performance, Geringer and Hebert (1991) develop and test several hypotheses regarding the reliability and comparability of a range of objective and subjective measures of joint venture performance. Glaister and Buckley (1994) extend the work of Geringer and Hebert (1991) by considering the effect of national cultural differences on the relationship between objective and subjective measures of joint venture performance. They develop their work by examining the ways measures of performance are affected by differences in perception on the part of the parent companies.

This chapter proceeds as follows. In the first section, a framework combining the goal and system performance criteria is described. This is followed by an analysis of the performance of the sixty-seven Sino-foreign joint ventures applying the goal and system criteria. Performance is regarded as a consequence of how well the ownership and control variables are matched. The performance effects of the fit between ownership and control are then examined. The final section discusses the results of testing with reference to the performance framework.

A PERFORMANCE FRAMEWORK

The distinction can be made, in evaluating joint venture effectiveness, between the goals contained in the investing companies' objectives and the system that is the joint venture itself – operating as a business system with reference to factors such as profitability, growth in sales, market share, technology development and the development of local managers and staff. The objectives set by the investing companies of a joint venture follow the goal perspective. The system perspective refers to the health or progress of the joint venture, which embraces mainly operational performance criteria (Etzioni 1960). The framework for performance analysis set out in Figure 8.1 draws upon both Pfeffer and Salancik's (1978) goal model and Seashore and Yuchtman's (1967) system analysis. It also distinguishes between objective and subjective measures of performance.

Figure 8.1 A framework for joint venture performance analysis

		Perspective on performance	
		Goal	System
Nature of data used	Subjective	Assessment by managers of how far joint venture partners' objectives have been achieved	Assessment of joint venture profitability, growth, technology development, development of local staff and managers
	Objective		Hard data on items such as profitability and growth in sales

One approach to performance assessment in the organisational literature is goal-oriented, referring to the preferences, goals, values and needs of organisational members. Expectancy theory (Vroom 1964) argues that people undertake actions according to the probability that these actions will lead to some instrumentally valued outcome. Goal theory (Locke 1968) argues that people undertake actions to achieve their goals. Needs theory argues that people act purposefully to fulfil their needs or to overcome need deficiencies (Maslow 1943, Alderfer 1972). Political theories (Pfeffer 1977, 1981a) assert that individual action is motivated by the need to achieve some desired outcome such as more resources, promotion or additional power. Pfeffer argued that the theories share some common elements.

Most research in organisational behaviour tends to treat goals, needs, attitudes or intentions as the selection of some actions from a set of possible options. There are some distinctions among the options reviewed. Expectancy theory (Pffeffer 1981b) presents one of the more elaborate models of the development of both attitudes and behaviour in the context of desired goals. Goal-setting theory predicts action solely in terms of intentions or goals, without the intervening calculus of expectations and instrumentality.

Although the goal perspective is the dominant one, at least in much work within organisational behaviour, the assessment of the achievement of objectives held by joint venture partners adds a new aspect. This endeavours to apply goal performance criteria to joint ventures, which are based upon subjective evaluations by the senior managers of those joint ventures, working as agents of the parent companies. Applying this subjective assessment to the present study would take account of the opinions of senior foreign and Chinese managers on the achievement of the objectives held by parent companies. However, this methodology could be criticised for being arbitrary, because different individuals are allowed to express values based on their subjective judgements.

Beamish (1984), Geringer and Hebert (1989) and Harrigan (1987) examined joint venture performance by using perceptual measures applied to partner goals. This approach allows managers to rate how effective a given joint venture has been in meeting the objectives established for it. Performance targets tend to be based on the perspective of an individual parent company, and are relevant to their own resource base and capabilities (Harrigan 1987, Doyle 1994).

The increased emphasis on joint ventures as an organisational form in a system context draws attention to variables that are descriptive of system performance, such as profitability, growth, market share, technology development and the development of local staff. Such measures refer to outputs and to various joint venture states and processes. These different indicators of system health have the merit of emphasising that no single criterion can reasonably be used alone to represent joint venture performance, and they thus emphasise that joint venture performance is complex. The measures are able to provide information regarding the extent to which the joint venture has achieved its overall objectives.

The reasons for using a holistic, system approach stem from the fact that each single performance measure may conflict with others. Maximising one measure may be to the detriment of others. Basically, it has been argued that the process of realising ownership commitments by the partners tends to generate a conflict of interest. Finding an appropriate measure of the relationship between ownership resourcing to a joint venture at its formation and its subsequent performance in the market is extremely difficult. The advantages of using system criteria in measuring joint venture performance are derived from two considerations. First, it avoids the complexity of applying goals to joint ventures, when two or more owning companies are involved. Second, many performance problems may be associated with a gap between the identification of long-term resources and capability needs *and* the actual commitment made by the partners to their joint ventures as a collaborative form. System criteria can reveal this gap. Overall, the goal model draws attention to criteria relevant to a long-term performance horizon, while many system measures, such as profitability, are more likely to reflect a short-term prospect.

A GOAL PERSPECTIVE OF PERFORMANCE ASSESSMENT

Identification of key variables associated with performance has been perceived very differently between partners of joint ventures. Most joint venture research in China has taken into account only the objectives of foreign partners, and has overlooked the objectives held by the Chinese partners, for example technology transfer (Davidson and McFetridge 1985). As a result, little is known about how the partners' diverse objectives evolve with the development of the joint venture over time, because of the interactions between them, the joint venture's competitive position and the performance it actually achieves.

The study described in this book has provided evidence of considerable differences in the objectives of the partners. Overall, foreign partners tend to concentrate on access to the Chinese market. Chinese partners focus on economic development criteria such as technology and management transfer and securing foreign capital investment. These large contrasts in objectives for engaging in joint ventures imply that performance assessment should be based on both partners' perspectives. In the author's study, foreign and Chinese senior managers were asked to rate how far the objectives they ascribed to their parent companies have been achieved since the formation of the joint venture. The analysis provides an insight as to how parent companies perceive joint venture performance. A combination of ratings of the achievement of Chinese and foreign partners' objectives proved to be a more effective empirical way of evaluating performance than using the single perspective of one partner only.

The Achievement of Foreign Objectives

Table 8.1 shows the ratings given by senior foreign managers of the extent to which they perceive that the foreign parent company's objectives have been achieved. Foreign managers were asked to assess performance along five-point scales in terms of their perceived achievement of the top five objectives ascribed by their parent companies when the joint ventures were formed. Chapter 6 reported the ratings of objectives given by the foreign partners, and it was clear that they value highly the establishment of a strong business presence and/or credibility, the gaining of a strategic position in China *vis-à-vis* competitors and access to the Chinese market.

Most foreign managers perceive that their parent companies have achieved their joint venture objectives to a satisfactory level. For each objective except one, the mean achievement score was above the mid point (3) of the five-point scale, although there are particular cases where achievement is reported as limited. Most of the foreign partners give high ratings to the achievement of a strong business presence, low labour cost, gaining a strategic position in China *vis-à-vis* competitors and benefiting from tax incentives.

The highest perceived achievement is in establishing a strong business presence. China is regarded as one of the main markets in global business. Establishing a business in China can be viewed as a strategic achievement, which facilitates international market expansion. Therefore, the criteria of success are measured according to the amount of global support, such as technical and marketing, contributed by the

Table 8.1 Achievement ratings of foreign objectives for joint ventures (N = 67 joint ventures)

Perceived achievement of foreign objectives, if among top five objectives. Scales range from 1 = not achieved at all, to 5 = fully achieved.

Items	*Foreign partners*	
	Mean	*Number of cases where the objective was included among the top five priorities*
Mean above 3.60		
Establish strong business presence	3.69	37
Low labour cost	3.68	28
Gain a strategic position in China	3.66	53
Benefit from tax incentives	3.62	17
Mean between 3.60 and 3.30		
Opportunity for quick profit	3.45	11
Low-cost sourcing	3.40	15
Benefit from advantageous transfer pricing	3.40	10
Learning how to do business in China	3.38	17
Mean below 3.30		
Access to Chinese market	3.21	51
Opportunity for good long-term profit	3.15	52
Facilitate international expansion	3.10	26
Diversification of products and service	2.67	6

parent companies to their subsidiaries and how these resource provisions are compared with their businesses elsewhere.

The reasons that foreign managers give high ratings are reflected in the strategic perspectives of the foreign partners. According to one respondent from an MNE in the fast-moving consumer goods sector:

> We need to develop new markets, particularly where there is a large market like China. As our business is labour intensive, it is also important to gain the benefit of cheap sourcing and labour from the local market. Both demand and supply economics will undoubtedly contribute to us establishing a strong business presence not only in China, but also in Asia Pacific region.

The finding is consistent with the indication by Beamish (1987) that many firms in developed countries look for local partners as a means of spreading the introduction of their technology to as many markets as possible.

Many respondents thought that low labour costs are of less strategic importance, although the satisfaction ratings tend to be quite high for this objective. The results indicate that foreign partners with shorter-term objectives, for whom low-cost sourcing, benefiting from advantageous transfer pricing and learning how to do business in China were deemed important, tend to be fairly satisfied with the extent to which their joint ventures have achieved those objectives.

Most foreign managers do not feel that learning how to do business in China from their local partner was an important objective in setting up their joint venture, and the perceived achievement of this objective is not very high, either. The reasons for this were expressed by a foreign operational manager in the electronics sector:

> It has taken much longer than we expected to understand so-called 'local' management practices. There is not much to learn from the Chinese in terms of 'management' knowledge. The Chinese managers in our plant lack technological skills and managerial know-how.

Foreign managers are, on the whole, moderately satisfied with the achievement of long-term profitability, but this satisfaction is not at the same level as with the business presence and strategic positions they have secured. This appears to be due to the fact that competition in the Chinese domestic market has increased. The overall pattern of foreign objective achievement ratings probably reflects the following factors.

First, there is a trend for the foreign partners to look to their local partners for a raw material contribution, and for the local Chinese partners increasingly to raise their localisation percentages. This reflects Chinese national policy to acquire raw materials locally. As a consequence of the rapid development of the Chinese economy, it has become increasingly possible to achieve low-cost local sourcing as long as quality criteria and delivery reliability are met. The relative importance of the Chinese contribution of special joint venture tax holidays plays a role on the joint venture's performance in its early years. The benefit from a tax holiday is strictly confined to joint ventures, and is guaranteed by the Chinese government without discrimination by region.

Second, most foreign investing companies can ultimately learn for themselves about the local economy, politics and culture. Their business scope enables them to have a wider range of opportunities to learn not only from their Chinese business partners but also from the local authorities and the business region. However, the opportunities acquired by foreign firms to use the areas of knowledge about and skills for dealing with the local government, and other institutional infrastructures, turn out to be a competitive advantage. Thus it will be increasingly difficult for foreign partners with only a limited financial commitment to cope with the areas of local sourcing, domestic distribution and personnel management.

Third, 76 per cent of foreign senior managers from the study felt that investment in China provided an important route to achieving long-term profitability. After several years of running joint ventures in China, most of the foreign respondents were only moderately satisfied with the extent to which their joint ventures had realised the attractiveness of the Chinese market in terms of securing a good rate of return. There was wide agreement that access to the potentially large Chinese market is negated by generally poor infrastructure, central and local government restrictions, poor quality raw material supply and poor training, especially a lack of expertise in marketing. Another reason requiring emphasis is that most joint ventures in the research sample are small to medium in size, and are on average only five years old. The accounting rules they use are highly varied, and there is no common basis for reporting profitability. In these circumstances, and in view of the tax advantages they offer, joint ventures tend to under-report their levels of profit, and this may have affected how foreign managers rated their joint venture's profit performance.

The Achievement of Chinese Objectives

Most Chinese senior managers tend to evaluate the performance of joint ventures on the basis of economic development criteria, including the acquisition of foreign capital investment, technology, management and employment creation. On the whole, Chinese partners rate the achievement of their objectives for the joint venture rather more highly than did foreign partners. Table 8.2 indicates that those Chinese partners for whom the joint venture objectives are employment creation, benefiting from tax incentives, import substitution and obtaining foreign cash investment give particularly high achievement

Table 8.2 Achievement ratings of Chinese objectives for joint ventures (N = 67 joint ventures)

Perceived achievement of Chinese strategic objectives, if among top five objectives scales: 1 = not achieved at all, 5 = fully achieved.

Items	*Achievement rating from Chinese partners*	
	Mean	*Number of cases where the objective was included among the top five priorities*
Mean above 4.00		
Employment creation	4.20	5
Benefit from tax incentives	4.15	13
Import substitution	4.09	11
Obtain foreign cash investment	4.00	41
Mean between 3.99 and 3.35		
Opportunity for good long-term profit	3.71	29
Opportunities for quick profit	3.67	9
Ability to import superior components	3.67	9
Assist diversification of products	3.67	15
Gain strategic position	3.50	27
Establish strong business presence	3.50	14
Technology transfer	3.40	41
Help expand in China market	3.36	10
Mean below 3.34		
Learning management expertise	3.35	52
Develop export opportunities	3.15	17
Help upgrade suppliers' technology	3.05	10
Opportunity to train Chinese staff	3.03	16
Foreign exchange generation	2.86	7

ratings. The ratings by the Chinese senior joint venture managers are fairly uniformly distributed. One of the relatively important areas of the foreign partner's contribution is capital in the form of cash. Because some Chinese firms encounter difficulties as a result of government capital restrictions, the achievement scores on foreign cash acquisition represent satisfactory attainment of an important objective for most Chinese partners. Although most Chinese senior managers give a satisfactory rating to the creation of long-term profit, other widely held goals such as technology transfer and learning management expertise obtain lower average ratings. For example, several Chinese managers from electronic firms commented on the difficulty of achieving technology transfer; one said:

> Foreign partners are very cautious about their technology when it is used in the joint venture. We encouraged our employees to learn more from them. They only allowed two Chinese technicians to visit their factory and stay there only for one month. Although the joint venture has been set up for five years, we still have not established a proper training programme for our employees.

The learning of management expertise, the development of export opportunities, help to upgrade Chinese suppliers' technology, the opportunity to train Chinese staff and foreign exchange generation were all given relatively low satisfaction ratings by the Chinese partners. Foreign partners, especially in electronics firms, tended to provide imported materials, channels for exporting the joint ventures' products and expertise in production management. They usually kept firm control of such business areas. Chinese partners gained very limited learning opportunities, and have had very little chance to access international markets in comparison with their foreign partners.

Several Chinese respondents commented on their ability to import superior goods and components and on the import substitution issue. For example,

> We don't think we know enough about what is going on within the international market. Basically we have very limited access to such information for our product. As you see, our marketing director is an expatriate manager. We are constrained on the goods and components that we import, as we are unable to get information on alternatives available on the international market.

One company admitted to being aware of the issues being tightly controlled by the foreign partners, but did not know how to solve the problem. The Chinese deputy general manager of a FMCG joint venture said:

> I want to achieve something on behalf of the Chinese parent companies, that is what I am here for. When I make any decisions I have to bear in mind the balance between the Chinese and foreign sides. I cannot put the joint venture itself as my priority as my

foreign partners do not. If the decisions are only minor issues, it normally turns out that there are no problems from my foreign partners. If the problem touches upon the so called 'corporate principles and polices', then it is up to the decision of my foreign partners. The Chinese parent companies hardly give us any support, as they do not have money or technology to back us up. It is very important to know which way we should go.

On the whole, Chinese top-priority objectives were the acquisition of technology and management expertise.

A SYSTEM PERSPECTIVE OF PERFORMANCE ASSESSMENT

The subjective measures of joint venture performance applying a system perspective are concerned with the five criteria of profit, growth, market share, technology development and the development of local staff and/or managers. These five variables represent performance at an operational level and criteria of joint venture development. Evaluations against these criteria were obtained from the most senior

Table 8.3 'System' assessment of joint venture performance ($N = 67$ joint ventures)

Subjective measures[a]	*Mean*	*s.d.*
Growth	3.38	1.07
Market share	3.36	1.03
Profitability	3.34	1.17
Technological development	3.25	0.96
Development of local staff/managers	3.07	1.00
Objective Measures[b]		
Growth in sales (annual increases over three years) $N = 47$[c]	2.10	2.13
Profitability (profits against sales over three years) $N = 39$	6%	0.58

[a]Subjective measures of five Likert-type, ranging from between 1 = not satisfied at all and 5= fully satisfied.
[b]Some joint ventures did not supply sales and profit data. Therefore numbers reported are below 67. In addition, when a joint venture had not been in operation for 3 years or had not attained profitability, it was excluded from the analysis
[c]Growth in sales is calculated over the three most recent years; profitability is measured as operating profit over sales for the three most recent years.

manager interviewed in each joint venture. Ideally, it would be desirable to measure performance in relation to the criteria directly. To this end, objective performance data on growth in sales and profitability were available.

In order to avoid bias in joint venture performance assessment towards the views of both foreign and Chinese partners, objective performance measures associated with the system perspective are included to complement the subjective assessments made by the joint venture general and deputy general managers. This perspective assumes that each joint venture can be evaluated primarily as a stand-alone business unit seeking to maximise its own performance, rather than from the perspective of its parent companies. Such an assessment gives an insight into the views of senior joint venture managers on the performance of their units. These can then be contrasted with the ratings of objective attainment. Table 8.3 suggests at least moderate satisfaction with the five system variables assessed by the joint venture managers.

Growth

Among the subjective system indicators of joint venture performance, growth on average secured the highest ratings from senior joint venture managers. The general satisfaction with joint venture growth is a reflection of the general potential growth of joint venture development in China. There are several possible explanations for the positive evaluation of growth performance. Discussions with both Chinese and foreign managers suggest that they see a link between profit, market share and the speed of Chinese market development. Foreign partners appear to take a view that the development of China's market is critical to the growth of their firms. They are very keen to increase their market share in the Chinese domestic market, owing to the size of the market, the low cost of labour and cheaper materials sourcing, and also to secure a strategic position in the market, which they value highly. Joint ventures that have been operating for several years appear to provide more opportunity for foreign partners to build up their own marketing and distribution systems than do start-up ventures. Many foreign managers intend to secure growth in their business by setting up multiple subsidiaries in China. Chinese managers tend to show more concern with 'growth' in relation to economic development criteria such as technology development and the development of local staff and managers.

Market Share

When asked about the market share of the joint ventures, respondents gave different answers. The achievement of market share is one of the most important objectives of most foreign companies. To secure it, foreign companies in China seek growth, the achievement of economies of scale, experience and strong control over markets and distribution channels. Some foreign investing companies own several businesses in China. Market penetration is enhanced by dealing with a wide range of business partners in China, in order to extend geographical coverage.

General comments made during the interviews suggest that market share objectives receive a lower priority from Chinese companies because, at least in the short term, these are perceived to be of lower priority than technology transfer, profitability and the development of local staff and/or managers. Chinese firms geared to market share are characteristically influenced by the old central planning system. Then, market segmentation was targeted and the central plan was related to the price and service expectations of target customers. This appears to be less distinctly correlated with the achievement of the longer-run market share objectives. A deputy Chinese general manager of an FMCG company commented:

> Of course, it is important to increase market share as soon as possible. Particularly as the existing Chinese market is developing dramatically fast. As our Chinese side has very limited resources in terms of capital, technology and management, we cannot extend or stretch our business too much, as that will affect the delivery of good-quality products and affect customer satisfaction. Our objectives should be the profit-oriented objective, which at least allows us to survive and stay in business. As our business faces the transition to a market economy, the rate of business failure is very high.

Comments made in interviews suggest that Chinese partners do not seem very concerned about the influence and domination of foreign partners in their domestic market. If the profit from the joint venture keeps increasing then Chinese partners will, it seems, be willing to allow the foreign side to have a large equity in the joint venture. Most Chinese partners seem content to have the foreign side manage the joint venture.

Profitability

As both an objective and a subjective measure of performance, profitability is by far the most common criterion among Western companies (Hamel *et al.* 1989). The majority of the sample joint ventures are satisfied with the level of profitability achieved. A general manager of a British FMCG company made the following comment:

> I did not expect that our business would grow so unbelievably quickly. We have not even got enough equipment and facilities to cope with the existing market expansion. The Chinese market accepts our product as a good-quality product. It is very popular in China. It is a good investment in China, and we got our money back very quickly.

Profitability is the basis for defining success in most previous studies (Doyle 1994). The choice of strategic objectives, ownership resources and the economic conditions appears to affect the judgement of a joint venture's profitability. High levels of diversity in objectives between Chinese and foreign managers appear to be the main factors affecting the performance criteria used by each side of the venture. Foreign partners seem to take a long-term view of profitability, while Chinese ones are more typically interested in annual dividends.

Some foreign partners have adjusted their prices of resource inputs downward or upward in order to generate more profits for their subsidiaries. One foreign electronics firm acknowledges that more than half the employees working in its joint venture are foreign. The main reason is to keep a strong managerial and technical team in that one joint venture, which looks after the rest of the other seven subsidiaries in China. It is notable that accounting profits are essentially an arbitrary factor, which are easily manipulated by foreign managers. Some respondents from electronic firms complain that manufacturing costs have been greater than anticipated because of low labour productivity and increased prices of electronic components. In 1994, the Chinese government introduced a new value added tax, which reduced joint venture profitability.

Evidence from the interviews suggests that Chinese partners attach most importance to joint venture profit, while foreign partners attach more importance to growth. Respondents were asked to identify areas of concern that exist for the joint venture as a whole, and also with regard to the regional offices and headquarters abroad. Several foreign managers mentioned the need to increase the foreign share of the equity so that the total foreign contributions can be more justly rewarded by a greater share of the joint venture profits.

Although, some years ago, Chinese joint venture partners and government authorities stressed developmental criteria for joint venture performance, Chinese managers have recently changed their performance criteria and become more like their foreign partners in that they now focus on the profitability of joint ventures. This is more likely to reflect the fact that China has made the transition to a market economy, and this encourages a more individualistic, profit-making orientation. It has resulted in less pressure from the Chinese side for joint ventures to export. The local Chinese government recognises that China can make more money from taxes and dividends by allowing joint ventures to sell locally rather than externally. It appears that, as long as the joint venture is generating a dividend stream for the Chinese side, there will be little resistance to having foreigners controlling it.

Technology Development

Technology transfer remains an important performance criterion for Chinese parent companies, as evaluated by Chinese joint venture managers. In contrast, foreign managers tend not to use economic development criteria to evaluate the performance of their joint ventures in China. Chinese managers appear to seek a faster pace of technology transfer than the foreign managers. Comments made in interviews suggest that some foreign partners prefer to provide their joint ventures with second-best technology, and with technologies that are not easily replicated illegally. Chinese managers are sensitive to the need to evaluate joint venture performance on the basis of the amount of management and technology that is transferred. Expatriate managers with lengthy experience in China have recognised the importance of transferring management and technical skills to their Chinese partners. This has certainly been true of Shanghai Yaohua Pilkington, a major British glass-making joint venture. However, only a few expatriates recognise that there is a need to evaluate joint venture performance on the basis of the pace and amount of management and technical skill that is transferred. The generation of the transfer of management technology provides mutual benefits to both the joint venture and the parent companies.

Most Chinese managers are seeking to transfer knowledge and skills from the foreign side to joint ventures. The joint ventures appear to vary in their ability to retain transferred technology within their boundaries. One problematic source of technology leakage has been the loss of trained people to other companies. The foreign side in joint ventures attempts to help their partners learn how to perform business activities through a variety of methods. These include on-the-job training led by expatriate managers at the joint venture site. Despite this, technology has not been transferred as quickly as the Chinese had hoped. Chinese partners regard the pace and extent of technology transfer as important issues for the development of joint ventures.

Development of Local Staff/Managers

The development of local staff or managers is given a lower rating. Foreign partners express fears of creating competitors in the near future. This is particularly the case in the Overseas Chinese joint ventures. Most of the training is only at the technical level. Very few joint ventures have taken management training seriously, and they do not let the Chinese managers get involved at the strategic level of decision-making. There is normally a symbolic appointment of the senior Chinese person as deputy general manager, but this position appears to have little influence.

Gaining decision-making control on critical business divisions is important to Chinese managers, because of the perception of a wide gap in experience and capability between Chinese and foreign parent companies. Chinese companies, unfamiliar with operating a business under competitive market conditions, or to current global business standards, are seen as unable to compete against foreign firms that are far more experienced in designing effective marketing strategies and in producing high-quality products. The performance criteria used by joint ventures are converging as foreign and Chinese partners work more closely together. Most of the Chinese functional managers felt they had learnt a lot more within a joint venture than they did in the parent company. Those Chinese managers that work frequently with expatriates have more opportunity to learn from them (Child *et al.* 1994).

The loss of newly trained Chinese managers, as well as experienced 'China hand' expatriates, was often mentioned as among the least satisfactory aspects of joint venture performance. Respondents from several joint ventures indicated that within a five-year time period there had been a significant loss of trained Chinese managers. One Hong Kong manager from an FMCG company mentioned his frustration at the loss of newly trained Chinese technicians and managers:

> We are not running a training school, but we certainly suffer a great deal by sending employees to get training. Our technical staff and managers either go to work at other joint ventures for immediate job advancement or they leave to set up their own business, after they have received training. Obviously we also have some people who are newly trained from elsewhere. But we have to pay a lot for those people.

The lack of diffusion of learning among Chinese technicians and managers and the loss of trained employees and experienced expatriate managers have increased dissatisfaction with progress in the process of the development of local staff and managers within joint ventures. In previous studies, there has been very little research into the evaluation of performance by joint venture managers. Shenkar (1990) suggests that the fact that partners tend to use different performance criteria based on their own interests has been the main reason for dissatisfaction within joint ventures in China. For example, although expatriate managers may wish foreign partners to provide them with varied experience and/or career development, the frequent replacement of expatriate managers appears to damage the performance of joint ventures, and is regretted by the Chinese side. A Chinese general manager from FMCG firms commented:

> My foreign counterparts have been replaced three times within four years. I was only informed of each new appointment without any discussion about why the foreign side wanted to replace the existing one. The obviously affects our business operation, particular if we lose some expatriates who have a rich knowledge of the joint venture and a good understanding of how to run a business in China.

Similar complaints were expressed by Chinese managers in about half of the sixty-seven sample joint ventures. Difficulties in developing a unified management and technical team for the joint venture appears to be one of the main factors adversely affecting the relationship between Chinese and foreign managers.

SUBJECTIVE AND OBJECTIVE MEASURES OF JOINT VENTURE PERFORMANCE

The extent to which there is an association between the measures of performance suggested, respectively, by goal and system models is examined by the correlation matrix shown in Table 8.4. Performance evaluation of Sino-foreign joint ventures incorporates multiple viewpoints – foreign and Chinese managers on behalf of their parent companies and the managers of joint ventures. Anderson (1990) argues that joint ventures should be evaluated primarily as stand-alone entities seeking to maximise their own performance, without reference to the parents. It can be argued that the performance of a joint venture cannot be assessed fully without reference to the objectives both of the partners' companies and of the managers of the joint venture. When the performance is assessed in relation to some general criterion set by the joint venture managers, as the agent of the owning partners, the objectives adopted by a joint venture tend to influence the level of achievement.

The problem stems from the fact that each one of these performance measures conflicts with others. Maximising one measure implies minimising others. Basically, it has been argued that the process of realising ownership commitments by partners tends to generate a conflict of interest. Finding an appropriate measure of the relationship between on the one hand the ownership inputs to a joint venture at its formation and on the other its subsequent performance in the market is extremely difficult.

Table 8.4 shows that of all the performance measures subjectively assessed, profitability evidences the most significant correlation with the perceived achievement of foreign and Chinese parent companies' objectives. With regard to current performance criteria, the subjective measures of performance tend to cluster together, but not often with objective measures of organisational performance such as profitability and growth in profit and sales. The results could be interpreted as supporting Geringer and Hebert's (1991) argument that objective measures have failed to reflect adequately the extent to which a joint venture has achieved its objectives. One reason may be that if joint ventures have exceeded the parents' expectations then they are considered successful by one or all of the parents. Another is that where objective and subjective measures of performance are barely correlated, this is because they capture different aspects of performance.

Table 8.4 Means, standard deviations and correlations between IJV performance indicators

Performance measure	*Mean*	*s.d.*	*2*	*3*	*4*	*5*	*6*	*7*
Achievement of Chinese parent objectives	3.56	0.68	0.39**	0.44***	0.28**	0.34**	0.17	0.11
Achievement of foreign parent objectives	3.41	0.75		0.40***	0.61***	0.49***	0.01	–0.08
Subjective assessment: profitability	3.34	1.17			0.49***	0.43***	0.56***	0.08
Subjective assessment: growth	3.48	1.07				0.51***	0.18	–0.05
Subjective assessment: market share	3.36	1.03					0.33*	–0.03
Objective assessment: profitability ROS ($N = 38$)[a]	0.15	0.12						0.19
Objective assessment: growth in sales ($N = 47$)[b]	2.18	2.18						

Notes:
[a]Number of cases is reduced, owing to incomplete data. Some joint ventures did not supply sales and profit data. Therefore numbers reported are below 67. In addition, when a joint venture had not been in operation for three years or had not reached profitability, it was excluded from the analysis.
$^{*}p < 0.05$; $^{**}p < 0.01$; $^{***}p < 0.001$

The subjective assessments regarding the achievement of foreign and Chinese objectives are correlated with the subjective measures of profitability. The foreign achievement of objectives is correlated more highly with the subjective assessment of growth. The Chinese achievement of objectives, on the other hand, is more highly correlated with the subjective assessment of profit. This suggests that no single strategic objective is adequate for judging the performance of a joint venture. Each parent objective concentrates on a limited perspective. For example, some foreign investing companies may focus on market share or growth. By contrast, Chinese objectives are oriented more towards profitability.

There are only two significant correlations between subject and objective performance indicators. One reason for this may be that subjective evaluations by managers tend to be oriented to the present time and recent past, whereas the objective measures are calculated over several years. Among the subjective measures, the achievement of objectives may be more appropriately used in this study to evaluate a very long-term performance horizon.

THE OWNERSHIP–PERFORMANCE RELATIONSHIP

The relationship between ownership and performance has taken on a new aspect in recent years, with the rapid growth in numbers of joint ventures. Ownership in joint ventures is typically concentrated, as ownership is shared between two, or a few partners, which will in most cases be legally formed companies rather than individuals. Performances are usually measured in relation to the various objectives established for a joint venture. As a result, it is necessary for joint venture research to examine performance-related issues from the perspective of the individual partners (Hill and Hellriegel 1994).

The empirical work of Schaan (1983) and Beamish and Banks (1987) measures performance on the basis of managerial assessment. These authors suggest that only when both partners are satisfied is the joint venture considered successful. In contrast, Anderson (1990) argues that joint ventures should be evaluated primarily as standalone entities seeking to maximise their own performance, without reference to the parents. The problem stems from the fact that each of this performance measures conflicts with others. Maximising one measure implies minimising others. Basically, it has been argued that the process of realising ownership commitments by partners tends to generate a conflict of interest. Finding an appropriate measure of the relationship between ownership inputs to a joint venture at its formation and its subsequent performance in the market is extremely difficult. This deficiency may be due to a number of reasons, such as the complexity of the structure of joint ventures involving two or more owning companies, or the lack of data available at industry and firm-specific levels. In addition, many problems may be associated with the gap between the identification of mutual long-term resources, capabilities, and the actual commitment of the partners.

The outcome of the ownership inputs between joint venture partners will only be satisfactory to the partners if contributions and expected benefits of the two companies are kept in balance.

Harrigan (1988) examined the control and influence of partner asymmetries on joint ventures on the basis of duration, survival, and managers' assessments. The results indicate that the joint ventures with symmetric partnerships tend to gain a better performance than those with asymmetric partnerships. Lee and Beamish (1995) found that the control was the most important factor in determining the performance of Korean joint ventures. Their results suggest that, in the case of Korea, the partners' needs regarding a joint venture were significantly related to joint venture performance. Beamish (1985) uses Killing's scale analysis in developing countries and finds that shared-control joint ventures are more successful. Similarly, Beamish also finds that partner needs and commitment are good predictors of performance.

THE UNIVERSALISTIC APPROACH

A Combination of Ownership Resourcing

The universalistic approach holds that high joint ventures performance will be the result of a combination of (1) equity inputs, (2) contractual inputs and (3) non-contractual inputs. The comprehensiveness of ownership resourcing committed by the partners, in equity, contractual or non-contractual forms, can be regarded as determinants of joint venture performance, because it may constitute the major resource for a firm's strategy in establishing its strategic presence in the foreign market.

Table 8.5 indicates that subjective and objective measures of performance yield different results for Chinese and foreign groups.

Table 8.5 Correlations between performance indicators and resource commitment to joint ventures ($N = 67$ joint ventures)

	Performance measures[a] *Subjective measures*		*Objective measures*		
	Achievement of objectives	*Profitability*	*Profitability ($N = 39$)*[b]	*Growth in profitability ($N = 47$)*[b]	*Growth in sales ($N = 47$)*[b]
Equity					
Chinese	0.34**	–0.12	0.07	–0.04	0.13
Foreign	–0.02	–0.11	–0.06	0.04	–0.14
Contractual input					
Chinese	0.12	0.03	–0.07	–0.04	–0.04
Foreign	–0.03	–0.02	–0.09	0.09	–0.04
Non-contractual input					
Chinese	0.10	0.04	0.07	–0.07	–0.04
Foreign	–0.04	–0.12	–0.21	–0.008	0.15

Notes:
[a] Achievement of Chinese objectives is correlated with Chinese ownership resourcing, while the achievement of foreign objectives is correlated with foreign ownership resourcing.
[b] Number of cases is reduced owing to incomplete data. Some joint ventures did not supply sales and profit data. Therefore numbers reported are below 67. In addition, when a joint venture had not been in operation for three years or had not reached profitability, that data was excluded from the analysis.
One-tail probabilities: $^{*}p < 0.05$; $^{**}p < 0.01$.

There is essentially no correlation between the six indicators of performance and the ownership commitments from both foreign and Chinese partners. Most of the correlation coefficients between Chinese ownership commitment and measures of joint venture performance are virtually zero. Among the correlations between each indicator of performance and the three subcategories of ownership commitments, there is only one positive correlation for subjective measures between Chinese strategic objectives and Chinese equity input.

This may reflect the fact that a higher equity share on the Chinese side is in most cases the only lever available for the Chinese partner to use to participate in steering a joint venture towards its objectives. The other interpretation is that most Chinese firms can achieve their objectives by equity investment, which often takes the low-cost form of land, existing buildings, plant and equipment, rather than cash. Chinese partners tend to contribute 'resource input', and, as this does not constitute a critical impact on the technology and management of joint ventures, it could eventually lead to the Chinese partners having a low level of bargaining power to establish priorities for technology and management.

The results imply that the provision of a more comprehensive range of ownership resources by each partner has no impact on joint venture performance. On the whole, the results suggest that a comprehensive range of ownership resources provided to the joint venture has no close relationship to the achievement of a good joint venture performance.

Transactional Resources

The transactional dependence of joint ventures on their parent companies indicates the importance of the inputs and outputs resources that the latter supply. With regard to transactional dependency, the proportion of resources inputs supplied by the parent companies, and outputs taken directly by them, can be examined. The intention is to test the extent to which supply uncertainties are reduced, and guaranteed outlets are provided, by the partners in the joint venture. The argument is that both will positively affect the performance of the joint venture. The decision on whether to source resources through the foreign or the Chinese parent company is decided largely by price. This determines the costs of raw materials, and also the quality of components supplied. This control facilitates the management of the costs of production, reduces the disruption of production, and leads to increased market performance.

Table 8.6 suggests that the impact on performance of resource inputs supplied by the foreign partners appears to vary between objective and subjective measures. The results suggest some evidence of enhanced joint venture performance when supplies from the parent companies (especially the foreign parents) account for a larger proportion by value of their joint ventures' resource inputs. The findings suggest also that the impact on performance of resource inputs supplied by foreign partners to their joint ventures appears to vary between objective and subjective measures. The percentage of resource inputs provided by foreign partners correlates with the subjective measures of joint venture performance, but not with the objective measures. Evidence gained from the respondents indicates that most of the foreign partners tend to have direct control over the resources imported from the international market. The results also indicate that when resource input is supplied by the foreign partners there is a greater likelihood of satisfactory performance.

This is consistent with the possibility that resource inputs supplied by foreign partners provide them with benefits from transfer pricing. Some Chinese managers admit that, when using existing foreign channels for resource inputs, joint ventures will benefit from improved quality control of those inputs and from lower transactional costs, and can gain a preference in claiming technological support from the foreign parent companies. Foreign partners appear to show a firm control of the international market outlets, and are also positively involved with domestic Chinese marketing.

As the Chinese domestic supply of materials and components improves, the foreign partners are able to have greater access to, and control of, the sourcing of material and components, even in the Chinese market. However, the extent of the proportion of resources supplied by the partners can affect the performance of a joint venture. When a higher proportion of the resource inputs is supplied by the Chinese partners, there is a positive correlation with the subjective indicators of performance, but not with the objective measures. Most of the respondents in this study shared the same belief that the Chinese partners are forced into a 'passive' position toward local sourcing issues by poor Chinese supplier capabilities. Several respondents acknowledge that Chinese local sourcing and domestic distribution in the past tended to be based on personal relationships. As localisation increases and the joint venture itself progresses, the joint

Table 8.6 Correlations between (1) indicators of transactional resources provided by the foreign and Chinese partners and (2) joint venture performance (N = 67 joint ventures)

Performance measures[a]	*Range of ownership resources*	
	Percentage of inputs by value supplied by foreign parent companies companies	*Percentage of outputs by value going directly to foreign parent*
Foreign objectives achievement	0.21*	0.17*
Subjective measures: profitability	0.30**	–0.16*
Subjective measures: growth	0.22*	0.16
Objective measures: profitability N = 39[b]	0.18	–0.36*
Objective measures: growth in profit N = 39[c]	–0.08	0.18
Objective measures: growth in sales N = 47[c]	–0.13	–0.08

Table 8.6 Continued

Performance measures[a]	*Percentage of inputs by value supplied by Chinese parent companies*	*Percentage of outputs by value going directly to Chinese parent companies*
Chinese objectives achievement	0.21*	0.10
Subjective measures: profitability	0.19*	0.30**
Subjective measures: growth	0.24*	0.10
Objective measures: profitability $N = 39$[b]	0.13	0.18
Objective measures: Growth in profit $N = 39$[b]	0.05	0.04
Objective measures: Growth in sales $N = 47$[c]	–0.23*	–0.08

[a]Achievement of Chinese objectives is correlated with Chinese resources inputs, while the achievement of foreign objectives is correlated with foreign resource inputs.
[b]Number of cases is reduced owing to incomplete data. Some joint ventures did not supply sales and profit data. Therefore numbers reported are below 67. In addition, when a joint venture had not been in operation for three years or had not reached profitability, that data was excluded from the analysis.
One-tail probabilities: $^{*}p < 0.05$; $^{**}p < 0.01$.

venture has to face the transition from dependence upon the existing Chinese partners for distribution to using the Chinese market network infrastructure.

Foreign partners also appear to control international distribution networks. The Chinese partner has a less aggressive attitude in terms of marketing, and less chance of access to international market outlets. This unbalanced manner of approach to distribution and marketing between the partners will eventually reflect in the output performance of the joint venture. The results evidence a significant imbalance in sourcing control, which appears to occur between the partners at an early stage in the life of a joint venture.

According to comments made during interviews, on the outputs side, joint venture profitability tends to be lower when a higher percentage of products go the foreign parent company, but higher when a greater percentage is supplied directly to the Chinese parent companies (normally to the domestic market). The correlations between the percentage of outputs taken directly to parent companies and the respective six indicators of performance are weak and not entirely consistent. One exception is that a moderately positive correlation is evident between the proportion of outputs taken by the Chinese partners and profitability assessed subjectively. A positive influence can be attributed to joint venture performance when the outputs account for a large proportion of the joint ventures' turnover. In short, the result receives some support in the case of joint venture transactional inputs supplied by the foreign parent companies.

Dominant or Shared Control

A distinction between dominant control and shared-control groups is made in order to focus on how a parent can use its resource and core competence to gain a higher level of overall control. The sample of joint ventures was divided into those in which one partner had dominant control and those where the partners shared control. Higher control by one partner is in turn hypothesised to lead to better performance.

The analysis is made as follows. The thirteen items of parent company influence over joint ventures management are taken as indicators of control. The scores for foreign and Chinese influence respectively in the thirteen areas are aggregated into the composite measures of control described in Chapter 6. Using this composite measure, 31 joint ventures out of 67 are identified as shared control joint ventures and 36 as dominant-control ones. Dominant control is when there are large differences in overall influence over the thirteen decision areas, as measured either by foreign influence scores minus Chinese influence scores or else by Chinese influence scores minus foreign influence ones. The shared control group can be distinguished by small differences in foreign influence scores and Chinese influence scores over the thirteen decision areas. The division of the sample in this way was made so as to provide as equal members as possible in the two groups. Using *t*-test analysis, Table 8.7 examines the extent to which the distribution of joint ventures between dominant and shared control predicts their levels of performance.

Of the seven indicators of performance used, only the objective measure of profitability is weakly related to dominant versus shared control. This measure indicates that dominant-partner joint ventures tended to be marginally more likely to have better performance than shared-management ventures. The performance mean score among the dominant group is higher than that for the shared group. If this difference has some validity, it would be consistent with Killing's (1983) finding that shared control constitutes a major source of management difficulties in joint ventures. The argument is that dominant partner joint ventures will find it easier to manage activities and consequently be more successful. The dominant control group displayed higher performance mean scores in 5 out of 7 instances, but all of these differences could easily have occurred by chance.

Duration

The duration of a joint venture refers to the number of years it has been in operation since its formation in China. The joint ventures examined were categorised into two groups according to their duration (length of operational history), that is: (1) less and equal to three years and (2) greater than three years. This was because in China joint ventures enjoy three years of tax exemption by law; it also happens that this criterion split the sample into two roughly equal groups.

The results (Table 8.8) indicate that joint venture duration has a significant relationship only with the objective measures of performance. The group of joint ventures with at least three years of operation has positive average profitability, while the other group does not. On the other hand, the longer-operating group has lower average rates of growth. An explanation could be that, with increasing experience in China, foreign firms acquire greater confidence in collaborating with

Table 8.7 Dominant vs. shared control in relation to joint venture performance (N = 67 joint ventures)

Performance measure	*Mean scores*		*t-test for Independent samples*	
	Dominant control (N = 36)	*Shared control (N = 31)*	*Value of t*	*Value of p*
Chinese objectives achievement	3.73	3.34	0.99	0.32
Foreign objectives achievement	3.40	3.42	0.61	0.44
Subjective measures: profitability	3.59	3.04	0.13	0.72
Subjective measures: growth	3.45	3.50	0.43	0.51
Objective measures: profitability (N = 39)[a]	16%	–9%	3.7	0.06
Objective measures: growth in profit (N = 39)[a]	1.84	1.79	0.12	0.72
Objective measures: growth in sales (N = 47)[a]	2.11	2.08	0.005	0.94

Note:
[a]Number of cases is reduced, owing to incomplete data. Some joint ventures did not supply sales and profit data. Therefore numbers reported are below 67. In addition, when a joint venture had not been in operation for three years or had not reached profitability, it was excluded from the analysis.

Table 8.8 Duration of joint venture operation in relation to performance

Subjective and objective performance measures	*Mean score*			
	Length of joint venture operation		*t-test for independent samples*	
	Less than and equal to three years (N = 30)	*Over three years (N = 37)*	*Value of t*	*Value of p*
Chinese objectives achievement	3.38	3.69	0.051	0.82
Foreign objectives achievement	3.29	3.50	2.09	0.15
Subjective measures: profitability	3.05	3.58	0.058	0.81
Subjective measures: growth	3.20	3.70	0.071	0.79
Objective measures: profitability ($N = 39$)[a]	–1.2%	1.5%	6.66	0.014
Objective measures: growth in profit ($N = 39$)[a]	2.56	1.49	8.59	0.006
Objective measures: growth in sales ($N = 47$)[a]	2.57	1.80	1.91	0.173

[a]Number of cases is reduced, owing to incomplete data. Some joint ventures did not supply sales and profit data. Therefore numbers reported are below 67. In addition, when a joint venture had not been in operation for three years or had not reached profitability, that data was excluded from the analysis.

their Chinese partners, understanding the Chinese market, gauging customer needs and estimating costs and returns. Uncertainty in the Chinese market is reduced only through actual experience. With increasing experience, foreign firms have more chance to secure the appropriate information to enable them to operate their business effectively. The results on the joint venture duration criterion imply that the longer a joint venture operates in China, the better the joint venture will achieve an understanding of local markets. This is perhaps not surprising, given that most of existing technology and most managerial expertise provided by the foreign partners are likely to be more efficient than the local staff with their technology purely from the local market itself.

THE CONTINGENCY APPROACH

The contingency approach postulates that a better 'fit' between a greater range of ownership resourcing committed by the partners and the extent to which level of control exercised by the partners, then a better level of performance will result. This study has drawn attention to ownership resource complementarity between partners at operational and strategic levels in joint ventures. Taking up this notion, the concepts of ownership resourcing and control can be integrated.

The Fit Between Non-capital Resources and Control

Higher- and lower-performing joint ventures are distinguished and the sample is divided into two sub-samples on the subjective and objective indicators of growth and profitability. Four performance measures, namely subjective assessments of growth and profit, and objective assessments of growth in sales and profitability, are used to compare the performance of those joint ventures achieving higher and lower ownership and control matching. Table 8.9 indicates that a better fit between them positively influences joint venture performance. As shown in Table 8.9, there are high correlations between the four indicators of performance and the strength with which the ownership and control variables are correlated. Higher-performing joint ventures are identified as those given above the scale midpoint (3) on the subjective performance measures of growth and profit (1 = not achieved, 5 = fully achieved) and above 1.12 times growth in sales and above

Table 8.9 Fit between ownership resourcing and control in relation to joint venture performance (N = 67 joint ventures)

	Ownership inputs correlation with overall control[a] for different performance groups			
	Subjective		*Objective*	
	Growth	*Profit*	*Growth in sales*	*Profitability*
	(N = 67)	*(N = 67)*	*(N = 47)[b]*	*(N = 39)[b]*
Higher-performing joint ventures				
Foreign equity	0.68***	0.74***	0.64**	0.58**
Foreign contractual resources	0.37*	0.60**	0.09	0.31
Foreign non-contractual resources	0.46**	0.49**	0.43*	0.12
Chinese equity	0.72**	0.81***	0.71***	0.76***
Chinese contractual resources	0.17	0.37*	0.14	0.33
Chinese non-contractual resources	0.51**	0.47**	0.65**	0.65*
Lower performing joint ventures				
Foreign equity	0.49**	0.48**	0.68**	0.48*
Foreign contractual resources	0.19	0.06	0.62**	0.54*
Foreign non-contractual resources	0.35*	0.36*	0.11	0.31
Chinese equity	0.62**	0.57***	0.63*	0.23
Chinese contractual resources	0.25	0.09	0.39*	0.42*
Chinese non-contractual resources	0.54**	0.58***	0.37*	0.21

[a]Correlation is respectively for foreign ownership resourcing with foreign influence and control, and Chinese ownership resourcing with Chinese influence and control, categorised by higher- and lower-performing joint ventures.
[b]Number of cases is reduced, owing to incomplete data. Some joint ventures did not supply sales and profit data. Therefore numbers reported are below 67. In addition, when a joint venture had not been in operation for three years or had not reached profitability, that data was excluded from the analysis.
One-tail probabilities: $*p < 0.05$; $**p < 0.01$; $***p < 0.001$.

1.63 times return on sales. The aggregated scores for foreign and Chinese influence in thirteen areas of joint venture management are used as measures of control. Correlations between foreign ownership resourcing and foreign control, and Chinese ownership resourcing and Chinese control, are compared for each of the 4 performance indicators, with the sample of joint ventures divided into higher- and lower-performing categories.

The results indicate that higher-performing joint ventures tend to have stronger correlations between ownership and control. This is consistent for both the subjective profitability measures and objective measures such as growth in sales and profitability as the performance criterion. When the equity committed by the foreign and Chinese partners is presented in terms of lower- and higher-performing joint ventures, there is a fairly consistent pattern among the variables.

It seems reasonable to suggest from evidence of the contrasting levels that, when a more comprehensive range of ownership resources committed by the partners is matched by a correspondingly higher level of control, this in turn will lead to a better performance. Correlations between foreign equity and control variables are positive and significant among the higher-performing joint ventures. The main exception concerns the objective measure of growth in sales, for which higher-performing joint ventures tend to show lower levels of resourcing control fit when contrasted with the lower-performing group. There are also clear indications that when the Chinese ownership resources valued as equity are more closely matched to the local Chinese control policies, the Chinese partners will then perceive a better performance of joint ventures. Overall, it can be suggested that, when the range of contributions, valued as equity committed by the partners, is matched to the level of control perceived by the partners, a better joint venture performance will result.

The correlations between foreign contractual resources and control measures show a clearer distribution between higher- and lower-performing joint ventures in comparison with the pattern results for Chinese contractual ownership resourcing. The results may reflect the fact that there is a significantly lower reliance on contractual resources from Chinese companies in joint ventures in terms of technology and management. The performance results indicate that, when foreign contractual resourcing fits or matches the overall foreign control and influence, the joint venture will have a better performance.

When the level of fit is tested between foreign non-contractual resources and the foreign control and influence, there is a clearly differentiated pattern as between higher- and lower-performing joint ventures. Most of the correlations are stronger and significant at the 0.01 level or less in higher-performing joint ventures. There are two correlations between the subjective indicators of growth and profit and the Chinese non-contractual resourcing, which state that there is less consistency in the higher-performing joint ventures. The findings associated with Chinese non-contractual resourcing are surprising, in that the correlations between the control and Chinese non-contractual resources in lower-performing joint ventures show slightly higher significant correlations.

On the whole, the contractual and non-contractual resources committed by foreign partners show a more clearly distinctive pattern as between higher- and lower-performing joint ventures by comparison with the Chinese group.

The Fit Between Transactional Resource and Control

The relationship between sourcing and distributional transactions with the partners and joint venture performance, and the influence of control on this relationship, is examined in this study. Both subjective and objective indicators of joint venture profitability and growth are employed to test this result, because as system performance criteria they bear most closely on the joint venture operational level.

Correlations are given respectively for foreign resourcing inputs and output percentages with foreign influence and control, and Chinese ownership inputs and output percentage with Chinese influence and control. Table 8.10 indicates the relationship between the dimensions of performance (growth, profitability) and business strategies (proportion of sourcing supplied by the partner). The results from applying both subjective and objective performance measures suggest an association between the percentage of outputs by value taken by the foreign and Chinese partners and overall control in the higher-performing joint ventures. As suggested by Porter (1980), when the bargaining power of partners is high then joint ventures tend to use internal sourcing via the partners. The results shows that if that percentage of resources transacted by the foreign and Chinese partners and respectively their overall control over joint ventures can be categorised.

This is because the partner may provide lower-cost raw materials and other resource inputs by using existing networks and distribution mechanisms. The partners in turn have more control over the price and the supply of components. A relatively lower degree of association was found between the output taken by the partners and overall control in lower-performing joint ventures. The findings indicate that there is a stronger correlation between the resource inputs supplied by foreign partners and their overall control among joint ventures with higher (objective) profitability. Foreign resource output correlations are positive, and there are statistically significant subjective performance

Table 8.10 Comparison of (1) the fit between transactional dependency and overall control and (2) performance of joint ventures ($N = 67$ joint ventures)

Performance measure	*Correlations between intensity of parent–joint venture transactions and for different performance groups' overall control*[a]			
	Subjective		*Objective*	
	Growth	*Profitability*	*Growth in sales ($N = 47$)*[b]	*Profitability ($N = 39$)*[b]
Higher-performing joint ventures				
% inputs from foreign partner	0.27	0.04	0.28	0.73***
% inputs from Chinese partner	0.18	0.15	0.56*	0.29
% output going to the foreign partner	0.35*	0.39*	0.44	0.41
% outputs going to Chinese partner	0.60*	0.36*	0.60*	0.39
Lower-performing joint ventures				
% inputs from foreign partner	0.17	0.27*	0.21	–0.04
% inputs from Chinese partner	–0.24	–0.13	–0.35	–0.31
% outputs going to the foreign partner	0.36*	–0.18	0.17	0.32
% outputs going to Chinese partner	0.33*	0.40*	0.37*	0.12

Notes:
[a]Correlation is respectively for foreign inputs and output percentages with foreign influence and control, and Chinese ownership inputs and output percentages with Chinese influence and control.
[b]Number of cases is reduced, owing to incomplete data. Some joint ventures did not supply sales and profit data. Therefore numbers reported are below 67. In addition, when a joint venture had not been in operation for three years or had not reached profitability, it was excluded from the analysis.
One-tail probabilities: $^{*}p < 0.05$; $^{**}p < 0.01$; $^{***}p < 0.001$.

measures on growth and profitability among higher-performing joint ventures. The fit between foreign transactional resource supply and foreign joint venture control is greater in higher-performing joint ventures than it is among lower-performing ones. With regard to Chinese transactional resource dependency, the results suggest a higher association between the output taken by Chinese partners and their overall control among the higher-performing joint ventures. On the whole, the fit of Chinese overall control with the level of resource inputs supplied by the Chinese partners is stronger in the higher-performing joint ventures than in the lower-performing ones.

The results from Table 8.10 can be interpreted as giving qualified support to the contingency argument regarding the fit between owning companies giving transactional support to their joint ventures and their achieving a good profits. Therefore, the findings suggest that the higher the proportion of a joint venture's inputs supplied by the parent companies, and outputs directly than taken by the parent companies, the better will be its performance. The finding are consistent with research done by Geringer and Hebert (1989) that partners are likely to focus control efforts in the areas critical to their company. The results for the matching of control with joint venture transactional dependency appear to fit the contingency testing of ownership and control.

SUMMARY

This study, by using both universalistic and contingency approaches, pursues a range of perspectives on joint venture performance. A universalistic approach postulates that joint venture performance improves when a greater range of ownership resourcing and higher transactional resources are supplied by parent companies. This performance is enhanced if one partner has greater control, and also when there is longer joint venture operational experience. Although the universalistic approach to performance receives little support, the findings related to the universalistic approach identify a number of issues.

The results suggest that when operational inputs are supplied directly by the foreign partners then joint ventures will enjoy better performance. Other evidence from the study suggests that when a higher percentage of inputs is supplied by foreign owning companies then the global sourcing strategies of those companies focus on the areas of quality control, product pricing and international sales. When outputs are taken by the Chinese partners, joint ventures tend to achieve a better performance, as the Chinese partners can reduce transactional costs, speed access to the Chinese domestic market and assist in the handling of local regulations. There is no clear performance difference between joint ventures having dominant and shared control. The results may imply that the development of joint ventures in China is still at too early a stage to judge their performance with regard to these two categories. The contrast between joint ventures in operation for, respectively, under and over three years is of some apparent consequence for their performance.

The support for the contingency approach suggests several managerial implications. First, a contingency approach postulates that joint venture performance will benefit from a matching of the levels of each partner's control over the joint venture and its resource provision. In other words, there may not be one best way to achieve a better joint venture performance, except where owners take special care on the resourcing they committed to the joint venture. It was found that the correlation coefficients for control over joint ventures, in relation to the range of ownership resources supplied by the partners, are, in general, higher and more statistically significant among better-performing joint ventures. Moreover, when transactional resources are supplied by the parent companies, rather than by the market, joint ventures tend to achieve better performance.

Second, a relatively high degree of correlation is found in higher-performing joint ventures between the resource inputs supplied by the foreign partners, resource outputs taken by the Chinese partners and their respective overall fit with control and influence. A matching of each partner's direct involvement in either joint venture input provision or output disposal, with its level of control, will be conducive to better performance. In other words, resource inputs and outputs, both supplied by or taken by the parent company, may require different sourcing strategies to achieve a better performance. Formulating a percentage of sourcing strategy at the joint venture level may restrict the flexibility of adjusting the strategy in the Chinese market, but it may, to a large extent, reduce the transaction costs for the joint venture.

Third, as businesses are dynamic in nature, what is considered at the present time an optimal strategy in terms of current 'goodness fit' between provision of ownership resourcing and control may not hold true in the future.

The Sino-foreign JVs studied appear in the main to have achieved a satisfactory level of performance. The mean ratings for the achievement of parent company objectives, and for the performance of the IJV themselves as business units, were all above the midpoints of the scales employed. Overall, Chinese parent objectives were seen to have been met to a rather greater degree than were foreign parent objectives. Judging by the ratings given, Chinese parent companies are content with the financial benefits offered by the IJVs, but they would like to see a more substantial transfer of managerial and technical knowledge from their foreign partners. Foreign parent companies appear in the main to have established themselves satisfactorily in the Chinese economy, but many are seeking better profits and a larger market share.

Part III
Conclusions

9 Conclusions: Implications for Theory and Practice

This chapter first brings together the main findings of the investigation. The contributions of the research are then discussed. The intention is to consider the extent to which the study reported here has been able to meet its original objectives. A third section discusses the limitations and theoretical implications of the study. The chapter closes with some of the practical implications for foreign and Chinese joint venture partners that may be derived from the research.

SYNOPSIS OF MAIN FINDINGS

This section summarises the findings and highlights the specific results. When the objectives of foreign partners are long-term, foreign investing companies tend to contribute a more comprehensive range of ownership resources and a higher value of equity capital to the joint venture. This tendency is not, however, either strong or clear-cut. The objective of establishing a strong business presence in China tends to be associated with the provision of a wider range of non-contractual resourcing by foreign owning companies. Also, most foreign partners with long-term objectives commit a relatively high level of capital to the joint venture.

There is no relationship between the prioritising of short-term objectives by foreign parent companies and (1) the range of their resourcing and (2) the level of equity capital they contribute to their joint ventures. If an owning company holds a greater share of equity of the joint venture then that company is likely to gain overall control in the joint venture. This overall control tends to be exercised through the rights to representation on the board of directors that are attached to equity share and the occupancy of key management positions. The holding of a majority equity share by foreign partners gives them control of the board and of the top management structure of a joint venture. Representation on joint venture boards closely reflects the equity position of the partners. Most expatriate managers are in favour of establishing a majority equity position, which, as this study has shown, facilitates their control over joint venture management and technology. This policy is being recommended by consultants such as McKinsey (Meier *et al.* 1995). The finding is also in line with the observation made by Harrigan (1986) that many multinational firms intend to gain a greater control over joint ventures by committing to a majority equity share.

Equity share is a stronger lever for strategic control over joint ventures than it is for operational control. The rights to control the appointment of a joint venture's board members and senior managers are derived from the proportion of equity share held by the partners of a joint venture. Control derived from a joint venture's board tends to focus on the strategic areas of decision-taking in a joint venture. Chinese control over strategic issues is somewhat more closely derived from their equity investments than is the case for foreign partners.

The ability to predict the relative levels of a partner's control in joint ventures is enhanced by the adoption of a definition of ownership that is broader than the purely legal one. When deciding on the amount of equity required, joint venture partners should not think that holding a majority equity share means that overall control necessarily follows. Sometimes, a foreign partner with a minority equity stake has achieved dominant control of a joint venture's operation. This has usually been because foreign partners bring to the joint venture expertise that the Chinese partners do not possess. An example is a Japanese electronics company that contributes high technology to the joint venture, and has secured a high level of operational control with a minority equity share. This finding reconfirms the conclusion reached by Lecraw (1984). He indicated that the relationship between a transactional corporation's overall management control of a subsidiary and its equity ownership in that subsidiary was roughly J-shaped. Lecraw concluded that:

> there was not a close relationship between percent equity ownership and effective control. Some multinational corporations with a low percent of the equity in their subsidiaries had a high degree of control over the critical success variables in their subsidiaries. Conversely, some multinational corporations with a high level of equity ownership had a low degree of control over these variables.
>
> (Lecraw 1984:38)

Schaan (1988) argued along similar lines. While the present study cannot support the view that equity share does not have a close relationship with control, it does at the same time point to the additional impact of non-capital, non-contractual resourcing for operational control in joint ventures, and possibly in joint ventures more generally.

Contractual resourcing is not strongly or consistently related to a parent company's overall control. A greater range of contractual ownership resourcing by foreign and Chinese partners does not on the whole lead to a correspondingly greater control over the joint venture operations. The difference between the range of contractual resources provided by Chinese and foreign parent companies bears some relation to differences in their control over the areas of technological innovation, quality control, reinvestment policy and purchasing policies. Most foreign partners tend to provide technological resources in order to establish their technology and brand name, and doing this through formal contracts enables them to maintain control within the joint venture in those areas. This is why the relationship between contractual ownership resourcing and parent companies' influence is confined to certain corresponding areas of management.

Drawing up relevant technology, sales, marketing and management contracts is a way for a foreign partner to establish legitimate influence in the corresponding areas of a joint venture, because these contractual resources are clearly perceived as valuable contributions to the joint venture by the local partner. The mechanism of control here is to maximise the fit between the critical resource inputs into joint ventures and then to establish corresponding management systems and technology systems to protect the implementation of these contracts. The data from the present study indicate that contracts can define boundary conditions for management influence within a joint venture, especially for influence over matters of technology. This, on the one hand, has an obvious added advantage in forcing the partners to follow the joint venture's articles of association. On the other hand, such a contract constrains joint venture management by virtue of its imposed obligations and responsibilities. This result is to some extent similar to the findings of Rugman (1981) and Agarwal and Ramaswami (1992). The latter reported in respect of joint ventures that 'Lack of protection would make the sharing of specialised knowledge risky in the long run, particular since it would limit the flexibility a firm has in adapting to future contingencies' (1992:9).

The impact of contractual ownership resourcing on operational control is limited to a link between technology provision *and* influence over technological innovation. A greater provision of technological resources does not, however, generally lead to correspondingly greater influence on joint venture operations as a whole.

The provision of ownership resourcing on a non-contractual basis adds significantly to parent company control over a wider range of joint venture management activities and decision-making, especially with respect to operational issues. Non-contractual resourcing offers a basis for operational control. Such resourcing tends to be provided on a continuing basis during the life of a joint venture. Non-contractual ownership resources denote more of a continuous commitment by the partners to their joint ventures than is usually the case with resources provided on the basis of one-off contracts. They therefore represent the basis for a more ongoing relationship between the partner companies and the joint venture. Non-contractual resources also tend to be directed at enhancing the on-going process of management in a range of areas, and thus add to the breadth of the control leverage provided by this category of resources.

Most of the non-contractual resources, such as technical assistance, management and training, are oriented towards improving the ongoing operation of joint ventures rather than with establishing their basic infrastructure. This result has gained some level of indirect support from the recent work of Hill and Hellriegel (1994). They indicated that a good-quality working relationship leads to similarity in operating philosophies. Yan and Gray (1994a) in turn reported a strong positive association between inter-partner consensus and the venture's overall performance. Transferring non-contractual resourcing represents a long-term commitment on the part of the foreign investing companies, and it tends to generate the goodwill of the Chinese parent and relevant government authorities.

The configuration of a partner's equity and non-contractual resourcing is reflected in the pattern of the overall control in a joint venture. Both equity share and non-contractual resourcing had independent contributory power in the prediction of joint venture control. That of equity share was the stronger for strategic control, while that of non-contractual resourcing was stronger for operational control. A more comprehensive range of ownership resourcing committed by a partner of the joint venture is thus likely to enable the partner to gain overall control in the joint venture.

A more comprehensive range of ownership resources does not necessarily lead to higher performance by the joint venture. An implication of this finding may be that it is the distinctiveness of ownership resourcing that produces higher performance rather than its range. Even when combining capital, and all non-capital resources (contractual and non-contractual), the range of ownership resourcing does not contribute to joint venture performance. However, when the items of non-contractual ownership resourcing are examined in detail, with reference to control over each operational area, the provision of product design and management services is found to relate positively to a higher joint venture performance. This latter result may be compatible with Geringer and Hebert's (1989) suggestion that, when joint venture partners focus their control efforts in decision areas significant to those ventures, their performance will benefit.

The higher the proportion of joint venture transactional operational inputs supplied by the parent companies, and outputs taken by them, the greater the likelihood of satisfactory joint venture performance. Most foreign partners have direct control over inputs to joint ventures from the international market. Foreign parent companies have relatively more chance to control the international purchasing and sales distribution of joint ventures. There is the possibility that resources supplied by foreign partners enable them to benefit from transfer pricing. The result suggests that when using existing foreign channels for resource inputs, joint ventures will benefit from improved quality control of resource inputs, lower transactional costs and preferential technological support from the foreign parent companies. Evidence also suggests that when a higher percentage of resource inputs is supplied by the foreign partners, their sourcing strategies appear to focus on the areas of quality control, product pricing and international purchasing and sales. When output goes directly to the Chinese parent companies, joint ventures tend to achieve a higher performance, because Chinese parent companies can use their existing distribution networks to reduce transactional costs. These networks speed up access to the Chinese domestic market, and assist in the handling of local regulations.

There is no systematic evidence from this study that a joint venture will achieve higher performance if control is dominated by one partner. Nevertheless, the impression gained from less structured sections of the interviews was that the dominant partner in a joint venture would find it easier to manage the joint venture business and consequently would have more chance to achieve a higher performance for it.

The greater the length of time the joint venture has been in operation, the better tends to be its profitability. The results imply that the accumulated business experience of joint ventures increases the confidence of both foreign and Chinese partners in the venture. This is supported qualitatively by the comments received in many interviews.

Joint ventures that have a relatively shorter experience are not expected to have sufficient skills to deal with operational problems in the Chinese market. Therefore, their chances of obtaining higher returns are not as good. This result is consistent with the previous findings of research by Contractor and Lorange (1988), Fayerweather (1982) and Agarwal and Ramaswami (1992).

The more ownership resourcing and control are matched, the better tends to be the joint venture's performance. This result indicates that a joint venture parent needs to have control proportionate to its ownership resourcing in order to secure higher joint venture performance. This need for joint venture control to match resourcing fits with the previous finding that there is no significant effect from the range of ownership resourcing *per se* on achieving higher performance.

When a joint venture parent company exercises more control than its partners in areas that reflect its relative strengths in the provision of resources and competencies, this usually leads to the achievement of a better performance of the joint venture. Foreign partners usually exert substantial control over joint ventures by managing the financial, production and sales areas. Global strategic considerations lead foreign investors to control the pricing of a joint venture's products on the international market, as this will enable the foreign partner to minimise the difference between their own domestic and Chinese joint venture products. Most foreign partners can usually gather first-hand market information through their foreign sales teams, and this appears to give them a powerful competitive advantage over their Chinese partners. Foreign influence tends to be exercised in the areas of finance, technical innovation, quality control and marketing (which are critical for securing good market or customer information), also the updating of the levels of technology and management. The Chinese influence tends to be relatively greater over personnel matters, such as social welfare, than in other areas. The comments from joint venture managers also tended to support the view that if a parent company exercises more control in those areas that reflect its particular and relative strengths in the provision of resources and competencies then a joint venture will tend to achieve a better performance.

The closer the fit between a joint venture's transactional resource dependence on its parent companies and the level of parent company control, the better will be its performance. The higher the proportion of a joint venture's operational inputs contracted directly with its foreign parent companies, the greater the control that company exercises over the joint venture. (Ownership operational inputs are defined as the direct supply of materials and components to a joint venture.) The finding suggests that when transactional resource inputs are supplied directly by the foreign partners, the foreign partner will enjoy more control. The proportion of joint venture inputs supplied by the foreign investing companies appears to provide a leverage for control over joint ventures that is derived from the parent companies having control over their product brand name, pricing, technological content and market channels, including purchasing and distribution. There is a higher association between the output taken by Chinese partners and their overall control among the higher-performing joint ventures.

OTHER FINDINGS RELEVANT TO THE RESEARCH

Ownership Resourcing

Cash investment may give the capital provider a preferential position to exert control over the joint venture at its formation. Comments from the interviews state that a partner that provides cash investment to a joint venture tends to gain control over its budgets. If an insufficiency of capital develops after formation then the joint venture usually undergoes a reallocation of equity, the renegotiation of the contract regarding composition of the board, the renegotiation of rights to control, and a search for a new investor or bankruptcy. This finding is consistent with that from Yan and Gray's (1994b) research on Sino-US joint ventures. They reported that the firm that commits the greater amount of capital resources gains an advantage in strategic control in the joint venture. However, they found no significant effect of capital provision on operational or structural control. The author's finding here is also consistent with several empirical studies on the relationship between the bargaining power of owners and control. These show that capital resourcing is critical to the joint venture's success and enhances a partner's bargaining power (Pfeffer and Salancik 1978, Harrigan 1986, Yan and Gray 1994a).

Very few foreign partners capitalise technology as an equity input in the Sino-foreign joint ventures studied. The foreign company's trademark or brand name, technical know-how ('soft technology') and goodwill are rarely capitalised. There are three probable reasons for this. First, it is difficult to agree on the capital value of technical know-how, because it is intangible and it is dependent on a company's business reputation. Second, when foreign technology assets are capitalised into joint venture assets according to Chinese law, the power to control the use of these technological assets is threatened, because the local partner may then assume it has been empowered with the right to use them via its participation in the joint venture. Third, negotiations on the valuation of technology assets often encounter difficulties, because they necessitate the local Chinese authority paying attention not only to the business reputation of the joint venture, but also to those of their foreign parent companies. There is pressure from Chinese local authorities and partners to undervalue technology assets, so as to increase their own share of joint venture equity. Thus, foreign firms find it is problematic to capitalise their technology as equity investment.

Most foreign investors contribute cash as their equity investment. A joint venture is a separate new business entity, and usually needs a large amount of capital to meet its start-up costs for construction, acquisition of equipment, provision of plant, and operational cashflow. It is very difficult for foreign partners investing in a new joint venture to get approval from local Chinese authorities to contribute equity in any form other than cash. In the present study, no firm used a loan from a source in China or an international bank to get the joint venture started. Most foreign partners appear to have less difficulty in committing funds than do their Chinese partners, even when the latter can spread their payments over several tranches.

The Chinese side tends to bring land, buildings, existing equipment and plant as its contribution to the joint venture equity. These assets do not convey any strong leverage for exercising management control over joint ventures, except over facilities such as power and water. This indicates that the Chinese partner's strategic and operational control is not necessarily derived directly from the resources they contribute to joint venture equity.

When a joint venture is formed, the Chinese partner usually contributes local knowledge. This contribution of local knowledge falls into two stages. The first occurs during joint venture formation, when there is considerable involvement with legal, official planning and financial matters. The second occurs during joint venture operation, which is closely linked to domestic sales, supplies and infrastructure. However, once a joint venture is in operation, the foreign partner progressively gains sufficient access to the first category of local knowledge. How long a Chinese partner's possession of the second category of local knowledge, relating to operational networks, retains its importance will depend on both the criticality of that knowledge and how fast the foreign partner learns. On the whole, the results of the present study are consistent with Hamel's (1991) research on the linkage between learning and bargaining power. Hamel found from his several case-studies that the bargaining power of the Japanese firms grew as learning from their partners progressed.

Most foreign companies tend to inject technology as a separate contractual resource to joint ventures. Foreign contractual technology packages include product design, production technology and professional services (with provision for royalties and sometimes for a flat fee). The technology contract is normally an appendix to the main contract of joint ventures, and usually has a time-frame different from that of the main joint venture contract. As joint ventures by their very nature have an embedded potential for conflict, the technology contract may be drawn up so as to provide for safeguards in the application of technology to a joint venture's operation. Foreign control over the use of technology is usually related to the specification of the joint venture technology contract.

Control

Of general managers in the study, 88 percent were expatriate, nominated either by the board of directors of joint ventures or by foreign parent companies when the joint venture has a shared or dominant control. General managers of joint ventures often take on responsibility for recruitment and evaluation, with the board giving final approval. They always take responsibility for senior joint venture managerial appointments. This result is consistent with previous research, especially that of Killing (1983), Beamish (1993) and Schaan (1988), on management structuring in a joint venture.

The Chinese partner usually assigns all of the board representatives that its equity share allows, and indeed often has an equal number of directors even when its equity share is somewhat below 50 per cent. Well-connected Chinese board members can be constructive in helping the joint venture to deal with the local bureaucracy, and to facilitate local marketing and distribution. Alternatively, they can occasionally be obstructive. A few Chinese board members are more likely to be appointed by local government and to use the joint venture board to reflect the government's power or interests.

CONTRIBUTION OF THE RESEARCH

> The objective of this book is to make a contribution in the relatively unexplored conceptual territory of the relationship between objectives, ownership, control and performance of Sino-foreign joint ventures. The intention is to develop a categorisation of ownership resourcing, based upon the distinction between contractual and non-contractual resources, which may add to our understanding of the differences between conventional companies and international joint ventures in China. The study also explores the applicability of established Western theories to the Chinese business context.
>
> (Chapter 1:7)

This section considers the ways and extent to which the research has been able to meet the above aims. The contributions made by the research are examined with reference to (1) the threefold classification of ownership resourcing; (2) the separate examination of strategic and operational control in relation to the three categories of ownership resourcing; (3) the universalistic and contingency approaches to analysis of joint venture performance; and (4) the interrelationships between the components of the research framework. A discussion of the limitations of the work and the opportunity for further research then follows in a later section.

THE THREEFOLD CATEGORISATION OF OWNERSHIP RESOURCING

The research reported in this book has offered a more comprehensive understanding of how the range of ownership resourcing provided by the partners fits the internal control structure of a joint venture. This is achieved by the distinction between three categories of ownership resourcing. The ability of a joint venture's partners to work together effectively is largely dependent on their respective provision of ownership resources as they are configured in the joint venture at its formation. A joint venture's level of success can be depressed from the start, if the partner's objectives and priorities conflict. The partners' objectives, be they long- or short-term, are constrained by the level of contractual and non-contractual resourcing that they intend, and are able, to commit. Clarifying strategic objectives and financial priorities from the start can help to avert suspicions that a partner's unstated goals are in conflict with the objectives of the other investors in the joint venture. Different and conflicting strategic and financial priorities will lead to behaviour that each partner considers to be bizarre in the other. Equity, contractual and non-contractual ownership resourcing each have their distinctive and sufficient control power on the performance of joint ventures, because these powers can produce 'desired' results according to an investing company's strategic objectives and financial priorities.

In the joint venture form of business, equity constitutes the legal concept of ownership. Ownership rights are associated with the range of resources valued as equity investments committed by the owning companies. The equity proportion held by partners is used to predict the levels of control and influence ascribed to the relevant parent company, and their nominated managers. Equity share conveys certain legitimised legal rights to determine the overall direction of a joint venture. Assets such as technology, market channels and management expertise have become increasingly recognised as ownership factors. Ownership, in the context of joint ventures, can also be categorised in a way that goes beyond the conventional. This is especially true in the formation of joint ventures, where they may constitute more important complementary assets than can be measured purely by financial contributions.

When non-capital resources are provided through contracts, these can specify rights as to the use and the management of such resources. The structure of contracts governing the range of ownership resourcing committed by the partners usually depends on the local legal system and social customs, and the technical attributes of the assets involved in the exchange. Some non-capital resources may be provided under terms that are set out in formal contracts. Such contracts typically convey formalised rights to exclusive control over the use of, and/or benefit from, assets including technology and brands.

When non-capital resources are provided on a non-contractual basis, they may still confer powers to the providing company, either because they create intrinsically a dependency on its expertise, or because they generate the moral authority which derives from the way they evidence commitment, or both. The range of ownership resourcing provided on a non-contractual basis represents the level of continuing commitment by the owning companies to the joint venture. Joint ventures are especially suited to knowledge transfers. They may provide scope for learning and capability accumulation (Hamel 1991). The partners of joint ventures can extend those limits outward by building up trust, and learning, through offering non-contractual equity resourcing to a joint venture. As a joint venture generates exposure to different routines, through exchange of personnel and other forms of interaction between the partners, this can facilitate a higher level of learning between partners.

The non-contractual equity resourcing to joint ventures can be linked to the use of informal mechanisms to build a partner's motivation and commitment. Joint venture partners providing resources, skills and knowledge additional to their equity and contractual contribution enjoy *de facto* property rights, through the expertise and moral influence these inputs generate. It is suggested that non-contractual ownership resourcing committed by partners mediates the relationship between the distinctive characteristics of a joint venture's cooperative arrangement. Non-contractual ownership resourcing can both reduce transaction operating costs and increase innovation between the partners of a joint venture. In addition to its mediating effects, this may increase partner specialisation and efficiency.

Resourcing by owners on a contractual and non-contractual basis in turn feeds back into the joint venture's performance. The distinction between these three categories of ownership resourcing is likely to be a significant one for the understanding of joint venture performance, because of the nature and scope of the power that stems from each of them.

STRATEGIC AND OPERATIONAL CONTROL IN RELATION TO THE THREE CATEGORIES OF OWNERSHIP RESOURCING

Recategorisation of non-capital ownership resourcing into both contractual and non-contractual resources adds significantly to an understanding of the influence and control that either the foreign or the Chinese partner can exercise over many areas of joint venture management. This distinction between contractual and non-contractual ownership resourcing links to that between strategic and operational control.

The ability to predict the relative levels of a partner's control in a joint venture is enhanced by the adoption of a definition of ownership that is broader in nature. The findings of this study indicate that equity share predicts both kinds of strategic and operational control. It is, however, a stronger lever for strategic control than it is for operational control. The provision of ownership resourcing on a non-contractual basis adds significantly to a partner's control over a wider range of joint venture management activities, especially with respect to operational issues. The provision of ownership resourcing on a contractual basis is limited to a partner's control in a narrow range of joint venture operational management activities, especially with respect to technology provision over technological innovation.

Drawing together the distinction between contractual and non-contractual ownership resourcing *and* their respective linkages to strategic and operational control has clarified the insights that several theoretical perspectives can provide on the relationship between joint venture ownership and control. First, with respect to the resource dependence perspective, if a partner contributes a range of contractual and non-contractual resources, and the other partner cannot provide those resources, then the first partner will gain power relative to the other. That first partner can exercise relatively greater control and influence over the joint venture, such control and influence accruing from the resources.

Second, the data indicate that the control employed is selective or focused on certain joint venture activities that, according to the level of substitutability of the resourcing, the other partners cannot provide. A partner, by emphasising non-contractual ownership resources, can have a direct influence over joint venture operations through technology, management transfer and learning from the joint venture's environment. Measuring the associations between non-contractual ownership resourcing and strategic and operational control is useful, because they can provide additional insights into the relationship between ownership and control of a joint venture. The distinction between contractual and non-contractual ownership resources gives rise to a corresponding distinction between 'boundary control' and 'operational control'. This adds to the analytical distinctions already made in the literature, such as those between focus, extent and control mechanism made by Geringer and Hebert (1989).

Third, the degree of operational control over the behaviour of a joint venture can be obtained by checking how the joint venture contracts are specified between the parent companies. The boundary conditions of contracts, such as total capital investment, contract duration and the proportion of equity retained by partners, is highlighted. The purpose is to understand how the operational control of the joint venture is influenced by the changes in the transformation of the host's perceptions of the foreign investing company's value added, and the implementation of the contract over time.

THE UNIVERSALISTIC AND CONTINGENCY APPROACHES TO ANALYSING JOINT VENTURE PERFORMANCE

If joint venture performance is measured in terms of the return on the partner's investment, this raises the question of which partner's resources should be used to assess performance. There is a possibility of the joint venture performing well, but only in terms of one partner's interests.

Universalistic and contingency performance approaches are used here to assess how well a joint venture meets both its subjective and its objective performance measures. The theoretical contributions of contingency and universalistic approaches of performance assessment are the following: (1) the extent to which the partners' desired objectives have been achieved in regard to their ownership resourcing investments; (2) the area of focus or selective control that the partners exercise in terms of matching their resourcing commitments. Because contractual and non-contractual resourcing have different impacts on the performance of joint ventures, the analyses related to performance vary according to the universalistic and contingency performance approaches under consideration. The intention in using a contingency approach to performance is to gain an insight into the dynamics of the matching between each partner's ownership resourcing and its respective area of control.

THE INTERRELATIONSHIP BETWEEN THE COMPONENTS OF THE RESEARCH FRAMEWORK

The research framework used in this study adopts a unidirectional view of the ownership–control relationship, with the main flow of influence assumed to pass from objectives, to ownership, to control and then to joint venture performance. The elements in this research framework shown in Figure 3.1 can interrelate in terms of three separate models.

Formation Model

This study has developed better working categories for each of the concepts of objectives, ownership and control – for example, classifying objectives based on the long or the short term, and whether they are financial or strategic in nature. Three ownership-resourcing categories have been examined, with their respective linkages to strategic and operational control of the joint venture. The classifications are useful for revealing the connections posited by this model in depth. Several results were derived from the formation model. First, joint venture objectives based upon the foreign and Chinese partners' strategic and financial priorities definitely show different patterns. Second, objectives based on long or short-term priorities can be traced from a partner's range of ownership resourcing and the level of value of equity capital the partner commits. Third, the objectives of the foreign partners in this study appear to be compatible with the resources and competencies that the company intends to and can actually commit.

Universalistic Model

The universalistic model is used to assess the presence of direct linkages between objectives, ownership and control variables over the performance of the joint venture. The interdependencies between the variables of the model can be evaluated to gain insights into the ownership–control relationship. The intentions in the universalistic model are the following. The first is to identify the comprehensiveness of ownership resourcing committed by a partner, in equity, contractual or non-contractual forms as determinants of joint venture performance. The second is to establish the extent to which the level of protection and guarantees are provided by the partners in the joint venture with respect to the proportion of ownership operational inputs supplied by, and outputs taken by, the parent companies. The third intention is the examination of the duration of the joint venture in relation to the achievement of overall Chinese and foreign objectives and some performance targets such as profitability and growth. Finally, shared and dominated control of the joint venture are categorised as parameters in order to gain different insights, as they are evidently different in joint venture operation.

The universalistic model receives varying degrees of support. The findings indicate that the higher is the proportion of a joint venture's operational inputs supplied by the parent companies, the greater is the likelihood of satisfactory joint venture performance. The greater the length of time the joint venture has been in operation, the better will be its profitability. However, a more comprehensive range of ownership resourcing committed by partners does not lead necessarily to higher performance. Dominant versus shared control does not have a clear impact on a joint venture's performance.

Contingency Model

The goodness of fit between joint venture ownership and control was assumed to bear upon joint venture performance. Contingency theory implies that that goodness of fit will enhance performance. In reality, it cannot be said that changes in ownership resourcing by the partners will cause predictable changes in joint venture control, but one can say that the need for such changes can be precipitated by anticipated changes in the strategic and operational requirements of the joint venture. With regard to interdependencies of each concept, the rationale is to view ownership in terms of areas to be influenced by a partner's strategic objectives and financial priorities over a certain range of ownership investments, and the ownership in turn is regarded as providing a leverage for the partner to manage the joint venture.

The results provide considerable support for the contingency model. They suggest that joint venture performance will benefit when the level of foreign and Chinese control is matched to their respective ownership resourcing commitments. When a match between foreign and Chinese ownership resourcing is achieved, the parent company's transaction costs are reduced. Correlation coefficients for control over a joint venture in relation to ownership resourcing are in general higher and more likely to be statistically significant among higher-performing joint ventures than among lower-performing ones.

THEORETICAL IMPLICATIONS OF THE RESEARCH

This research helps to clarify several important issues in the literature on the relationship between a partner's objectives, ownership, control and performance in international joint ventures. First, the results demonstrate that a partner's strategic and financial objectives have no direct influence on the commitment of the three ownership resourcing categories as applied to joint venture analysis. The findings broaden our appreciation of some aspects of the relationship between partner objectives and the consequent resourcing of joint ventures. For example, when the partners have divergent strategic and financial objectives, the configuration of ownership resourcing of the joint venture may be strongly influenced by the negotiation between them.

Objectives are viewed as emerging from a mix of strategic and financial motives at the time the partners enter into the joint venture agreement. There are very marginal links between the foreign partner's objectives and the ownership resourcing they provide, but not in the case of the Chinese partner. However, when distinguishing non-contractual ownership resourcing over the thirteen control areas, the objectives held by each partner of the joint venture do have some bearing on the resources they commit. In other words, non-contractual resourcing reflects the owner's objectives only in the operational areas of joint venture management. The result is significant to strategic management theory in considering choices of ownership investment in relation to perceived operational control and/or influence, and the desired integration of joint venture resourcing with their strategies.

Second, ownership affects strategic and operational control of the joint venture. The study has provided some theoretical and empirical support for the significance of non-capital ownership resourcing on strategic and operational control (Yan and Gray 1994a). The finding is significant, because it helps to explain that the nature and scope of joint venture control may stem from each of its ownership categories. Previous research examined ownership–control relationships by measuring the absolute amount of equity held by the partners as the sole control indicator. This research concluded that the ownership–control relationship evidenced high correlation when the linkages between three ownership resourcing categories and strategic and operational control are examined. On the basis of resource dependence theory, non-contractual ownership resources are demonstrated to have an important influence on the wider areas of joint venture operation.

Third, the study demonstrates that the positive relationship between ownership, control and performance holds only when the partners' ownership resourcing inputs fit their respective strategic and operational control modes. This finding contributes rather more to structural contingency theory (compare Donaldson 1995) than the strategic contingency theory of Hickson *el al.* (1971), by addressing the fit between a partner's ownership resourcing and its corresponding control. It has broadened the argument regarding the relative power and control that are derived from command of critical resources and the adaptation of those resources to the environment.

The results show that a joint venture's transactional resource dependence on a parent company enhances the latter's control over it. As expected, control derived from the transactional resource dependency is particularly significant in the areas of purchasing, marketing and sales distribution. With regard to the performance of a joint venture, this study demonstrates that there is no apparent impact of contractual and non-contractual resourcing in themselves on performance. However, once efforts are made by each partner to ensure that the resourcing is properly used in terms of establishing a control structure, then resourcing is found to have a positive role in the performance of the joint venture. In other words, development of a control structure to match the specific resourcing contributed by the partners does have a positive effect on joint venture performance. There is support for the contingency hypotheses, but not for all of the universalistic ones.

Fourth, the research shows the need to develop a better model of the relationship between joint venture objectives, ownership, control and performance. New dimensions of the relationship between partners' ownership resourcing and their respective control of joint ventures are captured from the empirical research on linkages between the three ownership resourcing categories and strategic and operational control. This has not been studied in the previous research. Resource dependency theory is particular useful in providing insights into the linkages of the analytical framework employed in this dissertation (Figure 3.1).

LIMITATIONS

Four limitations of this study should be mentioned. First, although a sample of 67 joint ventures is adequate for statistical analysis, a study with a larger sample would allow greater confidence in its results. This research is based on only two business sectors. As the study is associated with the relationship between ownership and control, findings drawn from the FMCG and electronics sectors may not wholly apply to other sectors. For example, companies investing in mechanical engineering joint ventures may have a different range of preferences in terms of strategic priorities, the range of ownership resources, and control mechanisms. Moreover, evidence has been presented to suggest that there are some variations in the results reported in this dissertation between the two sectors. It has been beyond the limits of the present work to consider these in detail.

Second, the pattern of Chinese ownership resourcing for joint ventures is likely to be influenced by the regional context of Chinese economic institutional settings, the stage of economic development, local cultural practices and regional development policies. The present study of Chinese ownership resourcing would be enhanced by taking into account the effects of changing industry development priorities and regional policies as inputs affecting constraints on the Chinese partners.

Third, regarding the data collection methodology, the interviewing of an average of three respondents from each joint venture and of seeking both foreign and Chinese perspectives has been beneficial. However, very often reliance had to be placed on only one respondent for certain categories of data. Securing information on ownership and the perceptions of influence from more than two joint venture managers could benefit the quality of future research, especially in order to take detailed account of the implication of ownership resources for the range of management activities. Reliance on either Chinese or foreign parent company respondents, as a data source for an overall view, including the scaling of objectives, control and performance of the joint venture, needs to be justified. Because the opinions of any joint venture respondents is constrained by their position, there may be biases derived from the differences between one respondent's and the next's knowledge and experience of setting up the joint venture. The experience of such interviews suggests that some expatriate managers, who lack experience and knowledge of the Chinese way of doing business, but who are granted autonomy by the foreign parent company, may be over-confident about their ability to control the joint venture, and possibly also about its performance. The tendency has been noted in the study for foreigners to respond by giving higher ratings for foreign control of the joint venture, and lower ratings for Chinese control, than do Chinese respondents.

Finally, there is concern associated with the limitation of the development of a logic of ownership resourcing based on the three categories. For example, the logic of the resource dependence perspective implies that a joint venture parent company will exercise more control in those areas that reflect its relative strength in the provision of resources and competencies. The logic in this study has some limitations, because it failed to distinguish the influence areas of joint venture, when both partners started with the same strength in the provision of resource and competence. In another example, an assumption is made that a parent company that contributes critical resourcing such as technology, know-how and management expertise will have more chances to exert control and influence in these corresponding areas. However, this assumption can be challenged on the basis of the fit between the joint venture and the parent company being limited by the institutional setting and government policies.

THE NEED FOR FUTURE RESEARCH

A number of suggestions for future research may be derived from this study. First, it would be valuable to conduct further comparisons of the findings on foreign ownership rationales, since these may vary by nationality. Moreover, different national preferences may be reflected in specific configurations of joint venture investment. It would also be interesting to see if the emerging forms of foreign ownership rationale in Sino-foreign joint ventures that have been identified in this study would apply to investors coming from other economies. The cultural distance between foreign and host country joint venture partners may play an important role in terms of the decisions to invest in the foreign countries. Taking account of cultural match (compare Child *et al.* 1994) would add usefully to insights provided by the existing literature on the relationship between ownership and control. Our understanding of ownership strategies could be complemented by examining national culture as a potential determinant of ownership decisions. New research on the perceptions of differences in national cultures concerning the ownership–control relationship would contribute to theory development and management practice.

Second, it would be worth while to investigate further the configuration of ownership variables themselves, given that the correlations between them are positive, but not high (see Note 1 in Chapter 6). This indicates that there is therefore scope for considerable variation in ownership resourcing configurations. Further investigation is also required into the relationship between the range of ownership resourcing provided and the proportion of equity held by the joint venture partners. This study has not distinguished between the ownership resourcing provided to a joint venture at its formation and subsequent investments by the partners, and whether or not these have led to revisions of equity share. Existing studies of foreign partner ownership decisions have assumed that the preservation of a firm's specific competitive advantage is necessary to avoid or overcome the disadvantage of not possessing local market resources and knowledge. However, this assumption may have its limits in terms of joint venture management over the long term. For joint ventures established in foreign countries, the assumption of a foreign firm's long-term disadvantage may not be valid, as the foreign partner can reduce this through learning. The idea of firm-specific advantage may also be questionable, because joint venture investment could be motivated by enhancement of an advantage. In such cases, where joint ventures are long established in a foreign country, reinvestment of ownership resourcing in terms of its range of equity and contractual and non-contractual resources can be strategically important for enhancing the competitive advantage of the parent companies.

Third, the results from this research indicate that equity and non-contractual (and, to a limited degree, contractual) resourcing have their independent effects on control, which highlights some important questions to consider in future research. It would be important to go into the details of equity composition, especially the value of the contributory elements. The reason is because investment in developing countries such as China is sometimes made 'in kind' – that is, technology, brand name or trademark, and equipment. Local partners tend to contribute their land and existing plant as equity investment. Over- or under-valuation is related to discrepancies between the book value and the real value of assets that investing companies actually bring to a joint venture. Information on equity composition and its values can be used to throw more light on the share of dividend polices, tax structure on capital expenditures, depreciation credits and control over strategic and operational areas of a joint venture.

Fourth, the finding that the provision of ownership resourcing on a non-contractual basis adds significantly to parent company control over a wider range of joint venture management, especially with respect to operational issues, highlights its importance to issues of learning and trust development. The relation between learning, trust and partner control in a joint venture has rarely been studied. It would be particularly interesting to view the partnership from a non-contractual resourcing investment perspective. The non-contractual resources contributed by joint ventures partners indicate how joint ventures achieve better performance through improved knowledge, skills and competence. To both foreign and local partners, a joint venture will bring unique features, which the partners must learn to manage. With regard to learning, partners of a joint venture are usually in the best position to conceptualise their firm's resource and capability. They tend to readjust and modify their strategic and financial objectives to the new investing environment through the transfer of knowledge and experience accumulated from their own past working experience. Non-contractual resourcing also gives rise to goodwill on the part of the other partner, and thus lays a foundation for the development of trust-based cooperative relationships (Kramer and Tyler 1996). Such relationships are crucial for the success of joint ventures (Faulkner 1995), and the role of non-contractual resourcing in fostering them is therefore an issue deserving further research.

With regard to the specific nature of learning and trust-building requirements between joint venture partners, it would be worth while to connect prior interactions and past relationships between partners with present non-contractual ownership resourcing. This is because these may be some of the most important factors impacting upon the relationship between ownership and control of joint ventures. Past association creates a good base of trust and credibility, and it is considered important to get a good feeling of each other before engaging in joint venture partnership. The potential cost of conflict in collaboration can be reduced through building on long-standing relationships that are investments from the past. With regard to non-contractual ownership resources, the important point is that trust tends to develop over time and emerges from working together in the daily running of a business. Non-contractual ownership resourcing appears to reduce transaction costs, and should thus eventually reduce investment in control. It also appears to readjust and modify each partner's objectives to the new investing environment, through the transfer of knowledge and experiences accumulated from its own past. There is a need for more research to understand the process of non-contractual provision via managerial and technical assistance and contacts, and its wider ramifications for inter-partner cooperation. Non-contractual resourcing may be an important basis for the development of inter-partner trust, which in turn reduces transaction costs. The learning that may be promoted by this closer contact between parent companies and the joint ventures adds further insight into the ramifications of the objective ownership–control relationship.

IMPLICATIONS FOR CHINESE AND FOREIGN POLICY

China is a large and diversified economy, which presents a particularly complex investment environment for foreign investing companies. This combines with a strong, traditional, multilayered cultural heritage, different regional identities, and rapid changes that have accompanied modernisation over the years since 1978. Child (1994:285) has described how China's social and political discipline has been maintained throughout the country by a comprehensive system of state and party leadership. The high degree of state control and influence, combined with the significant impacts from FDI, has enabled the authorities to build up its modernisation with 'Chinese characteristics'. This section takes some initial steps towards presenting the implications for policy and practices for both Chinese and foreign parties, which are derived from examining the relationship between ownership and control of Sino-foreign joint ventures.

For the Chinese Side

The Chinese government has shown its consistent interest in encouraging foreign investing companies to provide technology, management expertise and access to export market. With an increasing numbers of joint ventures in China, it should be noted that the government and Chinese joint venture partners have gained more knowledge and experience in dealing with joint ventures. The nature of the government intervention has changed from placing restraints on joint venture boards and top management structures to a more targeted policy of encouraging foreign direct investment in China. The degree of governmental influence is determined by a trade-off between benefits and the costs of developing and protecting Chinese national firms. This can be compared with alternative ways of accessing capital, technology and management expertise through the equity joint venture. The results of this study provide some food for thought to Chinese policy-makers with respect to using the government function as leverage for joint venture management control. Three broad suggestions for policy and management practices can be made for issues relating to the subject of this dissertation.

First, the powers of government can be used to adjust the relationship between ownership and control of joint ventures by setting instructions for locational priorities, industrial priorities and the range of ownership resourcing priorities to ensure Chinese internal control over joint ventures.

Chinese governmental policies, rules and regulations on joint ventures are continually changing to meet the development needs of the country. The need to control FDI with respect to locational and industrial priorities stems from the changes in the social, political and economic environment of China. Joint ventures can help to establish a new relationship between the government and Chinese joint venture partners through the changes in the nature of management resulting from a shift from state-owned enterprise to ventures jointly owned with foreign partners. This does raise some issues for Chinese policy-makers, including the effects of competition from joint ventures on the development of indigenous Chinese industry, domestic industry market share, regional development plan and the percentage of equity share held by the foreign partners in strategic important projects. Once the government is proactive in promoting investment in certain regions and industrial sectors, it is very important to target that investment in the most appropriate way so as to connect the Chinese control derived from the joint venture organisation with Chinese strategic and financial priorities. Selecting target business sectors and locations for joint ventures involves a number of choices: local source availability, good sector candidates and kinds of activities that allow Chinese partners to engage in joint venture management.

The recategorisation of ownership resourcing employed in this research indicates that certain investment conditions set by the government could impact on the opportunities for Chinese influence over joint venture management. Ownership resourcing on a non-contractual basis provided by the partners is gradually changing in nature, from providing local knowledge to dealing with bureaucracy, personal relationships, local distribution, training and local marketing. The Chinese partners can develop their technological and organisational capabilities effectively through the non-contractual resources committed by their partners. The government can use incentives to encourage training in technology and in management, which provides a positive demonstrable effect in facilitating the diffusion of learning, so that it is not held only at the senior manager level, but is also diffused at joint venture staff level. Paradoxically, however, it appears that this training adds to the capacity of the foreign partner to control joint venture operations. There is a need to add a partnership premium, so that Chinese managers and staff share in the non-contractually transferred know-how.

Chinese partners should encourage foreign investing companies to provide technological know-how and professional services on a contractual basis, because contractual ownership resources can be constructed as an effective way to transfer technology, management skills and knowledge between partners. As long as joint ventures operate in technology-led business sectors, Chinese policy decision-makers will have to face a trade-off between introducing advanced technologies and managerial expertise on the one hand and developing a corresponding management system to monitor the technology transferred on the other. Contractual technology packages will play a positive role in avoiding unnecessary competition in certain technological areas. In order to improve joint venture performance, attention should be made to complement foreign resource provision with control. Or, in other words, when foreign investment is protected or safeguarded by foreign control over technology and management standards, joint venture performance appears to benefit.

Second, for internal joint venture management, the most important determinant for designing an effective policy is to gain more autonomy for the local Chinese partner. The problem of ensuring joint venture management control by the Chinese side still remains. Indeed, the trend for multinational partners is to enlarge their equity shares.

More decision-making autonomy should be granted to Chinese joint venture managers. It will assist the development of their capabilities and the opportunities to experience both Chinese and Western management practices. The government should encourage local managers to have equal opportunities to be appointed to the senior positions in joint ventures. The present study has indicated that equity investment from the Chinese side does not give equivalent control and power in comparison with the foreign equity investment. This can be better explained by the appointment to senior positions within the joint ventures and also by the generally inferior quality of non-cash Chinese contributions to equity share. No matter what proportion of equity shares the Chinese partner may hold, the results indicate that the position of general manager is overwhelmingly occupied by expatriates. Also, respondents are normally of the view that the foreign partner exerts the greater influence over a joint venture's management. The senior positions held by Chinese staff tend to be in the areas of personnel, domestic sales, purchasing and deputy general managerships, and in the post of joint venture board chairman. This configuration of top management positions makes it very difficult to represent Chinese interests. For example, once technology and management systems are introduced into a joint venture, the foreign partner usually has considerable influence, both because of the management positions they occupy and because of the technology and competence they own. As Pearson (1991) noted, foreign dominance is inevitable so long as there is a lack of well-trained and competent managers from the Chinese side.

With regard to the higher authorities of the Chinese joint venture management, the local authorities should be granted strong autonomy to develop their regional economies. Local government autonomy over development policies, resourcing, and import and export networking could constitute an important advantage to the local partners of joint ventures. Foreign parent companies tend to have two tiers of foreign management control above their joint venture, namely, regional offices and headquarters. Joint venture managers appeared to have a very clear upward reporting line on the foreign side, but this is less clear on the Chinese side. As a result, some joint ventures have been totally neglected by their Chinese higher authorities. Because production is now entirely separated from the Chinese government planning administration system, strategic interactions between local government and Chinese partners should be strengthened, in order to enhance internal joint venture control on the Chinese side.

Third, when upgrading local content in terms of substituting imported resource components, the government should use incentives and tax mechanisms to control transactional resources supplied by local or foreign investing companies.

Chinese policy-makers should be concerned with the percentage of resource components imported and exported through joint ventures. Emphasising a low percentage of imports and a high percentage of exports for current joint ventures is crucial, because this could enable local business to get involved in the creation of access to international markets, together with the acquisition of more international market information on product pricing. Also, the results suggest that more sourcing from or via the Chinese partner will enhance its control – that is, participation in management in the joint venture.

For the Foreign Side

When managing joint venture operations in China, foreign investing companies must be aware of the traditional characteristics and the transitional nature of China's economy. Significant management barriers in reporting systems, information diffusion, administrative efficiency, status awareness and personalised relationships are still having a great impact on current business activities in China. These barriers stem from traditional management practices, which need to be recognised alongside the great economic system transition in China. Several suggestions for policies and practice, stemming from the present research, are the following.

First, foreign partners should aim to have substantially more than a 50 per cent equity share, while giving priority to a long-term involvement in China, rather than short-term profit.

In view of the historical tendency of Chinese authorities, present and post-1949, to take an active interest in the policy of firms, a substantial foreign equity majority is required to establish rights of control. Even so, however, active involvement via non-contractual resourcing provides a further guarantee of foreign influence over joint venture management, as well an giving attention to appointments to key joint venture management positions. Legal provisions designed to ensure that joint ventures operate according to acceptable rules, regulations and policies are still lacking in China. Therefore, it is all the more important that foreign partners know where they stand in joint ventures, particularly where they may not have the equity share to ensure control. The issue of ownership rights in China can be analysed using a framework derived from Western management thinking. However, it has been noted that in China the concept of ownership rights over property is different in terms of implementation. The local government can legitimately bring its authority to bear on property, if its interests are involved. Second, for internal joint venture management, foreign partners will gain more control and influence in the operational areas in joint ventures via investing more non-contractual ownership resources.

Foreign investing companies should provide technology and management training on a continuing non-contractual basis. This will enable them to exercise more control and influence in the operational areas of joint ventures.

Control of strategic and operational decisions is not necessarily derived from majority equity share. Some control and influence in joint ventures lies in the provision of critical resources and the holding of key management positions.

Most foreign partners dominate the appointment of senior positions in joint ventures, especially the general manager, finance manager and technology manager. The organisational structure of the joint venture and its context of reporting to the joint venture board appear to be organised by the foreign partners to fit with their existing foreign parent organisational structures. Their control and influence will be stronger and more consistent if foreign representatives are assigned to joint ventures from regional offices or headquarters, and job contracts are for more than three years. Controlling the key positions, and keeping expatriate managers in position for a longer period, are ways to ensure foreign control and influence.

Third, the foreign investing company should encourage its horizontal links with the local Chinese institutional system.

The present power structure of the joint venture imposed by the foreign side appears to address only an individual joint venture's internal management system. Long-term interconnections between the representatives of foreign partners from regional offices and headquarters and the Chinese higher authorities will have a positive result for any joint venture's strategic management. Foreign MNEs can use their international standing and prestige to secure influence with the Chinese authorities and can also have an advantage in creating a holding company when running several joint ventures.

It is very important to distinguish the vertical boundary between the Chinese partners and their respective higher authorities. The key point here is to clarify the boundary conditions between the ownership resourcing contributed by the Chinese partner and that partner's underlying power base provided by their higher authorities.

Fourth, working equally with local partners at an operational level is consistent with local Chinese culture and management practice.

Foreign investing companies should use their accumulation of experience as a basis for getting to know the local management, technology system and markets. The organisational structures of a joint venture can be configured in such a way as to build up career development opportunities for the Chinese managers and employees. This will be perceived as having great advantages for the Chinese individuals working in the joint venture.

References

Agarwal, Sanjeev and Sridhar N. Ramaswami 1992. Choice of foreign market entry mode: impact of ownership, location and internalisation factors. *Journal of International Business Studies,* 23: 1–28.

Aiello, P. 1991. Building a joint venture in China: The case of Chrysler and the Beijing Jeep Corporation. *Journal of General Management,* 17: 47–64.

Alderfer, Clayton P. 1972. *Human Needs in Organizational Settings.* New York: Free Press.

Alston, Jon P. 1986. *The American Samurai.* Berlin: De Gruyter.

Anderson, Erin 1990. Two firms, one frontier: on assessing joint venture performance. *Sloan Management Review*, 4, Winter: 19–30.

Anderson, Erin and Barton Weitz 1986. Make or buy decisions: A framework for analysing vertical integration issues in marketing. *Sloan Management Review*, 27: 1–26.

Anderson, Erin & Hubert Gatignon 1986. Modes of foreign entry: A transaction cost analysis and propositions. *Journal of International Business Studies,* 17: 1–26.

Aswicahyono H.H. and Hill Hal 1995. Determinants of foreign ownership in LDC manufacturing: An Indonesian case study. *Journal of International Business Studies,* 26: 139–58.

Barney, Jay 1991. Firm resource and sustained competitive advantage. *Journal of Management,* 17: 99–120.

Bartlett, Christopher A. 1986. Building and managing the Transactional: The new organizational challenge, in M.E. Porter (ed.) *Competition in Global Industries.* Boston Mass: Harvard Business School Press: 367–401.

Beamish, Paul W. 1984. *Joint Venture Performance in Developing Countries.* Unpublished PhD dissertation, University of Western Ontario.

Beamish, Paul W. 1985. The characteristics of joint ventures in developed and developing countries. *Columbia Journal of World Business,* 20: 13–19.

Beamish, Paul W. 1987. Joint venture in LDCs. Partner selection and performance. *Management International Review,* 27: 23–37.

Beamish, Paul W. 1988. *Multinational Joint Ventures in Developing Countries.* London: Routledge.

Beamish, Paul. W. 1993. The characteristics of joint ventures in the People's Republic of China. *Journal of International Marketing,* 1: 29–48.

Beamish, Paul W., J. Peter Killing, Donald J. Lecraw and Allen J. Morrison 1994. *International Management: Text and Cases.* Homewood, Ill: Irwin.

Beamish, Paul W. and Andrew C. Inkpen 1995. Keeping international joint ventures stable and profitable. *Long Range Planning,* 28: 26–36.

Beamish, Paul W. and J.C. Banks 1987. Equity joint ventures and the theory of the multinational enterprise. *Journal of International Business Studies,* 18: 1–16.

Beamish, Paul W. and H.Y. Wang 1989. Investing in China via joint ventures. *Management International Review,* 29: 57–64.

Bergsten, C. Fred, Thomas Horst and Theodore H. Moran 1978. *American Multinationals and American Interests*. Washington, DC: Brookings Institution.
Berle, Adolf A. and Gardiner C. Means, Jr 1932. *The Modern Corporation and Private Property*. New York: Macmillan.
Bjorkman, Ingmar 1995. The board of directors in Sino-Western joint ventures. *Corporate Governance*, 3: 156–66.
Bleeke, Joel and David Ernst (eds) 1993. *Collaborating to Compete: Using Strategic Alliances and Acquisitions in the Global Marketplace*. New York: Wiley.
Blodgett, Linda Longfellow 1991. Partner contributions as predictors of equity share in international joint ventures. *Journal of International Business Studies*, 22: 63–78.
Boisot, Max and John Child 1996. From fiefs to clans and network capitalism: explaining China's emerging economic order. *Administrative Science Quarterly*, 41: 600–28.
Borys, Bryan and David B. and Jemison 1989. Hybrid arrangements as strategic alliances: theoretical issues in organizational combinations. *Academy of Management Review*, 14: 234–49.
Bottomore T.B. and M. Rubel 1956. *Karl Marx: Selected Writings in Sociology and Social Philosophy*. London: Watts.
Brittain, Jack W., and John H. Freeman 1980. Organization proliferation and Density dependent selection in John Kimberly and Robert Miles (eds.) *Organizational Life Cycles:* 291–338. San Francisco: Jossey-Bass.
Bryman, Alan 1989. *Research Methods and Organization Studies*. London: Unwin-Hyman.
Buchel, Bettina, Prange, Christiane, Probst, Gilbert and Ruling, Charless-Clemens (1998) *International Joint Venture Management: Learning to Cooperate and Cooperating to Learn*. Chichester: John Wiley.
Buckley, Peter J. 1983. New theories of international business: some unresolved issues', in M.C. Casson (ed.) *The Growth of International Business*. London: Allen & Unwin pp. 34–50.
Buckley, Peter J. 1985. *The Economic Analysis of the Multinational Enterprise*. London: Macmillan.
Buckley, Peter J. 1988. The limits of explanation: testing the internalisation theory of the multinational enterprise. *Journal of International Business Studies*, 19: 181–93.
Buckley, Peter J. 1990. Problems and developments in the core theory of international business. *Journal of International Business Studies*, 21: 657–65.
Buckley, Peter and Mark Casson 1976. *The Future of the Multinational Enterprise*. New York: Hoimes and Meier.
Buckley, Peter and Mark Casson 1988. A theory of co-operation in intentional business. In Farok J. Contractor and Peter Lorange (eds.) *Co-operative Strategies in International Business*. Lexington Books, Lexington.
Burch, P. H. 1972. *The Managerial Revolution Reassessed*, Lexington, Massachusetts: Lexington Books.
Campbell, Nigel 1986. China Strategies, The Inside Story. Working paper, University of Hong Kong.

Carver, Anne 1996. Open and secret regulations in China and their implication for foreign investment, in John Child and Yuan Lu (eds) *Management Issues in China: International* Enterprises. London: Routledge.

Casson, Mark 1982. Transaction costs and the theory of the multinational enterprises, in A.M. Rugman (ed.) *New Theories of the Multinational Enterprise*. New York: St Martin's Press.

Casson, Mark 1979. *Alternatives to the Multinational Enterprise*. London: Macmillian.

Caves, R.E. 1971. International corporations: The industrial economics of foreign investment. *Economica*, 38: 1–27.

Caves, R.E. 1982. *Multinational Enterprise and Economic Analysis*. Cambridge University Press.

Child, John 1969. *The Business Enterprise in Modern Industrial Society*. London: Collier-Macmillan.

Child, John 1972. Organizational structure, environment and performance – the role of strategic choice. *Sociology*, 6: 1–22.

Child, John 1974. Managerial and organizational factors associated with company performance – Part I. *Journal of Management Studies*, 11: 175–89.

Child, John 1975. Managerial and organizational factors associated with company performance – Part II. A contingency analysis. *Journal of Management Studies*, 12: 12–27.

Child, John 1984. *Organization: A Guide to Problems and Practice*. London: Harper & Row.

Child, John 1994. *Management in China during the Age of Reform*. Cambridge University Press.

Child, John, Max Boisot, Zhaoxi Li, Jill Ireland and Jane Watts 1990. *The Management of Equity Joint Ventures in China*. Beijing: China-EC Management Institute.

Child, John and Lívia Markóczy 1993. Host-country managerial behaviour and learning in Chinese and Hungarian joint ventures. *Journal of Management Studies*, 30: 611–31.

Child, John, Lívia Markóczy and Tony Cheung 1994. Managerial adaptation in Chinese and Hungarian strategic alliances with culturally distinct foreign partners. *Advances in Chinese Industrial Studies*, 4: 211–31.

Child, John and Yuan Lu 1996. Introduction: China and international enterprise, in Child John and Yuan Lu (eds) *Management Issues in China*. London: Routledge

Child, John and Sally Stewart 1997. Regional differences in China and their implications for Sino-foreign joint ventures. *Journal of General Management*, 23: 65–86.

Child, John and David Faulkner 1998. *Strategies of Co-operation*. Oxford: Oxford Univerity Press.

Child, John, Yanni Yan and Yuan Lu 1997. Ownership and control in Sino-foreign joint ventures. in P. Beamish and P. Killing (eds) *Co-operative Strategies: Asia-Pacific Perspective*. New York: New Lexington Press.

China Economic News 1995. The developments of IJVs in Beijing. China Economic Daily Publisher. 25 April, p. 2.

China Statistical Year Book 1997. Beijing: State Statistical Bureau
Collis, David J. 1991. A resource-based analysis of global competition: The case of the bearings industry. *Strategic Management Journal,* 12 (Special Issue): 49–68.
Contractor, Farok J. and Peter Lorange 1988. Why should firms co-operate? The strategy and economics basis for co-operative ventures, in Farok J. Contractor and Peter Lorange (eds) *Co-operative Strategies in International Business Studies.* San Francisco: New Lexington Press.
Contractor, Farok J. 1989a. Contractual and co-operative modes of international business: Towards a unified theory of model choice. Working Paper, Rutgers University.
Contractor, Farok J. 1989b. Inter-firm technology transfers and the theory of multinational enterprise. The *International Trade Journal,* Fall: 1: 21–48.
Contractor, Farok J. 1990. Ownership patterns of US joint ventures abroad and the liberalisation of foreign government regulations in the 1980s: Evidence from the benchmark surveys. *Journal of International Business Studies,* 21: 55–73.
Creswell, John W. 1994. *Research Design Qualitative and Quantitative Approaches*. Thousand Oaks, CA: Sage.
Crozier, M. 1964. *The Bureaucratic Phenomenon.* London: Tavistock.
Cullen, John B., Jean L. Johnson and Tomoaki Sakano 1995. Japanese and local partner commitment to IJVs: Psychological consequences of outcomes and investments in the IJV relationship. *Journal of International Business Studies,* 26: 91–115.
Daniels, J.D., J. Krug and D. Nigh 1985. US joint ventures in China: motivation and management of political risk. *California Management Review*, 27: 46–58.
Davidson W. H. 1982. *Global Strategic Management*. New York: Wiley.
Davidson, W.H. and D.G. McFetridge 1985. Key characteristics in the choice of international technology transfer mode. *Journal of International Business Studies,* 16: 5–21.
Davies, H. 1977. Technology transfer through commercial transactions. *Journal of Industrial Economic,* 26: 161–75.
Demirag, Istemi S. 1988. Assessing foreign subsidiary performance: the currency choice of UK MNCs. *Journal of International Business Studies,* 19: 257–75.
DiMaggio, P.J. and Powell, W.W. 1983. The iron cage revisited: institutional isomorphism and collective rationality in organizational fields. *American Sociological Review,* 48: 147–60.
Donaldson, Lex 1995. *American Anti-Management Theories of Organization: A Critique of Paradigm Proliferation.* Cambridge: Cambridge University Press.
Doyle, Peter 1994. Setting business objectives and measuring performance. *European Management Journal,* 12: 123–32.
Doz, Yves 1986. Government policies and global industries, in M. Porter (ed.) *Competition in Global Industries*: 225–66. Boston: Harvard Business School.
Doz, Yves, Gary Hamel and C.K. Prahalad 1986. Strategic partnerships: Success or surrender? The challenge of competitive collaboration. Working paper, University of Michigan.

Dunning, John H. 1980. Toward an eclectic theory of international production: some empirical tests. *Journal of International Business Studies,* 11: 9–31.

Dunning, John H. 1988a. *Explaining International Production.* London: Unwin-Hyman.

Dunning, John H. 1988b. The eclectic paradigm of international production a restatement and some possible extensions. *Journal of International Business Studies,* 19: 1–31.

Dunning, John H. 1989. The study of international business: a plea for a more interdisciplinary approach. *Journal of International Business Studies,* 20: 411–36.

Dunning, John H. 1993. *The Globalization of Business: The Challenge of the 1990s.* London: Routledge.

Dunning, John H. 1995. Reappaising the eclectic paradigm in an age of alliance capitalism. *Journal of International Business Studies*, 26: 461–91.

Dunning, John H. 1977. Trade, location of economic activity and the multinational enterprise: A search for an eclectic approach, in B. Ohlin. P.O. Hesselborn and P.M. Wikman (eds) *The International Allocation of Economic Activity,* pp. 395–418. London: Macmillan.

Dunning, John H. and Alan M. Rugman 1985. The influence of Hymer's dissertation on the theory of foreign direct investment. *American Economic Review*, 75: 228–32.

Dunning, John H. and M. McQueen 1981. The eclectic theory of international production: A case study of the international hotel industry. *Managerial and Decision Economics.* 2:197–210.

Edstrom, Anders and Jay R. Galbraith, J. 1977. Transfer of managers as a co-ordination and control strategy in multinational organizations. *Administrative Science Quarterly,* 22: 248–63.

Eisenhardt, K.M. 1989. Building theory from case study research. *Academy of Management Review*, 14: 532–50.

Emerson, Richard M. 1962. Power-dependence relations. *American Sociological Review*, 27: 31–41.

Emmanuel, Clive and Otley, David 1985. *Accounting for Management Control.* Wokingham: Van Nostrand Reinhold.

Erramilli, M. Krishna 1996. Nationality and subsidiary ownership patterns in multinational corporations. *Journal of International Business Studies,* 27: 225–48.

Etzioni, Amitai 1960. Two approaches to organizational analysis: a critique and a suggestion. *Administrative Science Quarterly*, 5: 257–78.

Fagre, Nathan and Louis T. Wells 1982. Bargaining power of multinationals and host governments. *Journal of International Business Studies*, 13: 9–23.

Fama, E. F. and M. C. Jensen 1983. Agency problems and residual claims. *Journal of Law and Economics*, 26: 327–49.

Faulkner, David O. 1995. *International Strategic Alliances.* London: McGraw-Hill.

Fayerweather, John 1982. *International Business Strategy and Administration.* Cambridge: Ballinger.

Franko, Lawrence G. 1976. *The European Multinationals.* Stanford, Conn: Greylock.

French Wendell L. and Raven, B. 1959. The Bases of Social Power, in D. Cartwright (ed.) *Studies in Social Power*. Ann Arbor: Institute for Social Research, University of Michigan.

Friedman, Wolfgan G. and Beguin, Jean-Pierre 1971. *Joint International Business Ventures in Developing Countries.* New York: Columbia University Press.

Gatignon, H. and E. Anderson 1988. The multinational corporation's degree of control over subsidiaries: An empirical test of a transaction cost exploitation. *Journal of Law, Economics, and Organization,* 4: 305–36.

Geringer, J. Michael 1988. *Joint Venture Partner Selection: Strategies for Developed Countries*. Westport, Conn.: Quorum .

Geringer J. Michael 1991. Strategic determinants of partner selection criteria in international joint ventures. *Journal of International Business Studies,* 22: 41–62.

Geringer, J. Michael and Louis Hébert 1989. Control and performance of international joint ventures. *Journal of International Business Studies,* 20: 235–54.

Geringer J. Michael and Louis Hébert 1991. Measuring Performance of International Joint Ventures. *Journal of International Business Studies,* 22: 249–64.

Ghoshal, Sumantra 1987. Global strategy: an organising framework. *Strategic Management Journal,* 8: 425–40.

Ghoshal, Sumantra and Christopher A. Bartlett 1990. The multinational corporation as an inter-organizational network. *Academy of Management Review,* 15: 603–25.

Glaister, Keith W. and Peter Buckley 1994. Measures of performance and success factors in UK international joint ventures, unpublished paper.

Glaister, Keith W. 1995. Dimensions of control in UK international joint ventures. *British Journal of Management,* 6: 77–96.

Gomes-Casseres, Benjamin 1987. Joint venture instability: Is it a problem? *Columbia Journal of World Business*, 22: 97–102.

Gomes-Casseres, Benjamin 1989a. Ownership structure of foreign subsidiaries. *Journal of Economic Behaviour and Organization,* 11: 1–25.

Gomes-Casseres, Benjamin 1989b. Joint ventures in the face of global competition. *Sloan Management Review,* 3: 17–26.

Gomes-Casseres, Benjamin 1990. Firm ownership preferences and host government restrictions: An integrated approach. *Journal of International Business Studies,* 21: 1–22.

Gullander, Staffan 1976. Joint ventures and corporate strategy. *Columbia Journal of World Business*, 11: 104–14.

Guo, Aimin and Robert Ackroyd 1996. Overcoming barriers to technological transfers into China, in John Child and Yuan Lu (eds) *Management Issues in China: International Enterprises.* London: Routledge.

Hage, Jerald and Michael Aiken 1967. Relationship of centralisation to other structural properties. *Administrative Science Quarterly,* 12: 72–92.

Hall, Wendy and Jan D. Eppink 1992. Strategic alliances in the airline industry. *Journal of Strategic Change*, 1: 341–48.

Hamel, Gary 1991. Competition for competence and inter-partner learning within international strategic alliances. *Strategic Management Journal,* 12: 83–103.

Hamel, Gary, Yves Doz and C.K. Prahalad 1989. Collaborate with your competitors and win. *Harvard Business Review,* 5: 567–75.
Harrigan, Kathryn R. 1984. Joint ventures and global strategies. *Columbia Journal of World Business,* 19: 7–15.
Harrigan, Kathryn R. 1985. *Strategies for Joint Venture Success.* Lexington, Mass.: Lexington Books.
Harrigan, Kathryn R. 1986. Matching vertical integration strategies to competitive conditions. *Strategic Management Journal,* l9: 141–58.
Harrigan, Kathryn R. 1987. Joint ventures: A mechanism for creating strategic change, in Andrew Pettigrew (ed.) *The Management of Strategic Change.* Oxford: Blackwell.
Harrigan, Kathryn R. 1988. Joint Ventures and Competitive Strategies. *Strategic Management Journal,* 9: 141–58.
Hennart, Jean-François 1982. *A Theory of Multinational Enterprise.* Ann Arbor: University of Michigan.
Hennart, Jean-François 1988. A transaction costs theory of equity joint ventures. *Strategic Management Journal,* 9: 361–74.
Hennart, Jean-François 1989. Can the 'new forms of investment' substitute for the 'old forms'? A transaction costs perspective, *Journal of International Business Studies,* 20: 211–34.
Hennart, Jean-François 1991. The transaction costs theory of joint ventures: An empirical study of Japanese subsidiaries in the United States, *Management Science,* 37: 483–97.
Hickson, D.J., C. R. Hinings, C.A. Lee, R.E. Schneck and J. M. Pennings 1971. A strategic contingencies' theory of intraorganizational power. *Administrative Science Quarterly*, 16: 216–29.
Hickson, David J. and Derek S. Pugh 1995. *Management Worldwide: The Impact of Societal Culture on Organizations around the Globe.* London: Penguin.
Hill, Robert C. and Don Hellriegel 1994. Critical contingencies in joint venture management: some lessons from managers. *Organization Science,* 5: 594–607.
Hofstede, Geert 1991. *Cultures and Organizations: Software of the Mind.* London: McGraw-Hill.
Holt, David H 1998. *International Management: Text and Cases.* New York: Dryden Press: Harcourt Brace College Publishers.
Hwang P. 1988. *Multinationals' Strategic Choice of Institutional Mode: A Decision Model for Market Entry.* Unpublished PhD dissertation, Michigan State University.
Hymer, Stephen H. 1960. *The International Operations of National Firms: A Study of Direct Foreign Investment.* Unpublished PhD Dissertation, MIT.
Hymer, Stephen H. 1976. *The International Operations of National Firms: A Study of Direct Foreign Investment*. Cambridge, Mass.: MIT Press.
Itaki, Masahiko 1991. A critical assessment of the eclectic theory of the multinational enterprise. *Journal of International Business Studies,* 22: 445–58.
Janger, A. R. 1980. *Organization of International Joint Ventures*. New York: The Conference Board.

Jensen, M.C. and W.H. Meckling 1976. Theory of the firm: managerial behaviour, agency costs, and ownership structure. *Journal of Financial Economics,* 3: 305–360.

Johanson, H. 1970. The efficiency and welfare implications of the international corporation, in C.P. Kindleberger (ed.) *The International Corporation* Cambridge: Mass.: MIT Press.

Kerlinger, F. N. 1979. *Behavioral Research: A Conceptual Approach.* New York: Holt, Rinehart & Winston.

Kilduff, Martin 1992. Performance and interaction routines in multinational corporations. *Journal of International Business Studies,* 23: 133–45.

Killing, J. Peter 1982. How to make a global joint venture work. *Harvard Business Review:* 120–27.

Killing, J. Peter 1983. *Strategies for Joint Venture Success.* New York: Praeger.

Kim, W.C. and P. Hwang 1992. Global strategy and multinationals' entry mode choice. *Journal of International Business Studies,* 23: 29–53.

Kobrin, Stephen J. 1982. Global strategy and multinational's entry mode choice. *Journal of International Business Studies,* 13: 29–53.

Kogut, Bruce 1988. Joint ventures. Theoretical and empirical perspectives, *Strategic Management Journal*, 9: 319–32.

Kogut, Bruce and Harbir Singh 1988. Entering the United States by joint ventures: Competitive rivalry and industry structure, in Farok J. Contractor and Peter Lorange (eds) *Co-operative Strategies in International Business.* San Francisco: New Lexington Press.

Kogut, Bruce and Udo Zander 1993. Knowledge of the firm and the evolutionary theory of the multinational corporation. *Journal of International Business Studies,* 24: 625–45.

Kramer, Roderick M. and Tom R. Tyler (eds) 1996. *Trust in Organizations.* Thousand Oaks, Calif.: Sage.

Larner, Robert J. 1970. *Management Control and the Large Corporation.* New York: Dunellen.

Lecraw, Donald J. 1984. Bargaining power, ownership, and profitability of transactional corporations in developing countries. *Journal of International Business Studies,* 15: 27–43.

Lee Cho and Paul W. Beamish 1995. The characteristics and performance of Korean joint ventures in LDCs. *Journal of International Business Studies,* 26: 637–654.

Li Jiatao and Oded Shenkar 1996. In search of complementary assets: co-operative strategies and knowledge seeking by prospective Chinese partners, in John Child and Yuan Lu (eds) *Management issues in China: International Enterprises.* London: Routledge.

Lin, Damming 1996a. Hong Kong's China-invested companies and their reverse investment in China, in John Child and Yuan Lu (eds) *Management issues in China: International Enterprises.* London: Routledge.

Lin, Damming 1996b. *Sino-Hong Kong Joint Ventures: Strategies, Structure and Performance.* Unpublished PhD dissertation, University of Hong Kong.

Lincoln, James R., Jon Olson and Mitsuyo Hanada 1978. Cultural effects on organizational structure: the case of Japanese firms in the United States. *American Sociological Review*, 43: 829–43.

Liu Guoguang 1986. Changes in ownership forms: problems and possibilities, *Beijing Review,* 12 May: 17–22.

Locke, Edwin A. 1968. Toward a theory of task motivation and incentives. *Organizational Behaviour and Human Performance,* 3: 157–89.

Lorange, Peter and Johan Roos 1992. *Strategic Alliances: Formation, Implementation, and Evolution.* Oxford: Blackwell.

Louis Putterman 1996. The role of ownership and property rights in China's economic transition. In Andrew G. Walder (ed.) *China's Transnational Economy*. Oxford: Oxford University Press.

Lu Yuan and David Lake 1997. Managing international joint ventures: An institutional approach, in Paul Beamish and Peter Killing (eds) *Co-operative Strategies: European Perspectives.* New York: New Lexington Press.

Lyles, Marjorie A. and Rhonda K. Reger 1993. Managing for autonomy in joint ventures: A longitudinal study of upward influence. *Journal of Management Studies,* 30: 383–404.

Macintosh, Norman B. 1994. *Management Accounting and Control Systems: An Organizational and Behavioural Approach*. Chichester: Wiley.

Madhok, Anoop 1995. Revisiting multinational firms' tolerance for joint ventures: A trust-based approach. *Journal of International Business Studies,* 26: 117–37.

March, James G. and Johan P. Olsen 1976. *Ambiguity and Choice in Organizations*. Bergen, Norway: Universitetsforlaget.

Marris, Robin L. 1964. *The Economic Theory of 'Managerial' Capitalism.* London: Macmillan.

Mariti, P. and R.H. Smiley 1983. Co-operative agreements and the organization of industry. *The Journal of Industrial Economics,* XXX1: 437–51.

Maslow, A.H. 1943. A theory of human motivation, *Psychological Review*, 50: 370–96.

Meier, Johnnes, Javier Perez, and Jonathan R. Woetzel 1996. Solving the puzzle: MNC's in China. *The McKinsey Quarterly,* 2: 20–33.

Milliman, John, Mary Ann Von Glinow and Maria Nathan 1991. Organizational life cycles and strategic international human resource in multinational companies: Implications for congruence theory. *Academy of Management Review,* 16: 318–39.

Mintzberg, Henry 1983. *Power in and Around Organizations*. Englewood Cliffs, NJ: Prentice-Hall.

Monks, Robert A.G. and Nell Minow, 1995. *Corporate Governance.* Oxford: Blackwell.

Morrison, Allen J. 1994. Kentucky Fried Chicken in China, in Paul W. Beamish, Peter J. Killing, Donald J. Lecraw and Allen J. Morrison, *International Management: Text and Cases.* Homewood, Ill.: Irwin.

Murray, Janet Y., Masaaki Kotabe and Albert R. Wildt 1995. Strategic and financial performance implications of global sourcing strategy: A contingency analysis. *Journal of International Business Studies*, 26: 181–202.

Newman, William H. 1992. Launching a viable joint venture, *California Management Review,* 34: 68–79.

Nonaka Ikujro and Hirotake Takeuchi 1995. *The Knowledge-Creating Company.* New York: Oxford University Press.

Nolan, Peter 1995. Joint ventures and economic reform in China: A case study of the Coca-Cola business system, with particular reference to the Tianjin Coca-Cola plant, ESRC Centre for Business Research, University of Cambridge, Working paper no. 24, December.

Nohria, Nitin and Robert G. Eccles (eds) 1992. *Networks and Organizations – Structures, Form, and Action.* Boston, Mass.: Harvard Business School Press.

Ohmae, Kenichi 1993. The global logic of strategic alliances, in Joel Bleeke and David Ernst (eds) *Collaborating to Compete: Using Strategic Alliances and Acquisitions in the Global Marketplace.* New York: Wiley.

Osborn, R.N. and C.C. Baughn 1990. Forms of Inter-organizational governance for multinational alliances. *Academy of Management Journal,* 33: 503–19.

Osland, Gregory E. and S. Tamer Cavusgil 1996. Performance issues in US–China joint ventures. *California Management Review,* 38: 106–30.

Otterbeck, L. 1981. The management of joint ventures, in L. Otterbeck (ed.) *The Management of Headquarters Subsidiary Relationships in Multinational Corporations.* Aldershot: Gower.

Ouchi, William G. 1979. A Conceptual framework for the design of organizational control mechanisms. *Management Science,* 25: 833–49.

Ouchi, William G. 1977. The relationship between organizational structure and organizational control. *Administrative Science Quarterly,* 22: 92–112.

Pang, Yigan 1996. Influences on foreign equity ownership level in joint ventures in China. *Journal of International Business Studies,* 27: 1–25.

Parkhe, Arvind 1991. Interfirm diversity, organizational learning, and longevity in global strategic alliances. *Journal of International Business Studies,* 22: 579–601.

Parkhe, A. 1993. 'Messy' research, methodological predispositions, and theory development in international joint ventures. *Academy of Management Review,* 18: 227–68.

Pearson, Margaret M. 1991. *Joint Ventures in the People's Republic of China: The Control of Foreign Direct Investment under Socialism.* Princeton University Press.

Pfeffer, Jeffrey 1977. The ambiguity of leadership. *Academy of Management Review,* 2: 104–12.

Pfeffer, Jeffrey 1981a. *Power in Organization.* Marshfield, Mass.: Pitman.

Pfeffer, Jeffrey 1981b. *Organizations and Organization Theory.* Marshfield, Mass.: Pitman.

Pfeffer, Jeffrey and Philip Nowak 1976. Joint ventures and inter-organizational interdependence. *Administrative Science Quarterly,* 21: 398–418.

Pfeffer, Jeffrey and Gerald R. Salancik 1978. *The External Control of Organizations: A Resource Dependence Perspective.* New York: Harper & Row.

Pierce, Jon L., Stephen A. Rubenfeld and Susan Morgan 1991. Employee ownership: A conceptual model of process and effects. *Academy of Management Review,* 16: 121–44.

Porter, Michael E. 1980. *Competitive Strategy: Techniques for Analysing Industries and Competitors.* New York: Free Press.

Porter, Michael E. (ed.) 1986. *Competition in Global Industries*. Boston, Mass.: Harvard Business School Press.
Porter, M.E. and M.B. Fuller 1986. Coalitions and global strategy, in Michael E. Porter (ed.) *Competition in Global Industries*. Boston, Mass.: Harvard Business School Press, pp. 155–85.
Potter, Pitman B. 1995. Foreign investment law in the People's Republic of China: dilemmas of state control. *The China Quarterly*, no. 141: 155–85.
Poynter, T.A. 1982. Government intervention in less developed countries: The experience of the multinational companies. *Journal of International Business Studies*, 13: 9–25.
Prahalad, C.K. and Richard A. Bettis 1986. The dominant logic: A new linkage between diversity and performance. *Strategic Management Journal*, 7: 485–501.
Prahalad, C.K. and Gary Hamel 1990. The core competence of the corporation. *Harvard Business Review*, 68: 79–91.
Reichers, A.E. 1985. A review and re-conceptualisation of organizational commitment. *Academy of Management Review*, 10: 465–476.
Renner, K. 1904. *The Institutions of Private Law and their Social Function.* London: Routledge & Kegan Paul, 1949. A translation of the 1928 revised edition.
Reynolds, John I. 1984. The 'pinched shoe' effect of international joint ventures. *Columbia Journal of World Business*, 19: 23–29.
Robinson, R. 1969. Ownership across national frontiers. *Industrial Management Review*, 1: 41–65.
Root, Ferdinand R. 1988. Some taxonomies of co-operative arrangements in Farok J. Contractor and Peter Lorange (eds) *Co-operative Strategies in International Business*, Lexington, Mass.: Heath.
Rugman, Alan M. 1980. Internalisation as a General Theory of Foreign Direct Investment: A Reappraisal of the Literature. *Weltwirtschaftliches Archiv*, 116: 365–79.
Rugman, Alan M. 1981. *Inside the multinationals: The Economics of Internal Markets*. London: Croom Helm.
Rugman, Alan M. 1982. Internalisation and non-equity forms of international involvement, in Alan M. Rugman (ed) *New Theories of the Multinational Enterprise*. New York: St Martin's Press.
Rugman, Alan M. and Verbeke, Alain 1992. A note on the transactional solution and the transaction cost theory of multinational strategic management. *Journal of International Business Studies*, 23: 761–71.
Salancik, Gerald R. and Jeffrey Pfeffer 1977. Who gets power – and how they hold on to it: A strategic contingency model of power. *Organizational Dynamics*, 5: 3–21.
Schaan, Jean-Louis and Paul W. Beamish, 1988. Joint venture general managers in LDCs. In Farok J. Contractor and Peter Lorange (eds.) *Co-operative Strategies in International Business*, Lexington, Mass.: Health.
Schaan, Jean-Louis 1988. How to control a joint venture even as a minority partner. *Journal of General Management*, 14: 4–16.
Schaan, Jean-Louis 1983. *Parent Control and Joint Venture Success: The Case of Mexico*. Unpublished doctoral dissertation, University of Western Ontario.

Schneider, Susan C. 1988. National vs. corporate culture: implications for human resource management. *Human Resource Management,* 27: 231–46.

Schroath, Frederick W., Michael Y. Hu and Haiyan Chen 1993. Country of origin effects of foreign investments in the People's Republic of China. *Journal of International Business Studies,* 24: 277–90.

Scott, George M. 1973. An introduction to financial controls and reporting in multinational enterprises, *Studies in International Business*, University of Texas at Austin, Bureau of Business Research, Graduate School of Business. 1 August.

Scott, John 1979. *Corporations, Classes and Capitalism*. London: Hutchinson.

Scott, John 1985. Theoretical framework and research design, in Frans N. Stokman, Rolf Ziegler and John Scott (eds.) *Networks of Corporate Power,* Cambridge: Polity.

Scott, John and Michael Hughes 1976. Ownership and control in a satellite economy: A discussion from Scottish data, *Sociology,* 10: 21–41.

Seashore, Stanley and Yuchtman, Ephraim 1967. Factorial analysis of organizational performance. *Administrative Science Quarterly,* 12: 377–95.

Shapiro, Alan C. 1982. *Multinational Financial Management*. Newton, Mass.: Allyn & Bacon.

Shenkar, Oded 1990. International joint ventures' problems in China: Risks and remedies. *Long Range Planning,* 23: 82–90.

Shenkar, Oded and Yoram Zeira 1992. Role conflict and role ambiguity of chief executive officers in international joint ventures. *Journal of International Business Studies*, 23: 55–75.

Stopford, John M. and Louis T. Wells 1972. *Managing the Multinational Enterprise*. New York: Basic Books.

Teece, David 1976. *The Multinational Corporation and the Resource Cost of International Technology Transfer.* Cambridge, Mass.: Ballinger.

Teece, David 1986. Transaction cost economics and the multinational enterprise. *Journal of Economic Behaviour and Organizations,* 7: 21–45.

Teece, David 1992. Competition, co-operation and innovation. *Journal of Economic Behaviour and Organization,* 3: 1–25.

Teagarden Mary B. 1990. *Sino-U.S. Joint Venture Effectiveness.* Unpublished doctoral dissertation, University of Southern California, Los Angeles.

Thorelli, Hans B. 1986. Networks: Between markets and hierarchies. *Strategic Management Journal,* 7: 37–51.

Ting, Wen Lee 1988. *Multinational Risk Assessment and Management.* New York: Quorum.

Tomlinson, James W.C. 1970. *The Joint Venture Process in International Business: India and Pakistan.* Cambridge, Mass.: MIT Press.

Trompenaars, Fons 1993. *Riding the Waves of Culture*. London: Economist Books.

UNCTAD (United Nations Conference on Trade and Investment) 1997. World Investment Report 1997. New York: United Nations.

Vachani, Sushil 1995. Enhancing the obsolescing bargain theory: a longitudinal study of foreign ownership of US and European multinationals. *Journal of International Business Studies,* 26: 159–80.

Vanhonacker, W. (1997) 'Enterprising China: An Unconventional Approach', *Harvard Business Review*, Vol. 75, No. 2 pp. 130–140.
Vasconcellos e Sa, Jorge A. Sousa de. 1988. The impact of key success factors on company performance. *Long Range Planning*, 21: 56–64.
Vernon, Raymond and Louis T. Wells 1991. *The Manager in the International Economy*. Englewood Cliffs, NJ: Prentice-Hall.
Vernon, Raymond 1971. *Sovereignty at Bay*. New York: Basic Books.
Vernon, Raymond 1977. *Storm over the Multinationals: The Real Issues*. Cambridge, Mass.: Harvard University Press.
Vernon, Raymond 1983. Organization and institutional responses to international risk, in Richard Herring (ed.) *Managing International Risk*. New York: Cambridge University Press.
Vroom, Victor H. 1964. *Work and Motivation*. New York: Wiley.
Warner, Malcolm. 1986. Managing human resources in China. *Organization Studies*, 7: 353–66.
Warner, Malcolm 1993. Human resources management with Chinese characteristics. *The International Journal of Human Resource Management*, 4: 45–65.
Warner, Malcolm 1996a. Chinese enterprise reform, human resources and the 1994 Labour Law. *The International Journal of Human Resource Management*, 7: 779–96.
Warner, Malcolm 1996b. *Joint ventures vs. State-owned enterprises: management and human resources in China*, Research Papers in Management Studies 1996/9, University of Cambridge.
Weber, Max 1947. *The Theory of Social and Economic Organization*. Glencoe, Ill.: Free Press.
Wei, Liming 1994. Foreign investment priorities announced, *Beijing Review*. April, 18–24: 28–9.
Williamson, Oliver E. 1975. *Markets and Hierarchies*. New York: the Free Press.
Williamson, Oliver E. 1979. Transaction cost economies: The governance of contractual relations, *Journal of Law and Economics*, 22: 233–62.
Williamson, Oliver E. 1985. *The Economic Institutions of Capitalism*. New York: the Free Press.
Woodcock, Patrick C., Paul W. Beamish and Shige Makino 1994. Ownership-based entry modes strategies and international performance, *Journal of International Business Studies*, 25: 253–73.
Wright, Richard W. and Colin S. Russels 1975. Joint ventures in developing countries: Realities and responses, *Columbia Journal of World Business*, 10: 74–80.
Yan, Aimin 1993. *Bargaining Power, Management Control, and Performance in International Joint Ventures: Development and Test of a Negotiations Model*, unpublished doctoral dissertation, Pennsylvania State University.
Yan, Aimin and Barbara Gray 1994a. Bargaining power, management control, and performance in United Stated China joint ventures: A comparative case study, *Academy of Management Journal*, 37: 1478–1517.
Yan, Aimin and Barbara Gray 1994b. An empirical investigation of a negotiations model in American–Chinese joint ventures, paper given to the

Conference on Management Issues for China in the 1990s, St John's College, Cambridge, March.

Yan, Aimin and Barbara Gray 1996. Linking management control and interpartner relationships with performance in US-Chinese joint ventures, in John Child and Yuan Lu (eds) *Management Issues in China: International Enterprises.* London: Routledge.

Yan, Yanni 1994. *Ownership and Control in International Joint Ventures*, first-year report, Doctoral Programme, Judge Institute of Management Studies, University of Cambridge.

Yan, Yanni 1997. The effect of ownership on the performance in Sino-foreign joint ventures, *Advances in Chinese Industrial Studies,* 5: 219–47 Greenwich, Conn.: JAI Press.

Yan, Yanni, John Child and Lu Yuan 1995. Ownership and control in international business: An examination of Sino-foreign international joint ventures, Paper given to the Academy of Management Annual Meeting, Vancouver.

Yin, R.K. 1994. *Case Study Research: Design and Methods.* Beverly Hills, Calif.: Sage.

Zeitlin, M. 1974. Corporate ownership and control: the large corporation and the capitalist class, *American Journal of Sociology*, 79: 1073–119.

Zhou Wai Touzi Zazhi (Chinese Version) 1997. The Development of Equity Joint Ventures in China, *China-Foreign Investment Journal*, 8: 12.

Zhou, Xin. 1996. China's national economy grows well, *Beijing Review.* December 2–8: 21.

Zurawicki, Leon 1975. The co-operation of the socialist state with the MNCs, *Columbia Journal of World Business,* 10: 109–15.

Appendix I: A Summary of Managers Interviewed

	Chinese managers			*Foreign managers*		
Case	*GM*	*DGM*	*Functional managers*	*GM*	*DGM*	*Functional managers*
1			2	1		
2			2		1	
3			3	1		
4			2		1	2
5		1	2			1
6	1		2		1	1
7			2	1		
8		1	2			1
9		1	1			
10		1	2			1
11			2	1		
12				1		
13	1		2		1	1
14		1	1			1
15	1		2			
16	1		2			
17			2	1		
18		1	3			1
19			3	1		1
20	1		2			
21			2	1		
22			1	1		
23			1	1		1
24			2	1		
25		1	1			
26		1	2			1
27			1	1		
28			1	1		
29	1	1	2	1		
30			3	1	1	
31	1		1			
32			2	1		
33			2	1		1
34			2	1		

Case	Chinese managers GM	Chinese managers DGM	Chinese managers Functional managers	Foreign managers GM	Foreign managers DGM	Foreign managers Functional managers
35			2	1		2
36			1	1		
37			1	1		
38		1	2			1
39		1	1			1
40			2	1		1
41	1	2	1			
42	1		2			
43	1		2			
44		1	1			1
45	1		1		1	
46			1		1	
47			2	1		
48			1			1
49		1	1			
50		1	1			
51	1					
52		1	1			1
53			2			1
54	1	1	1			1
55			2	1		1
56	1		1	1		
57		1		1		1
58			3	1		1
59		1	1			1
60			1	1		
61			1		1	1
62		1	1			1
63			1		1	
64	1		2			
65	1		2	1		1
66			1		1	
67	1		1	1	1	1

Appendix II: Distribution by Sector and Nationality of Foreign Partner

	USA/UK	Continental European	Japanese	Overseas Chinese
Electronics 33	8	9	8	8
Fast-moving consumer goods 34	9	8	8	9

Appendix III: Interview Checklist for Joint Ventures in China

Name of joint venture

Name of interviewee:

Position of interviewee

Does the interviewee belong to the JV/affiliate board of directors?

Who formally employs the interviewee? (JV/affiliate, or a parent company?)

Nationality and ethnic background of interviewee:

[If foreigner] Number of years the interviewee has lived in China

Number of years interviewee has worked for the JV/affiliate:

Employment (position, company) of interviewee before joining the JV/affiliate:

Gender of interviewee:

Name of interviewer(s):

Date of interview:

Duration of interview:

Was the interview tape-recorded?

Language interview was conducted in:

1. Formation process

1.1 At what dates did each partner first search for a Sino-foreign alliance of any kind?
  # Chinese partner(s):
  # Foreign partner(s):

1.2 How were the partners brought into contact with each other?

1.3 Did the parent companies have alternative potential partners?

1.4 What were the issues on which it was most difficult to get agreement during the negotiation?

1.5 Did any of the owning companies have international venturing experience before they established this venture? If so, please tick the relevant type of experience.

Foreign partner –
Previous experience of:

(1) Joint ventures
(2) Technology collaboration
(3) Acquisition of foreign company
(4) International trading
(5) Investment in China
(6) Please specify any other international experience

Chinese partner –
Previous experience of:

(1) Joint ventures
(2) Technology collaboration
(3) Acquisition of foreign company
(4) International trading
(5) Investment outside China
(6) Please specify any other international experience

2. Ownership inputs

2.1 Total capital invested in this international venture by owning companies:

Registered capital

2.2 Owning companies which have an equity holding in this international venture:
Names of owning companies (Please note if part of a larger group) Nationality

2.3 Percentage equity share of registered capital held by each owning company in this international venture. Please mention in the same order as in Question 2.1.

	At formation	*Now*
Owning company 1		
Owning company 2		

2.4 Have the following items been valued as part of Chinese and foreign parents' contribution to equity? (If 'yes', record the value given)

Item	*Chinese parent*	*Foreign parent*
Capital		
Product design		
Production technology		
Land		
Existing plant, equipment and facilities		

Item	*Chinese parent*	*Foreign parent*
New plant, equipment & facilities		
Brand names/trade marks		
Goodwill		
Marketing support/distribution		
Others (please specify)		

2.5 *Contracted resources*

Please specify any inputs/resources which the parent companies have a contract to provide the JV/affiliate, in addition to their equity contributions.

Input	*Description*	*Which parent company provided?*
Management System		
Product design		
Production technology		
Professional services		
Training		
Other		

2.6 *Non-contracted Inputs/Resources*

Please specify any other inputs/resources which the parent companies have provided to the JV/affiliate on a non-contractual basis.

Input	*Description*	*Which parent company provided?*
Management systems		
Product design		
Production technology		
Professional services		
Technical know-how		
Training		
Other		

2.7 Date contract signed
2.8 Date that funds were first committed:
2.9 Were funds committed in one payment or in several tranches?
2.10 (If funds committed in tranches) Did the payment of any tranche cause problems to any of the partners?
2.11 If it did cause problems, what were the consequences? (E.g. realloca- tion of the equity, renegotiation of the contract regarding composition of the Board, rights to control, etc.)

2.12 Length of contract (years):
2.13 Does the JV/affiliate have its own legal identity? [If a contractual JV or wholly-owned subsidiary]
2.14 General comments on ownership:

3. Operational profile of the joint venture/affiliate

3.1 Date operations started: .... (month) .... (year)
3.2 Please mention the main products and services of the joint venture/affiliate:
3.3 Please tick one or more of the statements which most closely describe the operating facilities used by the joint venture/ affiliate:

- ☐ New facilities constructed on a new site.
- ☐ New facilities constructed on a site already used by one of the participating companies.
- ☐ Existing facilities previously used by one of the participating companies.

3.4 On which sites does the joint venture/affiliate operate?
3.5 Does the joint venture/affiliate have its own product and process development? If yes, please describe briefly:
3.6 Does the joint venture/affiliate itself commission or carry out any basic research? If yes, please describe.
3.7 Please indicate the names and nationalities of the suppliers of the following key operational items:

Item	*Brief description*	*Name of the supplier*	*Nationality of the supplier*
(1)	Key production technology		
(2)	Key product technology		
(3)	Professional services		

3.8 What percentage of inputs (i.e. materials and semifinished products) are actually supplied
(a) by foreign owners: .... (%) (b) by local owners: .... (%)
Percentage of inputs (i.e. materials and semifinished products) that are actually supplied by value:
Is there a contract specifying these percentages?
If yes, are the actual percentages the same as those contracted?
3.9 What percentage of outputs(end-products) actually go
(a) to foreign owners: .... (%) (b) to local owners: .... (%)
Is there a contract specifying these percentages?
If yes, are the actual percentages the same as those contracted?
3.10 Does the joint venture/affiliate produce any products that are not identical to those of the parent companies?

3.11 Operational trend of this joint venture/affiliate (last five years if applicable):

	1992	*1993*	*1994*	*1995*
Total employees				
No. of foreign staff working full time for this venture				
Sales turnover				
Proportion of sales exported by value (%)				
Proportion of inputs supplied within China (localisation %)				
Operational profit before tax (US$)				

4. Top management structure

4.1 Please complete the following profile for the managers in charge of each of the areas listed

Area	*Manager's nationality*	*Who manager reports to*	*Manager recruited from (please name owning company or state; 'E' if externally recruited)*
1. General manager (or CEO)			
2. Deputy general manager			

Area	*Manager's nationality*	*Who manager reports to*	*Manager recruited from (please name owning company or state; 'E' if externally recruited)*
3. Marketing			
4. R&D/technical			
5. Finance			
6. Production			
7. Quality control			
8. Personnel			
9. International sales			

4.2 Board of directors (check whether the company has a separate legal identity – see Q 2.10).
Please indicate board membership:

When the venture was created

(a) *Position*	(b) *Nationality*	(c) *Nominated by*	(d) *Length of appointment*

At the present time

(a) *Position*	(b) *Nationality*	(c) *Nominated by*	(d) *Length of appointment*

4.3 How frequently does the board meet?

4.4 Are there any advisers or consultants to the board or to the senior management? If yes, please indicate (a) their nationalities and (b) main areas they advise on:

	(a) *Nationality*	(b) *Main areas of advice*
Adviser 1		

4.5 Please enclose a chart of the senior management structure, if available.

5. Achievement of strategic objectives

5.1 Please choose and place in order of importance a maximum of five items from the set of cards that you think best describe the strategic benefits which *the major foreign and Chinese parent companies* sought from the JV/affiliate,
(1) when it was formed and (2) at the present time. *(Separate card for each item)*

FOREIGN PARENT

	Priority of goals (1) at formation	*Achievement rating (Q. 5.1) (2) now*
1. Gain strategic position in China *vis-à-vis* competitors		
2. Attraction of Chinese market		
3. Low-cost sourcing		
4. Benefit from advantageous transfer pricing		
5. Low labour cost		
6. Opportunity for quick profit		
7. Benefit from tax incentives		
8. Opportunity for good long-term profit		
9. Facilitate international expansion		
10. Learning how to do business in China		

	Priority of goals (1) at formation	*Achievement rating (Q. 5.1) (2) now*
11. Establish strong business presence/ credibility in China		
12. Diversification of products and services		
13. Other		

5.2 CHINESE PARENT

	Priority of goals (1) at formation	*Achievement rating (Q.5.1) (2) now*
1. Technology transfer		
2. Obtain foreign cash investment		
3. Benefit from tax incentives		
4. Develop export opportunities/ learning how to export		
5. Opportunity for quick profit		
6. Foreign exchange generation		
7. Gain strategic position *vis-à-vis* competitors		
8. Opportunity for good long-term profit		
9. Establish strong business presence/credibility in China		
10. Import substitution		
11. Employment creation		
12. Help expand in Chinese market		
13. Learning management expertise		
14. Help upgrade Chinese suppliers' technology		
15. Assist diversification of products and services		
16. Ability to import superior goods and components		
17. Opportunity to train Chinese staff		
18. Others		

5.3 How far do you think each of the strategic benefits you identified, both 'at formation' and 'at the present time', has been achieved? Please use the scale on the card to indicate your assessment. *(Show card with scale ranging from 1 = 'not achieved at all' to 5 = 'fully achieved'.)*

5.4 Please use the 5 point scale to indicate the extent to which you are satisfied with the JV's performance on the following criteria:

1 2 3 4 5

not satisfied at all |___|___|___|___| fully satisfied

Score

Profitability
Growth
Market share
Technological development
Development of local staff/managers

6. Control and influence

6.1 *Degree of influence*
In your view, how much influence is exercised by the foreign and local parties in each of the following areas of the international venture? Please insert the number closest to your view in each space, where 5 = dominant, 4 = considerable, 3 = some, 2 = minor, 1 = very little (*using the scale on the card*).

DEGREE OF INFLUENCE 5 4 3 2 1

|_____|_____|_____|_____|

Dominant Considerable Some Minor Very little

Areas	*Foreign party(ies) (or representatives)*	*Chinese party(ies) (or representatives)*
Allocation of profit		
Allocating senior managerial positions		
Setting strategic priorities		
Product pricing		
Training and development policies		
Reward and incentive policies		
Financial control		
Re-investment policy		
Purchasing policies		

Areas	*Foreign party(ies) (or representatives)*	*Chinese party(ies) (or representatives)*
Production planning		
Sales and distribution:		
international		
Far East region		
domestic		
Technological innovation		
Quality control		

6.2 *Extent of control*

Please give your assessment of the overall extent of control by the main Chinese parent, foreign parent and the JV/subsidiary using the 5 point scale. (*Show card.*)

Low control 1 2 3 4 5 High control

|____|____|____|____|

	Chinese parent	*Foreign parent*	*JV management/subsidiary*
Score			

6.3 *Mechanisms of control*

To what degree is control over the following areas in the JV exercised through the four approaches shown? (*Show four approaches and ask the interviewee to answer by reference to the following card.*)

To a very little degree 1 2 3 4 5 To a large degree

|____|____|____|____|

Score

Personal supervision
(personal on-the-spot checking)

Formal specifications
(rules, procedures, systems)

Evaluation against agreed targets
(e.g., targets for production, quality, sales)

Creating positive attitudes and motivations
(shaping employees' attitudes through training, campaigns, model worker schemes, etc.)

6.4 *Formal control*

CONTRACTS

Are there any contracts with parent companies or external bodies which limit what the joint venture/affiliate can do in the following areas? If 'yes', please describe briefly.

product design/content
production technology
brand names/trade marks
marketing and distribution:
suppliers:
provision of management and professional services:
any other activity limited by contract?

WRITTEN PROCEDURES

Are there any written procedures in place for the following activities and if so, (1) who laid them down and (2) who monitors their application in practice:

Activity	*Standard procedure?*	*Laid down by?*	*Monitored by?*
Marketing			
R&D/technical			
Finance			
Production			
Quality control			
Personnel/HRM			
Purchasing			

DEFINITION OF MANAGERIAL RESPONSIBILITIES

Area	*Are responsibilities formally defined*	*Who defines?*	*Who evaluates the manager's performance?*
General manager (or CEO)			
Deputy general manager			

Area	*Are responsibilities formally*	*Who defines?*	*Who evaluates the manager's performance?*
Marketing			
R&D/Technical			
Finance			
Production			
Quality control			
Personnel/HRM			
Purchasing			

FORMAL REPORTING

What has to be reported formally (via written reports and written information) on a regular basis to the following? [Also note frequency of the formal reporting]

(1) the parent companies directly
(2) the board of directors
(3) the GM/CEO

Who has the right to delay/veto decisions of the JV/affiliate?

6.5 *Process-oriented control*

In this section, the intention is to explore how control might be exercised via involvement of parent company managers in the process of JV/affiliate activity. The previous questions on the control of decisions and reporting relationships cover some of this ground. Further questions are:

Frequency of visits from parents to JV? (indicate which parent)

Frequency of visits of JV managers to parent companies? (indicate which parent).

Frequency of informal communication between the JV/affiliate GM and the parent companies? (phone calls, faxes, meetings, visits, etc.)

6.6 *Context-oriented control*

In this section, the intention is to explore any attempts to exercise control over the JV/affiliate via common culture and identity building:

Are there any symbols, slogans, rituals or ceremonies organised for the JV/affiliate by one or other of the parent companies?

Is the reward and incentive system under the control of one parent company?

Is there rotation of JV/affiliate staff into other units of a parent company?

7. Commitment

7.1 How much has been reinvested in the JV since its start?

7.2 Have the partners increased their allocation of capital to the JV over the amount originally committed (not including any reinvestment)

7.3 Is there a long-term vision statement for the JV/affiliate? If yes, please describe briefly (especially noting how many years ahead the statement extends) and who formulated it?

7.4 Have any procedures introduced by the parent companies been changed to suit the needs of the JV/affiliate? If yes, describe briefly.

7.5 Have the JV/affiliate's products been adapted to the needs of the local market? If yes, describe briefly.

7.6 Has the joint venture committed expenditure on employees' housing? if yes, how much?

8. **Mutual perceptions and working style**

8.1 In what respects do you see foreign and local managers in your international venture differing the most?
(a) in their approach to management:
(b) in their working style:
(c) in their attitudes:

8.2 How in a few key words would you describe the characters of each parent company?
(a) Chinese parent
(b) Foreign parent

9. Problems and developments in history of the JV/affiliate

9.1 *Questions for the foreign partner*
What have you learned from the experience of working with your international counterparts in the management of this venture?

What have been the main difficulties you have encountered operating in China?

Have there been any aspects of working with a Chinese JV partner which surprised you or which you did not expect? (Probe for perceived problems and differences of approach.)

Where have conflicts arisen between the local and foreign partners? The different attitudes toward welfare for the company's employees.

Do you see any requirements for change in local staff as to:

(a) how they manage the company's operations;

(b) their understanding of strategic issues;

(c) their culture (values and objectives)?

9.2 *Questions for the Chinese partner*

What have you learned from the experience of working with your foreign counterparts in the management of this venture?

What have been the main difficulties you have encountered working with a foreign partner?

Have there been any aspects of working with a foreign JV partner which surprised you or which you did not expect? (Probe for perceived problems and differences of approach.)

Where have conflicts arisen between the local and foreign partners?

Do you see any requirements for change among your foreign managers as to:

(a) how they manage the company's operations;

(b) their understanding of strategic issues;

(c) their culture (values and objectives)?

Appendix IV: A Summary of IJVs Visited

	Foreign equity share %	*Total capital investment (US$ 100 000)*	*Employees*	*Sector*
1	58	25.00	462	Electronics
2	40	5.00	50	Electronics
3	51	30.00	700	Electronics
4	40	62.64	1300	Electronics
5	40	170.00	1406	Electronics
6	40	20.00	700	Electronics
7	52	1.03	50	Electronics
8	50	500.00	3072	Electronics
9	50	113.00	50	Electronics
10	51	.38	150	Electronics
11	50	2.94	208	Electronics
12	40	1048.00	518	Electronics
13	25	4.00	177	Electronics
14	40	64.00	600	Electronics
15	28	198.70	50	Electronics
16	83	.49	34	Electronics
17	52	14.66	457	Electronics
18	44	8.00	250	Electronics
19	50	14.50	240	Electronics
20	51	3.00	60	Electronics
21	51	47.47	370	Electronics
22	65	26.00	590	FMCG
23	51	8.80	290	FMCG
24	50	13.00	200	FMCG
25	50	4.95	103	FMCG
26	60	60.24	191	FMCG
27	65	29.00	200	FMCG

	Foreign equity share %	*Total capital investment (US$ 100 000)*	*Employees*	*Sector*
28	85	30.00	150	FMCG
29	65	12.00	54	FMCG
30	38	.82	130	FMCG
31	55	28.19	250	FMCG
32	60	.85	70	FMCG
33	70	4.90	700	FMCG
34	50	3.0	70	FMCG
35	70	20.00	100	FMCG
36	90	10.00	900	FMCG
37	50	16.00	326	FMCG
38	60	2.80	80	FMCG
39	60	7.80	232	FMCG
40	64	30.00	200	FMCG
41	95	7.20	130	FMCG
42	70	15.00	208	FMCG
43	75	203.00	800	FMCG
44	55	2.20	99	FMCG
45	28	18.00	174	Electronics
46	90	8.00	472	Electronics
47	90	1.00	956	Electronics
48	50	13.00	1700	Electronics
49	43	1.00	50	Electronics
50	70	8.50	800	Electronics
51	34	5.00	80	Electronics
52	70	1.00	248	Electronics
53	50	4.00	90	Electronics
54	25	45.62	600	Electronics
55	56	7.00	90	Electronics
56	75	10.00	950	FMCG
57	70	10.00	64	FMCG
58	55	29.99	986	FMCG
59	50	8.42	160	FMCG
60	60	17.50	140	Electronics
61	51	1.70	50	FMCG
62	40	1.49	52	FMCG
63	50	7.20	500	FMCG

	Foreign equity share %	*Total capital investment (US$ 100 000)*	*Employees*	*Sector*
64	55	147.00	900	FMCG
65	90	2.44	400	FMCG
66	51	4.48	150	FMCG
67	55	6.50	120	FMCG
66	51	4.48	150	FMCG
67	55	6.50	120	FMCG

Index

LaVergne, TN USA
12 October 2009
160519LV00001B/10/A

9 780312 223014